Bleeding to Ease the Pain

BLEEDING TO EASE THE PAIN

Cutting, Self-Injury, and the Adolescent Search for Self

Lori G. Plante

Foreword by Chris Hayward, M.D.

ROWMAN & LITTLEFIELD PUBLISHERS, INC.
Lanham • Boulder • New York • Toronto • Plymouth, UK

Published by Rowman & Littlefield Publishers, Inc.
A wholly owned subsidary of The Rowman & Littlefield Publishing Group, Inc.
4501 Forbes Boulevard, Suite 200, Lanham, Maryland 20706
http://www.rowmanlittlefield.com

Estover Road, Plymouth PL6 7PY, United Kingdom

British Library Cataloguing in Publication Information Available

Library of Congress Cataloging-in-Publication Data

Plante, Lori G.
   Bleeding to ease the pain: cutting, self-injury, and the adolescent
search for self / Lori G. Plante; foreword by Chris Hayward.
       p.   cm. — (Abnormal psychology, ISSN 1554–2238)
    Includes bibliographical references and index.
    1. Self-mutilation in adolescence.   I. Title.

   RJ506.S44P43   2007
   616.85'8200835—dc22   2006038640

ISBN-13: 978–0–275–99062–6 (cloth: alk. paper)
ISBN-13: 978-1-4422-0394-5 (pbk: alk. paper)
ISBN-10: 0–275–99062–1 (alk. paper)

Printed in the United States of America

For my beloved Tom and Zach

Contents

Foreword

Cutting and other forms of self-mutilation have reached epidemic proportions among our youth. As psychiatrists, those of us in the mental health profession have witnessed this epidemic in emergency rooms and psychiatric hospitals where we provide care for increasing numbers of so-called cutters, many of whom are scarred from years of self-inflicted wounds. Why is this happening? In *Bleeding to Ease the Pain: Cutting, Self-Injury, and the Adolescent Search for Self*, Dr. Lori Plante skillfully weaves a way of understanding and intervening with adolescent cutting. Explanations for why a given teenager might engage in this "crazy" behavior are placed within the context of normal adolescent development along with dramatic new changes in youth culture. For example, in offering an account of why youth mutilate their skin, she writes: "Our society's ever-increasing focus on appearance makes the skin an ideal billboard for advertising identity."

For years we had associated cutting with borderline personality disorder. In fact, thirty years ago the phenomenon of cutting one's wrist to relieve emotional suffering was almost exclusively confined to patients with this diagnosis. Self-mutilation is occasionally seen in patients with psychosis or mental retardation, but until recently cutting to "feel alive" has been the sine qua non of borderline personality disorder. It is now the counterintuitive "creating pain to relieve pain" that has become pandemic in teenagers. Why has this bizarre behavior increased in our youth? Dr. Plante provides a compelling account of the cultural pressures that have broadened the cutting epidemic beyond these discrete diagnoses: Sensationalized media exposure to aberrant behavior, extreme pressure to succeed, and an exaggerated emphasis on physical appearance are all suspected factors behind this growing epidemic. Furthermore, the so-called contagion effect, known more commonly to occur in small outbreaks of adolescent suicides, is now enhanced by cell phones, instant messages, and other high-tech means that allow news of bizarre cutting rituals to spread like wildfire.

We do not know the exact relationship between societal forces and cutting behavior in youth, but Dr. Plante makes a strong case for understanding how they can exacerbate normal adolescent turmoil and result in self-injury. Whatever the cause, for a parent whose 14-year-old daughter has cut herself for the first time, or for an adolescent tormented by the compulsion to mutilate, it does not really matter. What parents, teens, and clinicians need to know is what to do to keep the youth safe and help them surmount this destructive behavior. Dr. Plante provides this important service in this book. She clearly understands how incomprehensible this kind of behavior is to most of us. Although sympathizing with parents' and clinicians' strong reactions to this behavior, Dr. Plante offers understandable explanations for why an adolescent might cut. The desperation to alleviate distress, control and regulate emotions, dramatize depression, cry out for help, or express anger and helplessness are some of the motives discussed. Dr. Plante cautions against overreacting, emphasizing a nonpathologizing approach. This is a refreshing counterpoint to the increasing tendency to describe everything out of the range of normal as a psychiatric illness. Diagnostic labeling cannot replace understanding. She rightfully tells us that it is essential to capture the meaning, context, and purpose of cutting behavior. Cutting needs to be understood in relationship to a larger context of an adolescent's developmental challenges and life circumstances. She then tackles how to get help.

Dr. Plante explains in detailed and understandable terms how to navigate the mental health system: what to expect, what treatments are available, how professionals differ, how treatments differ, when medications are appropriate, and how parents can help. These are important issues, and without such preparatory knowledge, parents and their children can react to the complexities of the mental health system with befuddlement and frustration and, worst of all, remain untreated.

This book departs from other accounts of adolescent cutting in that Dr. Plante gives hope, direction for action, and a perspective on cutting behavior in a larger context that will be comforting to parents and teens alike. Although providing a path for help, Dr. Plante emphasizes compassion and understanding. One feels while reading the text that Dr. Plante truly captures the emotional pain that teenagers can experience and that, unfortunately, now frequently leads to self-injury. It is Dr. Plante's ability to describe the essence of the psychological inner turmoil that leads to cutting that helps us all fathom why an adolescent might do this to herself and how to help her stop. We all owe Dr. Plante a debt of gratitude for providing understanding, compassion, and hope for these young people who are troubled and hurt themselves to show it.

Chris Hayward, MD
Professor and Chief of Hospital Services
Department of Psychiatry and Behavioral Sciences
Stanford University School of Medicine

Preface

At perhaps no other stage of life are we as exquisitely preoccupied with our flesh-and-blood selves than during the treacherous traverse of adolescence. This period of rapid physical, sexual, emotional, intellectual, and social development is a rallying cry for the adolescent to seek a renewed sense of self-identity. It is no wonder that the body, the most palpable engine behind all this change, becomes the battleground upon which this developmental struggle is fought. Cutting, with all its inherent pain, blood, scarring, and eventual healing, emblematizes the raw flesh-and-blood struggles and strivings of adolescence.

The twenty-first century is unfolding with an escalating epidemic of young people resorting to self-harm as a means of coping with pain and turmoil. Cutting serves multiple purposes, conscious and unconscious, such as the drive to express new emotions, the desire to control and punish the renegade adolescent body, and the longing for connection and empathy. Cutting, often referred to interchangeably in this book as *self-harm* or *self-injury*, is increasingly emerging in schools, hospital settings, and even the healthiest of home environments. Is it merely coincidence that witnesses the rise of cutting among adolescents alongside the widening worldwide focus on suicide and terrorism as weapons of the weak in search of power? What are the roles of teen culture, media sensationalism, technology, academic pressure, and changing notions of intimacy in exacerbating the challenges of today's adolescents? Most fundamentally, why would a young person inflict pain and bloody damage on themselves, and how can the youth's difficulties be given the needed dignity and attention to allow for healthier coping? This book addresses the reasons behind this painful, damaging act in adolescents and provides both a philosophy and a methodology for effective intervention.

The discovery that a child, a friend, a student, or even a patient is engaging in morbid, gory rituals of self-inflicted violence is always disturbing and deeply anxiety-provoking. Loved one's immediately fear the worst: Their son or daughter is suicidal, sick, crazy, or irrevocably lost to them. Teenagers themselves can feel deeply stigmatized and ashamed of their habitual cutting, realizing that they have crossed over the bounds of healthy behavior and fearing no return. The current wave of cutting among today's youth, however, is most often a misdirected effort to cope with and overcome normative conflicts inherent to adolescent development. I have worked with scores of adolescents who cut and burn and otherwise injure themselves only to eventually work through the underlying conflicts and proceed on a more mature, healthy, even thriving developmental path.

Clearly, though the specter of potential suicide warrants careful assessment and monitoring in each and every case of cutting, seeking to understand and engage the youth without panic or judgment provides the foundation of successful intervention. Professional help is essential in assisting the teen and the family to develop genuine insight and a range of new skills that can more effectively achieve developmental goals. No single, formulaic treatment program can address the unique needs of every adolescent, and clinicians and families must be equipped to utilize a range of intervention resources.

Many case examples are presented in this book to bring to life the real humanity of these struggling adolescents and illustrate how intervention can successfully unfold. In all of these cases, however, identifying information and particulars of history and treatment have been altered to diligently protect confidentiality. I owe a tremendous debt to the many adolescent patients, and their families, who have entrusted me with their highly personal struggles in overcoming the conflicts represented by cutting. It has been a privilege to accompany these adolescents in their always poignant search for self.

Chapter 1

Self-Injury on the Rampage

I thought I was unshockable after raising two challenging teenagers. But there she was, bleeding from her angry-looking wounds, wielding a razor blade, and screaming at me to leave her alone. To see my beautiful girl carving herself bloody before my eyes was just too much; I'm terrified of what else she might do.

Mother of a 13-year-old cutter

Adolescents are notorious for devising highly destructive outlets for their self-expression, their rage, and the ferocity of their teenage drives. Drug abuse, drinking binges, sexual risk taking, eating disorders, delinquent acts, and other undesirable behaviors seem to explode during the teen years. Tattoos, pierced body parts, risqué dress, and indiscriminate sex: Teens seem forever in search of dramatic actions that shock and stand out. A new behavior has increased in popularity with teens, as the phenomenon of adolescent self-injury has garnered heightened concern and attention in schools, institutions, psychotherapy offices, and the professional and lay literatures. The intentional infliction of cuts, burns, bruises, hair-pulling, deep scratching, needle pricking, and other nonlethal injuries is currently an alarming problem among an increasing number of youths.[1]

Self-injury refers to the intentional self-infliction of wounds by cutting, burning, or otherwise damaging the skin. Repetitive self-injury can create significant scarring, infection, or painful injury and grow into an essentially addictive and unremitting behavior. Self-injurious behaviors constitute an increasingly prevalent symptom among today's adolescents, providing a glaring emblem of a range of adolescent torments and clinical diagnoses.[2,3] Critical to the definition of self-injury, also referred to interchangeably as *cutting* and *self-mutilation*, is the deliberate infliction of wounds without the intent to kill oneself. Most commonly, adolescents will inflict non-life-threatening cuts or burns on their arms or legs in a complicated effort to alleviate intense distress. Only extremely rarely are such wounds lethal. As stated by Bina, age 16, "If I wanted to kill myself I wouldn't burn stupid holes in my skin. I want to kill the pain, and that's the only thing that helps."

Although teenagers are vulnerable to a range of high-risk behaviors, cutting is becoming an increasingly prevalent, even socially "contagious" syndrome among adolescents.[3] Understandably, the discovery of a teenager with self-inflicted wounds raises horrified alarm in parents, friends, and teachers and often requires immediate psychotherapeutic intervention. In the quintessentially adolescent manner of shocking, defying, and drawing attention, self-injury has become a new mode of not simply rebelling but of dramatizing inexpressible pain. A high school teacher I spoke with reflected the power of receiving this visual communication: "She was just a quiet, sweet, and hardworking student. I had no idea she had so much going on until she came to class with short sleeves; her scarred up arms really shook me up."

Who are the teenagers most prone to these self-injurious behaviors? First, females have typically been more likely to engage in self-injurious behavior of this kind than their male counterparts, consistent with patterns indicating that males tend to utilize more lethal methods than females in a range of self-injurious acts.[2,3,5] This assumption has recently been challenged by research, however, suggesting that males today may be self-injuring at a rate as high as their female counterparts.[6,7,8] Teenagers with depression, eating disorders, adjustment disorders, social difficulties, sexual conflicts, and often simply normative problems related to adolescent development all can seek catharsis, control, and communication through self-destructive physical acts. Few simple acts garner the type of immediate attention and response from others than the appearance of bloody, self-inflicted wounds in one's loved one, and few other signs so clearly articulate the depth of distress that plagues the teen.

Surprisingly, cutting is becoming an increasingly prevalent phenomenon that is plaguing teens, parents, and schools. The prevalence of cutting in adolescents has been estimated at occurring annually in approximately 1,000 per 100,000 youths. This number well exceeds estimates of self-injury at between 14 and 750 per 100,000 in the general population.[5] In a recent national study, cutting rates among patients presenting to community hospitals increased from 4.3 percent to 13.2 percent between 1990 and 2000.[2] The incidence among adolescent inpatients has been cited at a startling 40 percent.[9,10] So common has self-injury become in institutional settings that staff often largely ignore the behavior so as not to reinforce it, merely removing sharp objects and matches while encouraging the adolescent to verbally express her pain.

Self-injury is certainly not the sole domain of seriously disturbed teens. In a recent study conducted by researchers at Cornell and Princeton, 17 percent of almost 3,000 randomly selected Ivy League male and female college students reported having purposely injured themselves. Seventy percent of those had done so multiple times.[11] The researchers point to these data as an indication of cutting and other forms of self-injury representing an increasing phenomenon. Repeat self-injurers were more likely than noninjurers to be female and to report histories of sexual or physical abuse, eating disorders, and past suicide attempts. In a previous study by Gratz,[7] 35 percent of college students reported at least one incident of self-injurious behavior. The self-inflicted wounds and burns appearing on adolescents from all walks of life appear as a veritable silent scream of agony: "I don't even know why I do it. I just don't know what else to do when I'm freaking out like that."

Indeed, cutting is frequently the most visible sign of other severe associated problems. For example, females who repetitively cut themselves also suffer from an eating disorder such as anorexia or bulimia in 40 percent of cases. Similarly, 62 percent of self-cutters have a history of sexual or physical abuse.[12,13] Thus, cutting serves to subdue, communicate, and ultimately enact the suffering caused by a wide range of underlying emotional disturbances. As one bulimic patient put it, "Opening my skin and releasing my blood is soothing. It looks just like I feel: hurt, damaged, angry." Not only does cutting raise the specter of overt suicide risk, it also can result in infection, permanent scarring, social alienation, and an intractable pattern of self-mutilation. Ultimately, healthy development can be stalled by the reliance on self-injury, eclipsing healthy engagement in normative adolescent developmental challenges.

WHY ADOLESCENTS INFLICT SELF-INJURY: FINDING MEANING IN THE MADNESS

Why would a completely normal-appearing and -acting teenager choose to inflict cuts or burns on him- or herself? Why would a teen willfully choose pain and scarring over other forms of coping or communicating? What purpose could it possibly serve? Surprisingly, there are usually healthy strivings underlying these seemingly pointless acts, and untangling them becomes imperative in both understanding and intervening with the developmental struggle behind the self-destructive behavior.[14] Quite often, adolescents are as mystified by their behavior as the adults around them. A common refrain is, "I know it doesn't make any sense. I really don't know why I do it."

The need for both the teen and the adults in her life to understand cutting as not merely self-destructive but also ultimately in the service of the adolescent's emerging sense of self is critical to effective intervention. In other words, these destructive acts fall under the common adolescent theme of "doing all the wrong things for the right reasons." That is, self-injury is the wrong way to cope with all the right strivings related to independence, intimacy, and identity formation. It is these underlying and often unconscious conflicts that not only drive such behavior but also hold the keys to stopping it. The key to treatment often lies in helping adolescents use their minds to manage their emotions and conflicts rather than their bodies.

The vast majority of self-injurers report that they harm themselves in an effort to alleviate intense distress. Oddly, the infliction of pain is followed by a sense of relief and calm. In fact, cutting can work so well in quelling distress that an addictive cycle can develop. Self-injurers typically resort to cutting, for example, when their ability to cope with overwhelming emotional distress fails. Self-injury similarly provides teens with a sense of control, empowerment, cleansing self-punishment, or other remedy to their immediate distress. By making their inner pain visible, they can communicate their despair to others or keep it intensely private. Thus, self-injury is in itself a coping device, a means of controlling and communicating a confluence of overwhelming emotions.

Specific factors have been identified in studies utilizing the Self-Injury Motivation Scale (SIMS) to determine the reasons adolescents give for resorting to self-injury.[15] These factors and include (1) affect modulation, (2) management of overwhelming experience, (3) self-punishment, (4) influence or control of others, and (5) self-stimulation. Often, self-injury serves multiple purposes simultaneously.[16]

Another reason why adolescents appear to be self-injuring at such high rates is the classic phenomenon of "everyone's doing it." Social contagion appears to account for some of the increased prevalence of cutting,[17,18] and it seems to sweep through schools and hospitals in a fadlike fashion. Observation of peers engaging in self-injury can result in contagion through modeling of these behaviors as an appropriate coping device. Much like the social contagion aspects of overt suicide attempts and eating disorders, and the renowned suggestibility of teenagers, the increased awareness of self-injury among one's peers may provoke engagement in such acts. In fact, inpatient units are often hotbeds of self-injury as one after another of the patients observe and then imitate the dramatic behavior. Unfortunately, schools and other healthful teen environments are increasingly witnessing a rash of copycat cutters as teens adopt this unusual outlet that seems to eloquently articulate their distress.

FLAUNTING SUFFERING AND DYSFUNCTION

Happiness and health are perhaps not all that they are cracked up to be, at least in the mindset of today's youth. Perhaps these ideals seem too elusive or merely the domain of those with fame and fortune. Perhaps they meld too closely with adult values and parental admonitions, giving them an instantaneous taint of the dull and unimaginative mainstream. Finally, perhaps it is far easier to distinguish oneself through one's hardships than one's successes. After all, hardship is virtually everyone's potential domain, whereas success often seems increasingly elusive in this competitive world.

One's character is largely formed through confrontations with pain, loss, and disappointment, and it is perhaps the uniqueness and depth of each individual's difficulties that provide a foundation for distinguishing us as unique individuals. In teenagers' inexorable drive to individuate, the lurid display of human angst is in some ways an effective means of declaring a complex identity. Pain and struggle are also powerful sources of connection and identification between individuals and groups, simultaneously serving the adolescent's need to fit in and achieve intimacy. In a culture so focused on instant gratification and the expectation that happiness is a fundamental right, the value of painful struggle is easily overlooked. As teens confront all kinds of new challenges and experience adversity in a less sheltered and more palpable manner, cutting and its scars can represent the battle wounds of hard-won struggles. Seeking validation and even admiration for enduring character-building adversity can be sought in the stoic display of what are essentially developmental war wounds.

Visual cues are perhaps the best ways of displaying this angst. Although private disclosures between teens require trust and intimacy, visual symbols are often more comfortably employed and socially endorsed. The intricate language expressed through teen attire, hairstyle, makeup, tattoos, piercings, and flamboyant sexuality communicates identity, group affiliation, sexual availability, and level of alienation and rebellion. The scars that serve as evidence of self-injury and suffering, when revealed, similarly speak a thousand otherwise unspoken words and can be added to the list of the many regrettable manifestations of adolescent angst.

SPANNING HISTORY AND CULTURE: SELF-INJURY PAST AND PRESENT

Self-injury can be so shocking and horrifying as to make it seem beyond the pale of human logic. It is so foreign and so unpleasant that it is essentially a taboo topic. It can be invaluable for patients and their families, however, to look beyond the morbid aspects of self-injury in order to understand its broader context in history and culture. Cutting is not simply a bizarre new phenomenon of the twenty-first century. It has been deeply embedded in societies and entrenched with important meanings throughout human history. By appreciating the role of self-mutilation in a broader context, it is easier to grasp the mindset that drives today's youth to such grotesque acts.

Throughout ancient and modern history and across primitive and contemporary cultures, self-inflicted bodily damage has been an important and highly symbolic act. As stated by Enid Schildkrout,[19] "There is no culture in which people do not, or did not, paint, pierce, tattoo, reshape, or simply adorn their bodies." History abounds with innumerable examples of culturally sanctioned scarring, piercing, tattooing, and, in the view of many, frank self-mutilation. Although Western cultures may view many of these practices as primitive and tribal, they continue to manifest across the globe in urban, suburban, and rural cultures. In fact, modern movements have emerged with increasing visibility, from the popularity of tattooing and piercing to the painful rituals of bodily mutilation embraced by today's so-called modern primitives, urban aboriginals, and urban primitives, collectively referred to as *neoprimitives*.

Why is this history lesson important in the context of adolescents who self-injure? First and foremost, a broader understanding of the symbolic value of such human acts helps to destigmatize a seemingly horrific and senseless behavior. Most commonly, parents, teachers, and even clinicians recoil from the apparent perversity and violence of an adolescent's self-injurious behavior. If frightened, disgusted, or overly condemning, such reactions render the adult unable to effectively reach out to the teen and provide assistance. Although the intention is in no way to suggest that cutting is a positive, healthy, and benign enterprise, its compatibility with practices across vast spans of history and culture demand a deeper appreciation of its meaning.

Fakir Musafar,[20] who launched the modern primitive movement, draws parallels between the practice of primitive and modern self-scarification. He sees all cultures deriving important meaning from these acts, with commonalities that include self-injury performed as rites of passage; creation of lifelong peer bonding; symbols of status, bravery, or courage; initiation into greater mysteries of life; protection from evil or harm; rebalancing of the body; community connection; and the healing of a diseased body or self.[4] Similarly, anthropologists like Schildkrout conceptualize such modifications to the body as "a visual language." She views this language as a means of communicating a person's status in society, individuality, or "an irreversible life passage like the change from childhood to adulthood."

Favazza, perhaps the single most influential pioneer in the study and treatment of self-injury, echoes these conceptualizations, viewing scarification as a common adolescent rite in many cultures and as a symbol of the transition from childish to more mature concerns. He draws comparisons between shamanic healing, religious mortification, adolescent rites of passage, and today's cutting and other forms of self-injury. Furthermore, Favazza focuses on the significance of scar tissue in that it provides a visual representation of healing and survival and a record of one's personal struggles. The demonstration of strength and courage through the voluntary endurance of such pain further asserts the power and control of the self-injurer. Whether carried out in the socially sanctioned context of tribal initiation rites, such as the piercing and scarring of adolescent boys among the Guyaki of South America, the modern piercings common to Western adolescents, or the self-cutter's visual proclamation of internal struggle, the damaging of one's skin has spoken a common language across time and culture.

As Kiell[21] has pointed out, "The great internal turmoil and external disorder of adolescence are universal and only moderately affected by cultural determinants." Although adolescents from varying cultures have sought to rein in, symbolize, or otherwise mark this tumultuous life transition through a range of practices, cutting appears to be something of a modern rite of passage for some troubled youth. Yet in the universal context of adolescent turmoil and the almost instinctive use of the body as a billboard for self-expression, self-injury may not be as perverse or pathological as it might appear. In fact, many reasonably well-adjusted teenagers use cutting to communicate, catharize, or otherwise express themselves during periods of distress. Psychologist Scott Lines put it this way: "The skin becomes a battlefield as a demonstration of internal chaos. The place where the self meets the world is a canvas or tabula rasa on which is displayed exactly how bad one feels inside."[22] One need not have a mental illness to utilize this canvas in eloquent if bloody scars.

Historically, prior to the 1800s, Western cultures viewed self-injury as mortification of the flesh, a Christian concept practiced for religious atonement through suffering. In the nineteenth century, extreme forms are documented and largely attributed to madness. Eye enucleation, genital mutilation, bone breaking, and the burying of glass shards deep inside self-inflicted cuts are today referred to as *major self-mutilation*[5] and are not considered within the domain of the forms of self-injury discussed in this book. Although major self-mutilation results in the significant destruction of body tissue, moderate/superficial cutting involves minimal damage, low lethality, and an absence of suicidal intent. Numerous terms have been applied to this practice, including *delicate self-cutting, parasuicide, self-mutilation, intentional injury, symbolic wounding,* and *self-aggression.*

It was not until Karl Menninger's landmark 1938 publication of *Man against Himself*[23] that cutting was viewed not as a form of suicidal behavior but more as an effort to purge negative feelings and to self-heal. Gruenbaum and Klerman[24] followed suit in conceptualizing cutting as "self-prescribed treatment" of distress. Scar tissue ensued as a representation of healing, symbolizing an almost surgical removal of pain. In the 1990s, the most widely accepted classification of cutting was refined by Favazza and colleagues. Episodic and repetitive forms of moderate self-injury were seen as including a range of nonlethal behaviors such as cutting, burning, needle sticking, skin scratching, interference with wound healing, hitting, hair pulling, and the like. Many self-injurers use multiple methods, with cutting being the most prevalent method of harm. Significantly, this form of superficial/moderate self-injury is generally classified as an impulse control disorder in today's *Diagnostic and Statistical Manual of Mental Disorders* (4th ed.; DSM-IV).[25]

As eating disorders and body art have become better understood and increasingly regarded as cultural phenomena, so, too, should self-injury. Many comparisons can be drawn between the self-affliction of anorexia and bulimia with that of cutting, burning, or otherwise damaging the body. As stated by Cross,[26] self-cutting and eating disorders are "attempts to own the body . . . thinness is self-sufficiency, bleeding emotional catharsis, bingeing is the assuaging of loneliness, and purging is the moral purification of the self." Further, "Body and self constantly shift roles of victim and victimizer, master and slave."

Among the Kagoro of Papua New Guinea, scarification is used to initiate adolescent boys into adulthood. The boys undergo a period of fasting prior to the ceremony, in which they are then beaten with sticks by tribal elders. Subsequently, the boys endure an excruciating skin-cutting ritual that creates an elaborate pattern of scars across the entire upper body. After the scars heal, they are publicly celebrated as having proved themselves as men. As odd and cruel as this ritual may seem to Westerners, it is willingly engaged in toward the goal of casting off childhood and demonstrating inner strength in the eyes of oneself and one's community. Many cultures employ similar rituals that mark the end of childhood and the beginning of adulthood. In this relative context, today's explosion of self-cutting may represent a relatively mild initiation rite of its own.

SELF-INJURY IN MODERN PSYCHIATRY AND CULTURE: TODAY'S TEENAGE CUTTER

Although self-mutilation has been practiced by individuals and cultures throughout history, modern psychiatric attention to self-injurious patterns of cutting and burning emerged in the 1960s[24,27] and burgeoned in the 1980s.[4,28] Viewed by some as a discrete impulse-control disorder[4,29] and by others as just one of many impulsive behaviors exhibited by individuals with a range of disturbances such as anorexia nervosa, bulimia, eating disorders, depression, and borderline personality disorders,[5] the sine qua non of this form of self-injury is a repeated pattern of direct, intentional bodily harm without suicidal intent.

The most commonly cited purpose of self-injury is affect regulation, in that adolescents report reductions in anxiety, tension, depression, guilt, and loneliness after self-injuring.[9, 12] The syndrome most often begins in early adolescence at age 13 or 14 and often persists for many years, even well into adulthood.[12] It can become an intractable problem that leaves a legacy of permanent scars, both internal and external. This type of cutting has been classified as moderate/superficial[4] in that it has low lethality and involves relatively minimal tissue damage. Moderate/superficial cutting makes up the focus of discussion in this book and is distinguished from major self-injury that may involve infrequent yet dramatic forms of mutilation such as castration, limb amputation, or even the removal of one's own eyes.

The pattern of moderate/superficial cutting, also referred to as *delicate self-cutting*, is all too often dismissed as a nonserious, attention-seeking behavior devoid of any genuine suicide risk. Although only a small minority of cutters also make genuine suicide attempts, these teens can be difficult to identify. Hospital emergency rooms are plagued by the difficult decision as to whether teenage cutters should be discharged or hospitalized due to active suicide risk. Recent studies[30, 31] have found that surprisingly high numbers of persons who die by suicide have had a history of self-harm, with reports as high as 50 percent.[32] In younger age groups, this proportion jumps to two-thirds.[33] Yet, though many people who eventually commit suicide may have histories of self-harm, "cutting or self-mutilation is rarely associated with completed suicide in young people and also tends to be less lethal than other forms of self-injury."[2] In other words, though many people who commit suicide may have self-injured, cutting itself among teenagers has a very low potential for lethality.[34] In the United States during the year 2000, six adolescents (ages 15–19) committed suicide by injury with a sharp object.[35] Thus, teens who do in fact commit suicide use means other than cutting, such as drug overdoses or other highly lethal methods.

How can we understand this confusing array of statistics? First, any individual who self-injures must be evaluated on a continuum of lethality[36] and risk for further self-harm or suicide assessed. So, though a young person's cutting must be taken seriously and assessed clinically, parents and other adults should not panic given the lack of lethal intent that characterizes this growing population of self-injurers. Given the escalating rates of cutting among teens, we may be seeing a broader population that has not yet been studied longitudinally for eventual suicide risk. Thus, the key is to understand the broad syndrome of cutting as it applies to the vast majority of youths, identify the specific conflicts generating self-injury in each adolescent, while putting safeguards in place to minimize the ever-present risk of escalation to more dangerous acts of self-injury.

IDENTIFYING SUICIDE RISK

I live in constant fear that she'll kill herself. Anytime her door is closed I'm terrified that she's cutting herself or planning to commit suicide. I'm constantly waiting for the other shoe to drop.

Mother of a depressed 18-year-old

Is cutting a red flag signaling imminent suicide risk? This is naturally the pressing question asked by anyone confronted with a self-injuring teen. Although it is hard enough to bear the worry and heartache associated with self-injuries, the specter of suicide generates outright terror in parents and often in clinicians, friends, and teachers as well. How can the risk of suicide be carefully assessed and monitored? When is self-injury purely a coping mechanism and not in any way intended as a way to end one's life? How can families respond effectively to high-risk situations without being held hostage by artificial threats and fears? None of these questions can be easily answered, and each requires the ongoing involvement of a professional clinician to ensure safety and keep treatment from becoming derailed by false concerns.

Although the current phenomenon of self-cutting among teenagers is predominantly a strategy geared toward alleviating, communicating, and even advertising intense distress, the risk of suicide is not to be taken lightly. Approximately half of those who die by suicide have a history of self-harm.[32] Among younger age groups, the proportion reaches two-thirds.[33] This association is particularly high in individuals with borderline personality disorder,[31] a disorder discussed in more depth in the next chapter. Although self-injury may have occurred in many of those individuals who do eventually commit suicide, these statistics do not speak to the vast numbers of teenagers who self-injure but never contemplate, much less attempt, suicide. It is this rapidly growing group of self-injurious but not suicidal youth who constitute the focus of much of this book. The incidence of cutting is approximately 12 times greater than that of suicide among youths.[37]

Self-harm is regarded in more recent literature as a perverse but active coping mechanism, a self-help or life-sustaining act.[3] Thus, most self-harm defined as superficial/moderate is viewed as having decidedly nonsuicidal intentions and as being even a life-preserving coping strategy. Its level of risk is likened to that of bulimia, anorexia, and substance abuse by some authors.[3] Certainly these behavioral patterns are destructive and dangerous, but they are performed as misguided coping efforts rather than with any intent to commit suicide.

A number of demographic, behavioral, and psychological variables are associated with an increased risk of suicide. Teens are at a higher risk than the general population by mere virtue of their age, which speaks to the challenging and stressful aspects of adolescence itself. The Centers for Disease Control and Prevention reports that 17 percent of adolescents think about suicide each year, and about 2,000 youths aged 10 to 19 die from suicide each year.[35] Shockingly, suicide is the third leading cause of death among youths aged 15–24. In 2001, adolescents killed themselves at a rate of 8.2 per 100,000 teens aged 15–19. Five times as many males as females commit suicide. Among youths aged 20–24, the rate increases to 12.8 per 100,000, with seven times as many males as females killing themselves.[37] One positive development is the finding that the rate of youth suicide declined 25 percent during the 1990s, an improvement possibly attributable to the increased use of selective serotonin reuptake inhibitors (SSRIs).

Teens who engage in alcohol or substance abuse represent an additional risk. Obviously, drugs and alcohol impair judgment and impulse control, making it more difficult for the teen to control aggressive behavior and contend with distressing emotions. In addition, teens who utilize drugs and alcohol on an ongoing basis are likely self-medicating and acting out in response to preexisting emotional difficulties. Depression, loneliness, poor self-esteem, anxiety, and a host of environmental problems may be responsible for the teen's distress and consequent efforts to alleviate it through substance abuse. Drugs and alcohol make the likelihood of poor decisions, ranging from reckless driving to suicidal impulses, far greater. Teens with family histories of mental illness, substance abuse, suicide, or family violence are similarly at an increased risk.

Importantly, teens who cut versus teens who attempt suicide are often responding to different emotional constellations and motivations. Cutters are often seeking tension reduction, distraction from distressing emotions, self-punishment, or a sense of control. Teens overwhelmingly report feeling a great sense of relief following the painful self-inflicted action, thus serving as a stopgap measure that allows them to get on with their lives. Conversely, suicidal feelings are more classically experienced as a global sense of depression, hopelessness, and despair.[31, 38] In these cases, suicide is intended as a means of dying or, in the case of attempts or gestures, of at least eliciting vital care. In comparing self-injurers to adolescents who have attempted suicide, self-injurers were found to have fewer depressive symptoms, less suicide ideation, and more positive attitudes toward life.[39]

Many authors argue that self-injurious behavior deserves to be assigned a discrete diagnostic label as it "appears to be psychologically and phenomenologically different from suicide."[39] Individuals who self-injure often do not fit clearly into other diagnostic categories currently delineated in the DSM-IV-R (text revision), leaving the seeming so-called wastebasket category of impulse disorder not otherwise specified as the diagnosis of choice in many cases. Although self-injurious behaviors may exist on a continuum of suicidal behavior, what is emerging more and more clearly as a distinct syndrome demands a more clinically useful classification to aid treatment and research.

Monitoring the symptoms and severity of depression appears important in reducing suicide risk among adolescents. A number of psychological tests, both empirically based and more subjectively interpreted, specifically assess depression and overt suicide risk. Most authors and clinicians concede that both suicidal and self-injurious patients may differ in their intent but overlap a great deal in their common experience of distress. A careful diagnostic assessment can shed invaluable light on the patient's underlying conflicts and how best to provide treatment and ensure safety. As with suicide, individuals who are actively talking about their impulses to self-injure are less at risk than those who remain silent and hidden. The very act of revealing self-inflicted cuts, burns, and bruises to others in itself suggests a more positive prognosis against suicide.

WHO ARE THESE KIDS WHO CUT IN ORDER TO COPE?

Adolescents who cut defy easy definition. They come from diverse backgrounds, have unique strengths and limitations, and range in their behaviors and values from the stereotypical goody-goody to the archetypal juvenile delinquent. A brief description of three adolescents who presented for treatment as a result of repetitive self-injury can help capture at least a flavor of the types of circumstances that can lead to cutting as a strategy for coping with enormous developmental demands and difficulties.

Terra is a 17-year-old currently on home study due to her recent expulsion from school. Caught with a knife at school, Terra had been cutting her arms, legs, and abdomen both on campus and at home. Her academic performance had slipped dramatically in the past eight months, and she and her parents are discussing an alternative school or treatment center placement.

Terra was adopted as an infant, as was her older sister. Since turning 14, she has been in constant conflict with her parents, rebelling and defying them with poor grades, marijuana and alcohol use, disregard for rules and curfews, and rage-filled fights at home. She struggles with bulimia, hidden from her parents until just recently, and has repetitively and extensively cut herself in her frequent moments of turmoil. She is not shy about the many scars she bears, seeming to enjoy the shock and discomfort they provoke in others. Although her parents and peers see her as a cocky, angry kid, she struggles wretchedly with feelings of depression, worthlessness, loneliness, and despair.

For Terra, cutting is a means of both easing and fighting back against unwanted, uncontrollable emotions. When flooded with sadness and hopelessness, the act of cutting helps focus the pain and affords her a sense of control and containment. When angry and isolated, the blood provides a means of expressing aggression, against others or herself she is not always sure. Cutting is also a means of control and a declaration of autonomy; no one, not her parents, her therapist, or her friends, can make her stop.

Liz goes to an urban high school where gangs prevail and students must maintain vigilance over their personal safety. She is an average student, has a few close friends, and is part of a very nurturing family. Liz, a freshman, feels lost in the huge, frenetic, and overwhelming atmosphere of the school. Naturally shy, she finds herself withdrawing from all the tumult and simply getting through each day. None of her classes interests her, and she often feels bored and empty with only the warmth of her home to look forward to. She feels out of pace with her peers, who are focused on boys, and is frankly frightened by the overt sexuality that surrounds her.

Liz knows that she has a loving family and a "good life" and should not have anything to complain about. She has never been abused, her parents are not divorced or ill, and yet she does not understand why she feels so sad and alienated. She does not want to disappoint her parents or upset them with her mysterious troubles; they both work very hard to make a living and seek only her happiness. She outwardly pretends that all is well, whereas privately, her suffering is stifled by literally hitting and bruising herself. She bangs her head against the wall, punches her legs until they bruise, and pulls out small clumps of hair when she feels overwhelmed by self-hate and despair. She has no idea what is wrong with her and has no intention of letting anyone know about her unhappiness and painful self-injuries.

Rosa is a 16-year-old suburban teen with intense ambitions. She attends a private college preparatory high school where she takes several advanced placement classes, plays the clarinet in the school orchestra, and has won several fiction and poetry writing awards. She has always been the quintessential *perfect* child: cooperative, high achieving, responsible, sweet, and "never a problem of any kind." Despite all outward appearances of success and health, Rosa found the pressure to achieve her high goals in such a competitive environment a constant torment. Every test, every paper, and every performance caused her tremendous anxiety and fear, and no matter how well she did, she always dreaded a failure lurking just around the corner.

Rosa tried to perfect not only her grades and skills, but her body as well, allowing herself fewer and fewer calories in an effort to rid herself of all visible body fat. Sometimes she threw up after indulging in a forbidden treat, seeking to undo and punish herself for her transgression. Gradually she perfected her ritual of self-punishment in an effort to ease tremendous anxiety and feelings of unworthiness by stabbing herself repeatedly with a small pocket knife. These wounds were small but relatively deep, causing significant pain and more than just a few drops of blood. She always felt a sense of peacefulness as she watched the blood bead and drip from her stinging arm. These wounds eventually developed scabs which she picked and disturbed as a distraction from the almost constant psychic distress she felt, never allowing them to properly heal. Her best friend was shocked to finally discover her heavily scarred arms, and notified the school counselor when Rosa refused to talk to her about it at all.

Terra, Liz, and Rosa represent but three of the tens of thousands of adolescents who resort to self-injury. No two such individuals are alike, yet they all use self-injury to soothe, punish, control, communicate, and cope with their suffering. How to reach and intervene with these teens is a complex undertaking and involves delving deeply into the core adolescent self struggling to cope with the huge developmental challenges faced in establishing an acceptable and rewarding identity. Although the self-injurious behaviors themselves may seem perverse, frightening, or frankly disturbed, the critical goal is to focus on the healthy, age-appropriate strivings that inevitably underlie these symptoms.

CONCLUSIONS

This chapter has outlined the nature, prevalence, and risk factors that characterize the phenomenon of moderate/superficial cutting and self-injury in adolescents. Cutting is most commonly undertaken by teenagers without suicidal intent but can be intimately related to broader difficulties and diagnoses including eating disorders, personality disorders, and sexual abuse victimization. Self-injury is first and foremost a coping device, as it helps teens achieve a temporary sense of relief, calm, connection, or control in the face of intense emotional distress. As evidenced by the epidemic spread of cutting among middle school and high school populations, cutting has come to serve as an outlet for even normative adolescent conflicts and struggles.

Youth culture, with its premium on bold displays of identity, angst, and rebellion, has contributed through social contagion to the epidemic emergence of this powerful means of conveying suffering. Given the pervasive evidence of self-injury throughout history and culture, self-injury takes on a meaningful and highly compelling human character that can aid the teen and family in working through the difficulties posed by self-injury. Distinguishing the self-injurer seeking to cope with developmental difficulties from the actively suicidal teen at serious risk of harm is of tantamount importance in each and every case. In the next chapter, specific populations of teenagers most at risk for self-injury are discussed as the underlying complexity of these distressing actions are brought into clearer focus.

Chapter 2

Special Populations, Special Concerns: Teenagers Most at Risk

Everyone focuses on the cutting because they can see it and it freaks them out. It's just something I do to relieve all the pain. No one seems to care about all the other even worse stuff I've been dealing with forever.
    20-year-old struggling with bulimia and an early history of sexual abuse

Although all adolescents face a host of developmental stressors that may trigger problematic behaviors, certain teens are clearly at higher risk for self-injury. First, we know that females self-injure at higher rates than males, and the reasons for this deserve explanation. Second, females who have been sexually or physically abused are especially prone to self-harm behaviors and require interventions honed to their special concerns. Third, teens with eating disorders, anorexia nervosa or bulimia nervosa, frequently extend their bodily conflicts to overt self-harm. Cutting and other forms of self-mutilation often occur in concert with the nutritional destructiveness seen in malnourishment and excessive purging. Fourth, individuals who have been labeled as having borderline personality disorder (BPD) frequently exhibit self-injurious behavior. The emotional instability, relational conflicts, and impulsivity associated with this diagnostic classification appear to generate the angst and desperation associated with individuals who resort to cutting and the like to quell despair. Fifth, individuals in closed settings such as hospitals, prisons, and residential care facilities exhibit a high rate of self-injury. In fact, self-harm is frequently seen as a contagious phenomenon in such settings. This chapter will discuss the special issues associated with each of these five groups who are at the highest risk for self-harm.

THE GENDER FACTOR: WHY MORE FEMALES THAN MALES SELF-INJURE

Although estimates vary, it is generally agreed that self-injury occurs more frequently in females than males. Why might this be? First, males are more likely to act out their conflicts in externalized behaviors such as aggression, risk taking, alcohol and substance abuse, or overt defiance of authority at home and school. Males who have experienced childhood abuse are more likely to identify with the aggressor and turn their anger on others. Females, on the other hand, are more likely to exhibit internalizing behaviors that manifest in depression, withdrawal, repeated victimization, and self-destructive efforts to control the body, as seen in eating disorders. Self-injury is another form of turning one's pain on oneself. As stated by Miller, "Men act out; women act out by acting in."[40]

Males are also socialized to conceal feelings of pain or weakness; it is far more socially acceptable for women to express such vulnerabilities. Men's unwillingness to reveal self-injury may result in underreporting and, therefore, significant underestimates of these behaviors in men. Similarly, women are more likely in general to seek treatment for emotional problems, whereas men may feel more reluctant to reveal vulnerability and need. As one young male cutter said during a treatment session, "My friends would think cutting is really gay."

Many social and cultural observers have pointed out the changed roles of women in the twenty-first-century United States. More women are expected to work full time and raise children, meet ever-growing standards for beauty, and take on careers of tremendous responsibility. Today, more women than men are accepted into U.S. medical schools. Women have become more visible and influential on a political scale; witness, for example, Secretaries of State Madeleine Albright and Condoleezza Rice; the former television show *Commander in Chief*, which depicted the first female U.S. president; and high-profile members of Congress such as Hillary Rodham Clinton, Nancy Pelosi, and Olympia Snowe. The competing expectations to be competent and successful and yet still nonaggressive and nonthreatening to men place women in an often impossible dilemma. It is understandable that many young women find these expectations overwhelming and respond to their perceived inadequacies with depression, dysfunctional eating, or repetitive self-injury.

Nonetheless, young men do self-injure, do suffer from eating disorders, and do experience the same emotional turmoil and perceived inadequacy more commonly exhibited in women. These males have the added burden of feeling emasculated by a culture that values male strength, power, and stoicism yet deserve the same therapeutic attention afforded women. In young men, the same core adolescent themes of identity, independence, and intimacy are often at the root of the pain and conflicts that underlie their need to self-harm. Difficulties regulating painful emotions and a history of trauma similarly afflict males and females.

The most recent research is beginning to suggest that males are closing the gender gap in regard to self-injury. This may be a result of this newer wave of cutters and of more numerous and less gender-biased studies. For example, Gratz[7] reported finding equal prevalences of cutting in nonclinical samples of males and females. Briere and Gil[6] as well as Gratz, Conrad, and Roemer[8] similarly reported incidences of cutting among males and females in their sample. The metaphorical jury is still out on this issue, however, as evidenced by other studies that emphasize the dominance of females over males who cut, particularly among repeat self-injurers.[11]

Manny is 13. He is small for his age, shy, and decidedly nonathletic. He is used to being teased and feels deeply rejected by the so-called alpha-male culture in his school and community. It seems to him that if you do not play football, baseball, basketball, or soccer, you cease to be seen or valued. Most of the girls he knows also play sports, and he and his few friends feel marginalized and outcast.

Manny will be heading to high school in fall and dreads the transition to a bigger school with much older kids and a hugely athletic focus. In his junior high, he can avoid trouble and has learned to ignore the taunts and minor bullying. High school, however, seems overwhelming, with its aggressive, competitive, and sexualized atmosphere. More than anything, Manny would like to have a girlfriend, but he feels hopeless to compete with the hordes of more confident, physically mature boys around him. Adding insult to injury, because of his small and young appearance, peers frequently called him "a homo," which even had him wondering if he was "normal."

Manny pulls out his hair in clumps when he is overcome with despair and self-hate. It started with only a few hairs, but as he noticed the intense distraction it provided, he began to pull out larger clumps and create more pain. The searing pain would bring tears to his eyes, which would be followed by a flow of tears and a great catharsis. He would then carefully dab at the bloody wound on his scalp and apply antibacterial cream. Each time a scab would form, he found himself picking at it and then caring for the wound once again. This hair pulling persisted, and he also began to insert pins into his fingers until he could no longer bear the pain. Only when his parents brought him to therapy for apparent symptoms of depression did he reveal these behaviors.

SEXUAL ABUSE AND TRAUMA

Many experts have concluded that the most common causal factor related to cutting and other forms of self-injury is a history of sexual abuse and trauma.[3,5,12,41,42] One such study reported that female inpatients who self-injured had significantly higher frequencies of sexual abuse than noninjuring inpatients,[43] whereas another supports these data in reporting that the same was true among female adolescent inpatients.[9] Some authors have reported that 62 percent of sexual abuse victims also engage in cutting.[6,12] Sexual abuse has been reported in 60 percent to 80 percent of borderline patients[44] and in 50 percent of patients with eating disorders.[45] More to the point, among all adolescent psychiatric admissions to the University of California, San Francisco (UCSF) during a six-month period in 1998, 83 percent of patients with histories of sexual abuse also engaged in cutting. The correlations are unmistakable in their implications: Sexual abuse poses an early trauma that can later resurface in the form of self-injurious acts.

Why would childhood sexual abuse create such a legacy of mental illness and self-injury? The violation of sexual abuse can be emotionally devastating. Whether the abuser is a trusted parent, relative, or other adult, the exploitation of a child's body inflicts lifelong damage on emotional regulation, self-image, and relationships. Often the abuse is so traumatic that the child can only cope with the overwhelming horror of the act through dissociation, a form of psychological distancing that helps the child disconnect physically and emotionally from the experience as if in a dreamlike trance. Children often feel too guilty or frightened to report the abuse and bury its legacy in a constellation of depression, powerlessness, low self-esteem, body-image conflicts, and self-destructive patterns. Often these self-destructive patterns lead toward entering other abusive relationships or engaging in self-injurious acts.

Callie and her twin sister, Lucy, were sexually abused by a friend of their parents from ages five through eight. They were lured into this contact by an adult they trusted and who rewarded them with treats, attention, and special gifts. Neither was aware that the other sister was also being abused, and the confusion, shame, and fear kept either from speaking to anyone about it. It was not until they were both in their early twenties that Callie developed severe bulimia and Lucy, always the more subdued twin, became severely depressed. Amazingly, both had been cutters since high school and had hundreds of fortunately superficial scars. Eventually, Callie and Lucy were able to connect the dissociation they experienced during their traumatic history of sexual abuse with the numbing sensations and bodily punishment they reenacted with self-injury.

By no means, however, have all teenagers who exhibit cutting experienced sexual abuse. In fact, the false assumption or groundless suspicion of sexual abuse can severely impede treatment. Many psychological conflicts can be expressed in self-injury, often without any relationship to past victimization whatsoever. Truly, many women who have suffered sexual victimization (an estimated 25% of the population!) prove highly resilient and able to overcome long-term detrimental effects. It should therefore never be assumed that a self-injurer is somehow concealing a history of abuse. There are other forms of trauma in childhood that may be less dramatic yet equally damaging and insidious. For example, contending with an alcoholic parent, experiencing parental divorce, a major medical difficulty, or an ongoing assault on one's sense of competence or social acceptance can all lead toward many of the difficulties perhaps most profoundly seen in patients with overt histories of abuse.

EATING DISORDERS: ANOREXIA NERVOSA AND BULIMIA

Virtually synonymous with female adolescence, eating disorders almost always emerge in girls during the teen years. Both disorders are fraught with body-image and impulse-control struggles and can be quite debilitating and even deadly. In anorexia nervosa, girls essentially starve themselves by restricting their food intake and exercising excessively to the point of emaciation. This starvation can create grave medical instability and become a highly intractable problem. In bulimia, girls binge on large quantities of high-calorie foods and then vomit or abuse laxatives to avoid weight gain. This cycle can become an obsessive preoccupation and lead to numerous episodes of binging and purging each day. The medical risks with bulimia are also significant, as electrolyte imbalances can lead to fainting and heart attacks and the abused gastrointestinal tract can develop perforations and ulcers.

Beyond the medical risks, the social and emotional tolls of eating disorders are high. Anorexics typically become socially withdrawn and isolated as their flagging energy and sense of alienation intrude on their interest in peers. Depression can be significant, concentration wanes, and intense anxiety about gaining weight creates a fearful sense of slavery to the disorder. The psychological effects of starvation are well documented and include depression, obsessive rumination about food, compulsive behavior rituals, difficulty concentrating, and an overarching sense of intense physical and psychic discomfort. At worst, anorexics can die from starvation. There is a 5 percent mortality rate in anorexia nervosa, among the highest for any psychiatric illness.[46] Death due to either starvation or suicide are the two leading causes of death in patients with anorexia nervosa.[47]

Bulimics, who are sometimes seen as unsuccessful anorexics, succumb to their hungry impulses with a vengeance. Binges can involve huge quantities of food, and the purging rituals involve terrific misery, shame, and isolation.

Bulimics are often noted to have a variety of additional impulsive behaviors, which may include sexual indiscretion, alcohol or drug abuse, kleptomania, or self-injurious behaviors like cutting.

Teens with eating disorders frequently express their torment through cutting in an effort to punish, purge, and take control of their bodies. Thus, many teens who become repetitive cutters also struggle with ongoing eating disorders and require well-coordinated treatment plans with medical, psychological, and often pharmacological intervention. Bulimic patients in particular are frequently so distressed and disorganized by their lacking sense of self-control that cutting emerges as another form of self-punishment and desperation.

Lana has been secretly binging and vomiting for months. Since turning 16, and suffering a painful rejection by her boyfriend, Lana has become preoccupied with "hating" her body for being "so fat." She has tried to fast during the day, only to succumb to the hunger imperative that strikes her at night with a vengeance. She binges voraciously, secretly, and with a horrible sense of shame and self-loathing. An intensive purging process is her effort to reverse these awful feelings and regain a sense of esteem and calm. Sometimes she is so disgusted with herself that she augments the purging with angry stabbing wounds to her thighs and stomach. Although the wounds are shallow, inflicted with a pair of nail scissors, the pain and blood eloquently articulate her self-rejection and despair. Although she remains intensely secretive regarding the bulimia, she wishes that someone would notice her cuts and the cries of pain they represent.

BORDERLINE PERSONALITY DISORDER: WHAT IS IT AND WHY DOES IT LEAD TO SELF-INJURY?

The most common diagnosis associated with repetitive self-injury is borderline personality disorder. Borderline personality disorder (BPD) is defined in the *Diagnostic and Statistical Manual of Mental Disorders* (4th ed.) by the American Psychiatric Association (1994) as "A pervasive pattern of instability of interpersonal relationships, self-image, and affects, and marked impulsivity beginning by early adulthood. . . . Symptoms include strong fears of abandonment, unstable and intense relationships, identity disturbance, impulsivity, recurrent suicidal or self-mutilating behavior, affective instability, feelings of emptiness and intense anger, and sometimes, paranoid or dissociative symptoms." If this constellation of Sturm und Drang brings to mind the classic volatility of many adolescents, it speaks to the need to go beyond behavioral symptoms in assigning this diagnostic label to adolescents who are, by definition, often highly emotional and erratic.

Authors such as Otto Kernberg have stressed identity diffusion as the sine qua non of BPD.[48] Lacking identity integration leads to extremely contradictory behaviors, self-perceptions, and views of others as well as chronic feelings of emptiness and depressive loneliness. Borderline patients are viewed by Kernberg as having ineffective psychological defenses against the anxiety associated with their internal and interpersonal conflicts. Marsha Linehan[36] similarly stresses the inability of the borderline patient to modulate strong affects and subsequent tendency to become overwhelmed and seek relief through cutting.

Taken together, the concept of BPD has evolved to represent an emotionally volatile, insecurely attached, impulsive, and depressive individual, usually female, who is highly likely to engage in suicidal or self-injurious behaviors. Clearly, then, one would expect a high degree of correlation between the clinical presentation of the typical teenage cutter and the typical so-called borderline. Given that the typical cutter is in the throes of adolescent development with its inherent identity, relational, and independence challenges, however, it is important to realize that adolescents are in a time of immense transition and therefore should not be labeled BPD. Many teens, and many cutters, emerge from adolescence into healthy and satisfying adult lives.

Although a diagnosis of BPD should not be given to anyone under the age of 18, many of its core features can be extremely useful in understanding and relating to teens who self-injure. Self-injuring teens have tremendous difficulty managing intense emotions and developing a stable sense of self- and interpersonal connection. Given their turmoil and poorly developed coping mechanisms, they are therefore prone to acting out their distress in self-destructive behaviors.

The most problematic aspect of the BPD diagnosis is its stigma. To many, BPD is a highly pejorative label that ultimately interferes with patients accessing the optimal treatment they deserve. The BPD label often suggests to therapists both intransigence and emotionally demanding characteristics that merely cause therapists to hold little hope or desire to work with these individuals.

BPD also has been dismissed as a so-called wastebasket diagnosis for individuals with perplexing and troubling symptoms, often with pejorative overtones. It can be an ultimately unhelpful and even destructive term in that it can be code for *undesirable patient*. Individuals with the BPD constellation of symptoms experience significant distress and genuine pain in their own uniquely human manner, thus defying simple categorization. Clinicians and loved ones should never lose sight of these patients' courage in seeking help and change. This ability to persevere and reach out to professionals for help should in many ways be applauded and regarded as a truly hopeful sign.

Finally, BPD has been criticized as a term laden with sexism that is only rarely applied to men. Women are frequently dismissed as BPD in the same way that women in the early 1900s were viewed as so-called hysterics. Both labels conjure images of helpless, needy, overly emotional, and even childish behavior that is rarely attributed to men. It can be akin to dismissing a woman's honest anger and emotional distress as "just PMS," often an invalidating and condescending attribution. Thus, the diagnosis must be communicated to patients, professionals, and families in a meaningful way that does not convey the pejorative labels that so often do an immense disservice to individuals suffering with these difficulties.

Ann is undergoing her sixth inpatient hospitalization for suicide threats and intense symptoms of anxiety and depression. Her anxiety is palpable in her shaking legs, rapid speech, and pleading for extra doses of Ativan, an antianxiety medication. She has a long history of multiple self-injuries and has made two suicide attempts involving intentional overdoses of her medications. An extremely bright young woman no longer able to remain enrolled in the Ivy League university she attended for two years, Ann has been unable to manage her overwhelming feelings of emotional distress.

Ann forms intensely dependent relationships with therapists and has volatile, often angry relationships with friends and family. Despite her many accomplishments, she is racked with self-doubt and unable to secure a job due to her disabling anxiety. Cutting, burning, and even hitting her head against the wall are often her only means of calming the searing, panicky distress of despair and loneliness. After self-injuring, she often phones her therapist in search of some reassurance, empathy, and suggestions for getting through the day. She has carried the diagnoses of borderline personality disorder and generalized anxiety disorder, but to those who know her she is a highly likable but insecure, overly sensitive, and enigmatic young woman.

INSTITUTIONS AND SOCIAL CONTAGION

Adolescents, almost by definition, are vulnerable to peer pressure and peer norms. As anyone working with adolescents confined to an inpatient unit, residential facility, boarding school, or juvenile detention facility can attest, many negative behaviors become highly contagious. Not only can these include self-injury and suicide attempts, but bulimia, anorexia, drug abuse, and violence also can escalate quickly in closed settings.

Increasingly, self-mutilation has taken on an almost faddish quality in that many girls begin injuring themselves in direct imitation of others. Taiminen and colleagues[18] concluded in their study of adolescent female inpatients that a majority of deliberate self-harm incidents may be triggered by contagion. In fact, deliberate self-harm can spread through an inpatient setting, impacting even those patients who were previously unaware of its existence. Offer and Barglow[49] noted that self-mutilators were often group leaders, and their behavior was widely imitated with a "ritualistic exhibitionistic character." Rosen and Walsh[17] viewed self-mutilation as an outward display of affiliation and bonding. Their findings further demonstrated that self-mutilation incidents occurred in clusters throughout the year and were even more contagious than suicidal behavior among adolescent inpatients.

Hospitalized and incarcerated youth are most vulnerable to self-injury and contagion for a number of reasons. First, the dysfunction that led to their confinement may indicate underlying personality disorders, impulse-control disorders, or other difficulties that leave them more impaired than other youth in coping with emotions and peer influence. Second, institutional life is notorious for exacerbating underlying pathology in that individuals often feel stripped of their identity and sense of control, leading to intense despair and anger. By self-injuring, these adolescents can feel powerful, as staff members generally react with frustration and anxiety to these morbid actions.

Furthermore, a sense of belonging and connection to their peers is enhanced by what is often an initiation rite involving self-harm. Group acceptance in confined settings may feel tantamount to survival for the teen, isolated from familiar family and friends within an institutional setting. Even primates have been observed to engage in self-injury when stressful changes occur within the confined environment, such as a change in room population or overcrowding.[50] Taiminen et al. conclude that social isolation and social stress within an over-populated closed ward, combined with female adolescents exquisitely vulnerable to imitation, enhance the risk of contagion.

Although incarcerated and hospitalized youth are particularly susceptible to suicidal and self-injurious contagion, nonclinical settings also witness contagion of self-injury. Junior and senior high school settings are increasingly reporting self-injurious behavior, and contagion may be seen in settings as seemingly benign as summer camps. Episodes of suicide attempts increase among peers immediately following publicized cases. In fact, contagion increases following newspaper coverage and in accordance with the intensity of publicity surrounding the incident. Suicide watches are commonly undertaken in schools and communities after a youth has tragically killed him- or herself, as copycat suicides are often attempted by other vulnerable teens.

Similarly, many teens in my own practice have reported acquiring the notion to harm themselves only after learning about peers who have done so. Witnessing the scarring and dramatic evidence of internal pain and anger often speaks to a distressed teen's own despair, as she in essence thinks to herself, "That's exactly how I feel." Cutting becomes a form of identification with others who mark themselves as enigmas, misfits, sufferers, and bold renegades by virtue of their wounds. Teenagers often can list a number of fellow students identified as cutters, a group designation joining the ranks of jocks, geeks, stoners, and nerds in the adolescent nomenclature.

The psychologist at a private prep school contacted me regarding a rash of self-injuries among the female students. So far, six girls have been sent to the counselor by teachers noticing their scars, and word has spread that many other girls also have been cutting but have not yet been discovered. In speaking with each of the six girls, the school psychologist noted that all of them were aware of other cutters on campus but were adamant in dismissing any suggestion that they were imitating anyone else. All of the girls were defensive, and only a few admitted to emotional distress and life difficulties as prompting the cutting. The psychologist was seeking a means of addressing this growing destructive trend on campus and also of reaching these girls who were obviously expressing some pain and desire for attention and help.

The generation gap that exists between youth fashion, music, tattoos, icons, and the like similarly exists with cutting. Parents and other adults are often uniquely shocked and stunned by such behavior, whereas among teens it is becoming increasingly fashionable. Within certain populations of adolescents, self-injury poses an especially prominent threat and represents but one of a number of complex difficulties. Helping parents and teens understand the developmental conflicts and challenges that underlie self-injury is more important than focusing solely on a campaign to stop the behavior. In teens and young adults with histories of trauma and abuse, eating disorders, and borderline personality disorder, the deeper sources of their need to self-injure must be addressed in a sensitive and comprehensive treatment framework.

CONCLUSIONS

This chapter has described specific adolescent populations most at risk for self-injury. Teens who are female, eating disordered, struggling with borderline personality features, confined to institutions, or victims of childhood sexual abuse and trauma are at the highest risk for repetitive self-injury. Adolescents in closed settings, correctional or psychiatric, are particularly vulnerable to these behaviors and are also the most susceptible to social contagion. Given the epidemic spread of cutting among middle and high school populations, however, cutting has come to serve as an outlet for even subclinical adolescent conflicts and struggles, further popularized by social contagion. In the next chapter, the developmental challenges of adolescence are addressed as well as how these difficulties can manifest as self-injury in otherwise "healthy" adolescents.

Chapter 3

Developmental Challenges in Adolescence: The Agony, the Ecstasy, the Cell Phone, and the Internet

I have no idea who I am anymore. There's this whole dark side of me that's been taking over.

14-year-old self-injurer

One minute I can hardly recognize her for all the hostility and screwing up. Then the next minute she's sitting in my lap and wanting to be held like a little girl again.

Father of 15-year-old girl

Adolescence is first and foremost a cataclysmic transition. The wholesale transition from child to adult does not come easily or smoothly and can be fraught with tumult, pain, and conflict. The seemingly erratic and irrational manifestations of adolescent angst do in fact have rhyme and reason, and it is the identification of the healthy developmental goals underlying problematic behavior that holds the key to useful intervention. The inexorable drive toward adulthood competes with the tugs of childhood dependency and innocence, creating an ambivalence that can be maddeningly confusing for both the teens and parents.

The virtually universal challenges of adolescence can be summed up in three central themes: (1) identity formation, (2) independence, and (3) intimacy and sexuality. All of these developmental tasks involve lifelong struggles, yet adolescents face the onslaught of these challenges at a particularly unsteady time of life. The mammoth biological and emotional changes of puberty, the need to let go of parental dependencies in pursuit of intensified peer relationships, and the dual temptations and terrors of greater independence all collide during the teenage years. Imagine a rock climber about to repel down a massive cliff for the first time. She has been reassured that the rope will assure her safety, that all she has to do is fall back and allow the rope to catch and support her successive leaps during the descent. Yet there is that breathless moment of letting go, of feeling unsupported and at enormous risk, until the rope does indeed take hold. This combination of terror and exhilaration in the climber's moment of free fall can be likened to the confluence of emotions faced by the adolescent traversing the often steep terrain between childhood and adulthood.

PUBERTAL TIMING: THE NEGATIVE PSYCHOSOCIAL EFFECTS OF EARLY MATURATION IN FEMALES

Puberty is viewed as the pivotal developmental milestone marking the onset of adolescence. In addition to considerable physical and hormonal changes, puberty invokes major transitions in psychological and social development. Chris Hayward, MD,[51] has edited an in-depth and scholarly book that addresses gender-based biological and psychosocial consequences of puberty. Boys, for example, typically welcome the physical changes of puberty, as increased strength, height, hair growth, and voice changes are generally consistent with social expectations valuing these assets in males. Girls, on the other hand, frequently abhor the rapid changes in their bodies, experiencing unwelcome weight gain, menstruation, and feelings of vulnerability as newly visible, overt sexual beings. According to research, white and African American girls are developing secondary sex characteristics at an increasingly early age in the United States, with visual changes occurring at a mean age of 8.9 years in African Americans and 10.0 years in whites.[52] Other research using onset of menarche as the measure of pubertal onset, however, has found that the mean age has not changed from 12.2 years in African American girls and 12.9 years in white girls.[53] What remains less controversial is the consistent finding that girls who do mature earlier than their peers are at increased risk for a variety of difficulties. Girls who are forced to confront these developmental and social challenges at an earlier stage of psychological maturity are not surprisingly more susceptible to psychosocial difficulties than their on-time or late-maturing peers.

Specifically, early-developing girls have been found to show more internalizing problems such as depression, eating disorders, and low self-esteem. They are also more likely to interact with older-age peers, thus rendering them more susceptible to externalizing behaviors such as high-risk sexual contact, drug and alcohol abuse, and delinquency.[54] Many of the early-maturing teenage girls presenting to me for treatment are precociously sexualized and become targets for older males long before they are cognitively, socially or emotionally mature enough to make healthy decisions in matters regarding sex, drugs, and high-risk behavior. These heightened physical and social demands thrust upon girls at a younger age appear to overwhelm many adolescents' ability to cope in a healthy manner. Thus, early maturation in females represents a risk factor for a variety of emotional and behavioral problems.

Interestingly, one of the primary biological factors thought to influence early maturation is related to the chemical leptin produced by adipose tissue.[55] Moderate obesity has been clearly associated with earlier menstruation, and given the increasing rate of obesity in the United States, it is understandable that more girls are reaching puberty at an earlier age.[56] Dovetailing with this weight-related factor is the heightened aversion girls have to weight gain given the ever-oppressive cultural imperatives around thinness and beauty. Thus, girls who are confronted both with unwanted weight gain and with premature sexual development are subjected to additional tumult at puberty. Not only do early-maturing girls diet more and have more negative views about their bodies,[57] they also develop more problematic eating habits that can persist throughout adolescence.[58]

The following case history of an early-developing 13-year-old girl helps illustrate the pressure early puberty provokes.

Norma was referred for treatment after having been caught with marijuana at school. She admitted smoking numerous times, but never before at school. She had been suspended, and both she and her parents were highly motivated to address the difficulties this event exposed. Norma was a precociously developed girl with full breasts and a curvaceous build, conspicuously taller and more mature than her peers. It quickly became apparent in talking with Norma that the marijuana represented only the tip of the iceberg regarding the depth of troubles she was experiencing.

First, Norma revealed that she had been labeled a slut at school and felt crudely ridiculed by the boys and ostracized by the girls. She was sent lewd and offensive e-mails and found graffiti bearing her name and the words *school slut* throughout the school. She discovered her only form of connection and approval through providing oral sex to various boys in her school, seeming to adopt the identity that had been thrust upon her. She stated that she did not even know why she engaged in oral sex, did not like it, and had a strikingly blasé attitude toward it.

In addition, she had been chatting with various men over the Internet, as her parents were stunned to discover. Opening several highly provocative e-mails between Norma and seemingly random, lascivious men, her parents became alarmed. Again, Norma seemed nonplussed by these revelations, seemingly oblivious to any problematic implications of her burgeoning sexual promiscuity. Her primary concerns were feeling fat, lonely, and oppressed by her parents' mounting restrictions. She revealed a litany of superficial scratch marks on her arms, saying that they too were "no big deal." She also had been on a shoplifting spree, finding it "exciting," despite having little interest in the goods she stole. Altogether, her behavior was alarming, yet she remained oddly disconnected from the implications of her actions.

Norma's after-school time with friends was greatly restricted, and her computer was moved into the kitchen where she could be supervised. She felt angry and cut off from a social life, despite not feeling that she had any real friends. She began to cut herself more frequently and deeply, saying that she did not know what else to do when alone. Her behavior culminated one evening when her parents received a 3:00 A.M. phone call from the police stating that she had been located drinking in the car of a 22-year-old man. She admitted to having had sexual intercourse with this man but denied that it was forced upon her.

Clearly, Norma's behavior was out of control, placing her at serious risk for physical harm. Emotionally, Norma did not have the tools to comprehend the danger of the choices she was making, feeling driven purely by the excitement she felt with guys, drugs, and risk taking. Although cutting was a part of her symptomatic picture, all of these problematic behaviors pointed to a teen wholly overwhelmed by her precocious sexuality, powerful drives, and confusing social difficulties. For Norma, the adolescent tasks related to intimacy, identity, and independence were thrown off course by her early sexual maturation clashing against her ill-equipped psychosocial maturity.

IDENTITY FORMATION: WHO AM I BECOMING?

Identity formation is the ultimate development of an acceptable, realistic, and consistent sense of who one is, how one relates to others, and what roles, aptitudes, and values form the structure of one's life. Erik Erikson, in his seminal work on human development, defined the central task of adolescence as the establishment of identity.[59] Identity is rarely solidified by the end of the teen years, often evolving over the course of one's lifetime, but a consistent sense of self that can guide decision-making becomes more clearly integrated during the course of adolescence. Identity confusion can result in the appearance of troubling symptoms such as depression, anxiety, hostility, school failure, unsatisfying relationships, high-risk behavior, and self-doubt, even in seemingly well-adjusted and gifted teens. The types of ordinary conflicts confronted by ordinary teens illustrate the challenge of determining one's path in the face of competing emotions.

Krista has always been a good student, abiding by rules and seeking the approval of teachers and parents. Her best friend wants her to cut school this afternoon and go to the beach with two very attractive sophomore boys. She is torn between two competing desires: to bond with her friends and yet avoid getting in trouble. Is she someone who plays it safe and sticks to the rules or someone who takes risks and makes friends and fun a priority? She is not sure how she can accomplish both, so she takes off with her friends and will test the consequences later.

When later arrives, Krista learns that the school noted her absence and contacted her parents. She is suspended for two days from school, and her parents furiously read her the riot act, adding one week of being grounded for good measure. The next six months involve escalating conflict between Krista and her parents over time spent with friends. Krista sometimes gouges her fingernails into her thighs in frustration and loneliness, quietly leaving a patchwork of bruises and bloody punctures on her skin.

Angela is in love with Greg. He wants to have intercourse, and she is conflicted. Should she say no as her conscience tells her or say yes in response to her compelling sexual desire? What about pregnancy and sexually transmitted diseases? What about her virginity? She is not prepared to make such a complex decision. At the same time, she wants Greg to choose the same local college for next year, but he wants to accept admission to a college across the country. She thinks she wants to study communications, but she is not really sure. Also, should she play soccer in college or devote her time and energy to her studies? At home, her parents find her unusually hostile and do not know what to make of it. She seems tense and volatile and yet she will not tell them what is troubling her.

Angela does not begin cutting until her first year at college. She misses Greg and begins a series of unsatisfying, sexually exploratory relationships. With the added pressures of school, she feels her identity as a solid student and stable girlfriend threatened. She begins to diet in an effort to feel back in control and punishes herself with harsh exercise regimens and razor cuts when the impulse to give into her hunger feels overwhelming.

Even the healthiest of adolescents struggle with making choices consistent with their self-image. The increased complexity of choices during the teen years understandably creates confusion and conflict. In less well-adjusted teens, such as those who resort to cutting, these conflicts can prove overwhelming and result in problematic behaviors and unmanageable emotions. At the core is a struggle to integrate a satisfying identity amid a plethora of pushes and pulls.

This imperative is confronted at a time of life when adolescents are even more concerned about how they are viewed by others than how they view themselves, and this mutual process of establishing image and identity evolves within the complex social spheres of teens.

INDEPENDENCE: FREEDOM AND RESPONSIBILITY

Independence is achieved, however tentatively, in a tightrope walk between easing yet not severing parental attachments (the proverbial net) while establishing a sense of competent independence. The young adolescent is called upon to become less dependent on parents for both intimacy and decision-making assistance as she ventures more earnestly into friendships, sexual relationships, and autonomous pursuits outside the home. It is a seesaw of emotional peril and exhilaration for both the adolescent and her parents. Adolescents are called upon to demonstrate greater independence and responsibility, whereas their parents are required to relinquish control and tolerate the diminished closeness they can enjoy with their children. Joanna and Alicia, two adolescents grappling with their parents over issues of independence, provide two examples of this balancing act parents and teens must perform.

Joanna does not want to go along on her family's annual camping trip. She wants to stay home and be with her friends, as she insists any rational 16-year-old would want. Her parents are sad and hurt that she does not want to accompany them and simultaneously worried about her staying behind without their supervision. How can they negotiate a solution that maintains family relationships but allows Joanna increased independence with appropriate safeguards? They reach a compromise that enables Joanna to bring a friend along and a promise to stop at the outlet shopping center on the way home.

Alicia is sick and tired of her parents micromanaging her homework. They are constantly talking with her teachers, checking her work, and nagging her to study. She says she can handle her classes herself and wants to be independent. Yet her grades have been poor, and the school has been expressing concern about her incomplete homework and low exam scores. How can Alicia demonstrate an ability to be responsibly independent; that is, how can she convince her parents to back off yet improve her schoolwork on her own? They agree to back off from their involvement with her schoolwork and instead enlist a tutor to assist Alicia. They agree that she must show improvement in her work or she will face computer and cell phone restrictions and a resumption of her parents' anxious involvement.

These are common, age-appropriate parent-child conflicts over issues of increasing autonomy and independence. When parents insist on relentless control and unilateral decision-making, they risk alienating their teens by building a chasm of resentment and noncommunication. When parents too freely relinquish oversight, teens are at risk for exercising poor judgment and making deleterious decisions. Thus, a teeter-totter of negotiation must ensue in order to achieve a judicious balance between safe limits yet validation of the teen's increasing ability to handle greater levels of freedom. Mistakes and missteps must be tolerated by families and integrated into continued developmental aims. Similarly, emotionally enmeshed families risk smothering the teen's sense of confidence by fueling anxiety and preventing the teen from acting independently with success. In such cases, the teen can be stuck between anxious dependency and an attitude of rebellion that forcefully demands more autonomy.

The natural ambivalence experienced by adolescents between dependence and independence is often confusing and exasperating to parents. Adolescent conflicts are rife with contradictions. Proclamations and behaviors can seem utterly irrational, actions directly opposite the attitudes espoused. On the one hand, adolescents demand independence but, on the other hand, gripe that their parents forgot to put their essay in their backpack or demand that parents take responsibility for their schedule, transportation, and spending money. On the one hand, adolescents proclaim that they can handle things on their own yet betray that boast with school difficulties and, in the case of the self-injurer, wounds that speak volumes as much about helplessness as about autonomy. Decoding the conflict and simultaneously appreciating each side of the coin can greatly assist parents and clinicians in intervening evenly and effectively without tipping the balance of ambivalence to one extreme or the other.

Ambivalence refers to competing feelings, needs, or desires. For example, we may not want it to rain so we can be outdoors, but we do want it to rain for the sake of the plants and water supply. Emotionally, we may deeply love a friend yet at the same time deeply resent certain aspects of his or her behavior. With teens who self-injure, ambivalence is intense. Wanting freedom and independence yet fearing it, wanting emotional help but feeling humiliated by it, and yearning for romance yet feeling extremely anxious about intimacy are but a few examples of such ambivalence. The ritual of cutting seems to at once say, "I want you to understand me" and "Stay out of my business." Clinicians and parents must be equipped to negotiate such contradictions, fully understanding that both feelings can indeed exist simultaneously.

Sometimes, the louder and more urgent the demand made by the teen, the more anxious is the ambivalence that underlies it. Screaming "Stay out of my life," "I have everything under control," and "I don't need anything from you" with slammed doors and tearfulness may just as likely speak to adolescents' despair over their own neediness, dependency, and lack of control. Similarly, the adolescent who on the one hand adamantly maintains that her eating disorder is not a problem yet leaves flagrant evidence of binging and purging for her parents to find is having difficulty owning both sides of their ambivalence. Finally, the teen who insists on privacy and decorates her door with "Stay Out" signs in 12 different languages is just as likely to be the teen who "accidentally" leaves her diary in plain sight. One must often ask that if the teen is so confidently independent, so happy, and so fully in control, why must she so vehemently and desperately deny evidence to the contrary?

The flip side of these conflicts is also apparent. The adolescent who complains that she has no control over her behavior is refusing to take responsibility for the control she can in fact assert. The challenge in intervening with all of these mixed messages is to supportively acknowledge and make explicit both sides of the ambivalence.

INTIMACY AND SEXUALITY

Intimate and sexual relationships are, of course, lifelong themes for all of us, but adolescents are especially challenged as a result of pubertal changes and the onset of overtly romantic and sexual involvements. An imperative developmental goal is the ability to relate honestly and rewardingly with others and, where appropriate, integrate a responsible and healthy sexuality into one's intimate relationship. Adolescents are caught in the throes of intense sexual desires and demands, enormous needs for acceptance and affiliation, and the often confusing task of defining one's sexual orientation, identity, and boundaries. These challenges erupt during a time of increased freedom and decreased parental attachments, making for an often tumultuous and sometimes hazardous period of development.

Every era has its sexual norms and dating rituals. The beginning of the twenty-first century in the United States has witnessed a relational pattern newly labeled *hooking up*. Hookups are casual, no-strings-attached, sexual meetings between teenagers, usually devoid of emotional investment. Teens often will engage with numerous hookup partners interchangeably, and peer groups freely mix and match partners without apparent jealousies or expectations. This form of sexual exploration, though allowing immediate fulfillment of sexual impulses, fails to integrate feelings of affection, love, affiliation, or sometimes even genuine attraction. In fact, adolescents often will argue that it is exactly such vulnerable feelings that they want to avoid. Thus, a generation of young people is integrating a model of intimacy and sexuality that views attachment and commitment as anathema. As a result, teen sexual relationships are experienced by many as curiously empty and detached.

This free-for-all of sexual exploration is incumbent upon the peer group formed, and the attendant factor that dating as we know it is no longer standard practice. Teens go out in groups, split off briefly for rendezvous, and reintegrate back into the sense of group as opposed to individual affiliation. Many adolescents are intimidated by this type of sexual exploration and expectation, and others wonder how to understand and contend with bothersome feelings of longing and attachment that are no longer socially acceptable. Thus, teens are expected to jump into and out of sexual involvements long before they have the maturity or even minimal emotional connection to provide any semblance of security.

Thalia is 13 and wants desperately to be accepted by a group of friends at school. The girls in the group are "fast," and tell Thalia about their sexual exploits, mainly in providing oral sex to boys. The boys seek out these girls, and Thalia does not want to be left out. She finds herself in a series of sexual relationships that she finds degrading, lonely, and devoid of pleasure. She does not know how to integrate these experiences into her self-image and finds herself increasingly passive and unable to set appropriate boundaries. Before she knows it, she has a reputation at school as a slut, and she resigns herself to this label as a plausible new identity.

Jen has just been given the cold shoulder by a guy she has hooked up with on numerous occasions. Although she agreed to these hookups, she has developed real feelings of fondness and attachment. She feels rejected and unexpectedly bereft and becomes deeply depressed. She seeks solace in a series of new partners, which ultimately fails to bring her the sense of secure connection she craves.

Adolescents facing these conflicts increasingly resort to self-injury as a form of acting out, expressing and releasing unwanted distress in the crescendo of pain and defiance. All teens in treatment need to have their sexual and relational challenges acknowledged, dignified, and integrated into their conscious choices and identities. It is not uncommon for teens to find themselves flabbergasted to learn that these drives and dilemmas are entirely normal and yet may lie at the root of their self-destructive impulses.

DEVELOPMENTAL CRISES

All adolescents must grapple with life challenges related to identity formation, autonomy, and intimacy. Distress and confusion are virtually inescapable by-products of these struggles. For some adolescents, however, these challenges prove so painful and overwhelming as to compel them to act in self-damaging ways. Drug abuse, school failure, promiscuity, risk-taking, and rebellion are quintessential pitfalls of adolescence. Increasingly, self-injury is becoming a prevalent symptom of an adolescent in crisis and is no longer the sole domain of the severely pathological individual.

For teens experiencing a developmental roadblock related to intimacy, identity, or the quest for independence, their private pain can become unbearable. As we will discuss in the next chapter, cutting provides a perverse means of temporarily alleviating intense distress, of seeking control, and communicating internal complexities to others. Adolescents with conflicts related to their body image and appearance are especially vulnerable to inflicting punitive wounds rife with self-loathing, reducing a world of misery to the now visible and flagrantly legible blood and scarring.

Other teens seek to medicate their misery with drugs or alcohol. Some rebel against parents and school authority, resulting in academic suicide or police contact. Many teens express their turmoil in high-risk acts such as driving dangerously, running away, or stealing. Sexual indiscretions also can take on a frankly self-destructive tone. It is not uncommon to find teens in treatment engaging in many of these self-destructive acts simultaneously, and cutting may be just one component of a chaotic adolescence. Few red flags, however, so clearly scream distress than the appearance of self-inflicted, bloody wounds.

When self-injury (and other forms of self-destructive behavior) becomes an entrenched act that precludes the teen from progressing forward in their development, a crisis can ensue. They or their worlds can seem to be falling apart. Their behavior may bear little resemblance to their pre-adolescent functioning, and they can become fragile, volatile, violent, withdrawn, and stuck beneath collapsing academic, social, and familial structures. Every effort to help the teen progress in these real-life challenges should be made and the focus placed on their well-being and life goals as opposed to the cutting per se. Only once the teen has adequate supports, insights, tools, and motivations to meet their healthy needs and strivings can the crutch or coping mechanism of self-injury be weaned away.

Neil has seemingly quit participating in his life. Despite being threatened with expulsion from school due to academic failure, a complete withdrawal from social contacts and activities, and a seeming deterioration in his mood, health, and interest in life, he essentially has refused to discuss or make changes in his situation. Neil's peers seem to be moving on rapidly without him, and he feels more and more alienated and hopeless. No form of cajoling, reasoning, pleading, or threatening seems to engage or energize him. He smokes pot, uncaringly burns holes in his skin, draws morbid quotations and pictures on his bedroom wall, and passively listens to talk about being sent to a treatment school in Utah. Neil is deeply depressed and experiencing a pivotal developmental crisis.

DEFICITS IN ADOLESCENT SELF-CAPACITIES

Three so-called self-capacities, as defined within the constructivist self-development theory,[60, 61] are particularly relevant in teens who self-injure. These are the developmentally determined abilities to (1) tolerate strong affect, (2) maintain a sense of self-worth, and (3) maintain a sense of connection to others. Research has shown that individuals with histories of self-injury show greater impairment in these self-capacities than do noninjuring individuals.[62] Furthermore, individuals with a history of childhood abuse were found to have even greater impairments in self-capacities.

Given the central tasks of adolescent development, these three self-capacities have particular relevance to the understanding and treatment of self-injury. Virtually all adolescents who repeatedly engage in self-harm do so partially out of an inability to sufficiently manage, soothe, or tolerate strong negative emotions. Cutting and other self-injuries serve as a coping mechanism to compensate for this deficit, as cutting almost always results in a feeling of relief, numbness, or other suppression of painful affect. Thus, not only are adolescents who self-injure coping with the normal challenges of adolescence, they are doing so without the adequate skills to manage strong affect. These deficits in affect tolerance may be related to developmental conditions dating back to childhood, a disruptive history of abuse or trauma, or simply an overreactive nervous system that becomes rapidly overwhelmed by emotions. Thus, teens who cut may need to bolster their coping mechanisms when experiencing painful emotions as well as better understanding their own emotional and biological reactivity.

The second self-capacity, the ability to maintain a consistent sense of self-worth, is notoriously challenging for adolescents but especially for adolescents who self-injure. Frequently, the precipitant or trigger to an onslaught of distress involves a perceived loss of self-esteem, either from a peer rejection, an apparent inadequacy, a negative social comparison, or a direct criticism. The inability to weather a momentary disappointment or integrate one's limitations into the greater whole of one's healthy self-image accounts for much of the turbulence experienced by self-injuring youths. Such teens are often hypersensitive to the opinions of others and easily feel hurt, rejected, or otherwise inadequate. They rarely feel any control over their own sense of worth and are therefore vulnerable to real and imagined external judgment. These painful feelings of inadequacy and worthlessness often are cited by adolescents as a precipitant to the overwhelming emotions that lead to cutting.

The third self-capacity, the ability to maintain a sense of connection to others, is yet another sine qua non of adolescent development. Perhaps at no other time in the life span are interpersonal relationships as exquisitely important and daunting. Youths who harm themselves often seek such connection through the very act of cutting, signaling however cryptically their need for others to see them and care about them. Often a calculated secondary gain of self-injury, scars and wounds generally alert the cavalry to come to the aid of the overwhelmed teen. Frequently, however, self-injury is secretive and extremely private yet sparked by loneliness, despair, anger, or other painful emotions resulting from interpersonal disconnection. Heightened sexual awareness further complicates teens' experience of self and others, provoking an often daunting array of longings, fears, self-doubts, and confusion. Self-injuring adolescents need strong interpersonal support as well as guidance in more productively conducting their relationships. Much of treatment is therefore focused on assisting the teen in meeting his or her social needs.

The concept of self-capacities is helpful to the adolescent and her family in better understanding what deficits exist and where to focus support and intervention. Identifying specific self-capacities that interfere in the adolescent's coping abilities helps teens identify single issues or deficits as opposed to maintaining a global sense of inadequacy and helplessness. Treatment efforts can then be more readily structured and inviting to the teen when the potential payoff of personal effectiveness is made clear.

LARGER SOCIAL AND CULTURAL FACTORS

Since time immemorial, people have engaged in body art, adornment, scarring, and other symbolic rituals involving trauma or visible marking of the skin. In many U.S. cultures, tattoos and piercings are employed much like clothes or hair styles to signify affiliations with subgroups of peer culture and disassociation with mainstream mores. Self-injury can be a truly private act, but more often the evident scarring conveys significant meaning in each person's cultural context.

Although it is beyond the scope of this chapter to address the in-depth social forces acting upon youth in diverse socioeconomic and racial groups, clearly our broader society's ever-increasing focus on appearance makes the skin an ideal billboard for advertising identity. For youths who self-injure, the message is that of a sense of damage, daring, and exquisite pain. Fresh wounds scream more urgently and immediately than the gradually developing evidence of anorexia, bulimia, depression, or sexual abuse, therefore affording the teen immediate and urgent attention.

Media also increasingly highlight sensationalized, aberrant behavior. The explosion of reality television attests to the public's fascination with dysfunction, exhibitionism, and the exposure of private lives. Few behaviors are as shocking as a young person intentionally carving herself bloody, immediately declaring herself a spectacle of pain and fascination. In an ever-competitive society, it may be more difficult to distinguish oneself through one's accomplishments than through the demonstration of victimization or dysfunction. Body art consisting of tattoos or multiple piercings increasingly have become commonplace among adolescents and are generally a more socially acceptable means of self-expression than cutting.

Social contagion has been recognized as a significant influence in the spreading epidemic of cutting. Studies have concluded that even a majority of self-harm incidents on an adolescent psychiatric ward may have been induced by contagion.[12, 14] This spread of self-injurious behavior even was observed in adolescents who had previously been unaware of the existence of this behavior. Self-injury even may be more socially contagious than suicidal behavior among adolescent inpatients.[14] The compelling need for adolescents to identify with peers and try out all sorts of ill-fated activities readily explains the spreading use of cutting as a means of coping with and expressing pain.

TERRORISM AND THE POST-9/11 WORLD: ARE THEY RELATED TO THE UPSURGE IN SELF-INJURY?

The horrific events of September 11, 2001 (9/11), forever etched in the U.S. mindset the power of suicide as a weapon. Anyone who tried to explain to their children on 9/11 why people would kill themselves in an act of terrorism found it is at least as challenging and disturbing a concept to grasp as that of self-inflicted injury. Has the concept of suicide as a weapon, as terrorism, and as a desperate means for disenfranchised people to assert one's rage been hijacked (so to speak) by teenagers who similarly use cutting as a weapon in their battle with parents and development itself?

There are no clear data available on whether there is merely a spurious correlation between the explosion of suicide bombers and teenage self-injury since 2001. At the least, however, 9/11 forever illustrates the devastating power wielded by those threatening to harm themselves. In individuals who feel otherwise helpless and alienated, the destruction of their own bodies can sometimes be parlayed toward attention, extortion, revenge, or some other desired goal. The concept of the hunger strike performed by innumerable prisoners and self-perceived martyrs further illustrates this paradoxical truth.

In a modern world where terrorism prevails on the international stage as one of humanity's ultimate horrors, one must ask how this shifting climate has affected our youth. Where violence seems employed to resolve so many conflicts, would not these highly charged events speak to the increased tendency of youth to resort to self-directed violence as a means of contending with their own problems? The cultural impact of 9/11 and the explosion of world ter-rorism would intuitively seem to influence the mindset of teenagers struggling under the burden of such a violent and threatening world.

SELF-INJURY AND HEIGHTENED ACADEMIC STRESS: TWO INTERACTING EPIDEMICS

Why are cutting and other forms of self-injury becoming increasingly preva-lent in today's teens? One factor receiving recent attention is the phenomenon of multiplying pressures and expectations faced by today's students. Academic demands, competitive college admissions pressures, and the vast array of extra-curricular activities undertaken by middle school and high school students have become staggering in their intensity. High school students typically juggle an ever-increasing array of honors and advanced-placement courses, competitive athletics, and other extracurricular activities both inside and outside of school that places unrealistic demands on their time and energy. Arguing that this frantic pace values achievement over health and learning, researcher Denise Clark Pope, director of the Stressed-Out Students Project at Stanford Uni-versity, asserts, "Now more than ever before, pressure for high achievement in school has become a significant risk factor for adolescent mental and physical health, academic integrity and school engagement."[63]

Pope and a growing number of both academics and educators are leading a national outcry for educational reforms. Research has documented the delete-rious effects of school stress on adolescents, including an explosion in the inci-dence of anxiety and depression, physical complaints, cheating, and the abuse of so-called study drugs such as the stimulants Ritalin and Adderall normally prescribed for the treatment of attention deficit disorders.[64] The desperation to succeed at all costs contributes to the genesis of adolescent eating disor-ders, sleep disorders, clinical depression, somatic complaints (e.g., headaches, stomachaches, fatigue), and debilitating anxiety. Owing to the fact that adoles-cents also are contending with developmental imperatives related to peer rela-tionships, sexuality, identity, and independence, it is easy to understand how stressed and overwhelmed today's teens have become.

A seemingly benign local newspaper article[65] that recently appeared in a sub-urban community illustrates the superhuman expectations of today's college-bound students. In it, a graduating senior is celebrated for her achievements. And wow, what achievements: a 4.27 grade point average, a 1,405 on her SAT, top 10 percent in the National Math Olympiad, holder of four school swimming records, a black belt in jujitsu, and membership in the junior national water polo team. That is not all; this remarkable 18-year-old also teaches self-defense classes, works as a tutor, and received the California Interscholastic Federation Scholar-Athlete of the Year award. Although these exceptional accomplishments certainly deserve admiration, one has to wonder how most mortal teens can compete with such expectations. In fact, few can and, finding it impossible to distinguish themselves in the brutally competitive school environment instead opt for alternative identities, all but abandon their academic strivings.

School teachers and counselors have decried the increase is stress-related problems in their students. Self-injury is a prime example of this level of distress and desperation reaching out-of-control proportions. Adolescents may resort to self-injury to quell anxiety, numb depression, punish perceived failures, or cry out to others for intervention. For many, it is the only way they can communicate their distress and articulate the pressures that feel so all-encompassing. Reevaluating priorities and restricting the number of activities or advanced-placement courses can ease some of these pressures, but clearly, today's ever-growing academic expectations and frantic pace are insidious in schools, homes, and communities and call out for larger-scale intervention.

Case Example: Christina

Christina is a junior at a suburban public high school. She is an A student and closely tracks her grade-point average, which currently hovers around 3.8. She is enrolled in honors chemistry, history, and English and plays on the school water-polo team. She also is an accomplished musician, playing flute in the community youth symphony. Her schedule is a nightmare.

Christina typically rises at 5:30 A.M. for water-polo practice. She begins her classes at 8:00 and gets out of school at 3:00. Her day is long from over, however. After school she meets with her lab partner in chemistry to study for tomorrow's exam before rushing off to symphony practice across town. She returns home at 6:00, exhausted, irritable, and facing the prospect of studying late into the night.

She eats a hurried dinner while checking her e-mail and then tries to study; however, she feels tired and lonely and calls her friend Teresa instead. Teresa is having a crisis of her own regarding her older brother returning home from a drug rehab program, as she wants to go and live with her boyfriend's family while her parents noisily hash things out with him again. Her boyfriend, however, has started smoking pot every day, and she is freaked out by his erratic behavior. Teresa's own use of marijuana has increased along with her stress.

Christina tries to resume studying but only feels more alone after talking with Teresa. She feels she has to stay focused on her grades in order to get into the best college she can. But there is so much competition, and so much work to do, and she feels totally unprepared for her chemistry test tomorrow. The more anxious she feels, the more difficult it becomes to focus. She cannot get anything below an A– on this test or in any of her classes, and if she does not reach her

goal of getting into a prestigious college she will be devastated. Christina studies painstakingly until after midnight, and the whole exhausting, stressful cycle
begins anew the next day.

The meaning and message behind self-injury can only be deciphered in the
context of each adolescent's peer, family, and cultural milieus. This is precisely
why intervention often requires more than a laser focus on the teen's seeming pathology. Intervention is incumbent upon a broader understanding that
includes aspects of the teen's environment that can be drawn on as resources or
addressed as detriments. A biopsychosocial approach emphasizes the need to
integrate biological, psychological, and social factors into a meaningfully individualized treatment strategy. As a result, group psychotherapy, family therapy,
school consultation, and medication can be essential components of a truly
viable and comprehensive intervention strategy.

A NEW GENERATION OF TECHNOTEENS:
TECHNOLOGY AND ADOLESCENTS

Not a single parent of a teenager today grew up with the mass influence of
the cell phone or the Internet. Instant messages, chat rooms, e-mail, Black-
Berries, and the veritable umbilicus of the cell phone are all dramatically new
innovations in human history. It is impossible to discuss teenagers without
understanding the pervasive impact of such technology on the cognitive and
social development of this new age of so-called technoteens.

Consider the following scene. Five teenage friends are sitting together at
a Starbucks table with coffee drinks in hand. Surrounding them are all the
emphatic and spirited sounds of teens socializing: laughter, urgent mono-
logues, attentive "uh-huhs," and the intricate planning of meeting times and
places. Only one thing seems wrong with this picture: All five of the teenagers
are talking on their cell phones to friends other than those beside them. Is there
an odd lack of engagement and intimacy in this scene? Why are they not con-
tent to enjoy one another's company? How has the cell phone revolutionized
the way teens relate?

Similarly, parents are constantly bemoaning the tremendous amount of time
their teenagers spend on the Internet. Entire relationships are forged and extin-
guished online, whereas the threat of a crashed computer feels akin to being isolated on a desert island, cut off from immediate access to scores of people. Not
only can teens use the Internet as a telephone of sorts, but there are also the ubiq-
uitous chat rooms, MySpaces, blogs, and predatory threats that parents fear for
their naive and vulnerable teens. The seduction and actual rendezvous between

predatory adults and trusting teens are commonplace enough activities to cause police departments to employ officers specifically to ward off such attacks.

Even beyond the so-called time suck and potential dangers of the Internet, a generation of alienated youths is one of the potential dire results of this new way of relating through virtual as opposed to face-to-face relationships. Teenagers move much more quickly and comfortably toward sexualized and seductive conversations online than they would ever feel capable of engaging in face-to-face. Hookups and preplanned sexual rendezvous are matter-of-factly arranged online, bypassing the natural inhibitions around direct emotional expression and highly sexualized talk for which self-conscious teens are famous. Parents are frequently stunned by the raw and vivid sexual messages and photos they discover in their teenager's e-mail boxes. Just as destructive are the often vicious, slanderous, and manipulative messages that so devastate self-conscious teens that one angry peer with a personal vendetta can so easily unleash.

Furthermore, technology as a mediator or even as a substitute for real relationships is contributing to a generation of youths who learn to avoid conflict or unpleasantries with peers by simply logging off, ultimately failing to truly engage or build intimacy. The tendency to seek immediate gratification and a quick fix in communication fails to equip teens with the skills necessary for coping effectively with frustration tolerance, loneliness, or conflict. The great irony is that though teens insist that cell phones and the Internet enhance their social lives, research has determined just the opposite.

In a study conducted by researchers at the Carnegie Mellon University,[66] use of the Internet was found "to cause isolation, loneliness and depression." By monitoring the personal computer usage of 169 high school students with widely ranging demographic backgrounds, these researchers found a significant correlation between the amount of time spent on the Internet with "later declines in talking among family members, reductions in the number of friends and acquaintances they kept up with, and increases in depression and loneliness."[67] Of the different computer users studied within families, teenagers not only logged the most online time, they also proved to be the most vulnerable to negative effects.

The authors conclude that many teens substitute superficial online friendships for more meaningful real-life relationships that demand active engagement and both positive and negative interactions. Teens today appear to be poorly equipped and extremely hesitant to face difficult interpersonal situations and may become more easily overwhelmed by painful emotions. Most adolescents who self-injure experience such deficits in their interpersonal relationships, complaining of loneliness, an urgent need for contact, and a catastrophic response to the normal vicissitudes of friendship and romance.

In fact, a crucial aspect of treatment always involves assisting the youth in learning to brave direct communication and engagement with their peers. Instead of firing off eight e-mails to various friends regarding an interpersonal dilemma or frantically calling everyone and anyone on the cell phone to assuage loneliness or hurt, directly talking with the person at the source of their distress is the only way to attain genuine resolution or closure. In fact, teens are often shocked to find that many of their assumptions and fears are completely unfounded once they work through the concern directly with a friend or parent.

Negotiating the developmental challenges of adolescence with the added barriers imposed by technology is complicating the changing landscape for today's teens. The integral role of the cell phone and the Internet in confronting the agonies and ecstasies of teenage strivings toward maturity must not be overlooked in therapy. This dependency needs to be appropriately integrated yet also exposed as a potential insidious barrier to true intimacy.

CONCLUSIONS

Identity, independence, and intimacy are the three core challenges confronted by adolescents. Each presents its own conflicts, disappointments, and rewards. Many adolescents encounter internal and external obstacles as these processes unfold and a developmental crisis occurs. Self-injury is but one of numerous expressions of adolescent angst, as substance abuse, sexual missteps, risk-taking, or general rebellion also can mask the poignant underlying struggles. Self-capacities, the ability to tolerate strong emotions, maintain self-esteem, and feel connected to others, are compromised in self-injurers and provide an imperative focus for intervention.

The social and environmental context also plays a major role in adolescent expressions of identity and pain. Indeed, body art and even self-mutilation have been embraced across many cultures as hallmarks of developmental transition and individuality. Additionally, the teen's immediate familial, cultural, religious, economic, academic, and peer contexts can have powerful impacts on the development of self-injury. Although difficult to assess, even the notion of the post-9/11 world causes one to consider the impact on the teenage imagination of the use of suicide as a weapon. Resources and stressors within each of these contexts need to be thoughtfully integrated into understanding and treating each adolescent.

Finally, the age of the Internet and the cell phone creates additional challenges to adolescents. Teens are increasingly alienated as they substitute superficial and virtual relationships for true engagement and intimacy with peers. Despite finding these technologies essential means of communicating with peers, the pitfalls and the alternative value of engaging face-to-face need to be made evident. Teens who self-injure are frequently overwhelmed by interpersonal dilemmas and their emotional fallout and need to acquire courage as well as the skills to put aside technological barriers and actively engage with others.

Chapter 4

Why Teens Self-Injure: Doing All the Wrong Things for the Right Reasons

It seemed like a good idea at the time.

Sources too numerous to list

As perverse as it may seem, cutting is utilized by many adolescents in an earnest effort to overcome and ease the distress related to normative conflicts. Self-injury is often resorted to as a means of alleviating painful emotions, securing the help of others, rejecting negative parts of oneself, or striving toward greater self-control, autonomy, and independence. Although cutting is clearly a negative and destructive means of achieving these goals, the positive nature of the goals themselves must not be overlooked. The challenge for teens, parents, and clinicians is to appreciate the healthy strivings underlying the cutting and parlay this positive framework into the development of more constructive and effective means of attaining the desired goals. Not only can this approach avoid a power struggle surrounding the act of cutting itself, it also can help the adolescent gain insight and tools for surmounting obstacles that have up until now felt overwhelming. In important ways, many forms of adolescent self-destructive behavior represent wrong choices for coping with the right developmental goals.

ALLEVIATING DISTRESS

The desperation to quell intensely painful emotions is often cited as the most fundamental goal of self-injury. In fact, its actual ability to alleviate distress renders many teens highly reluctant to discontinue it. The adolescent who is overwhelmed by anger, sadness, longing, self-loathing, anxiety, or a

host of other emotions commonly resorts to cutting as a means of refocusing emotional pain into a physical act they can control. Cutters typically
report that they feel "numb," "calm," "in control," "strong," "relieved," or otherwise comforted by this act. Some early research even suggests that the pain
of cutting releases endorphins, chemicals that induce a feeling of well-being,
in the brain. Thus, ample evidence supports the adolescent's contention that
cutting does help them feel better, albeit temporarily.

Physiological studies have indicated a biological basis for this seemingly perverse effort to feel better. Endorphins and enkephalins, the natural opiate-like
chemicals in our brains that suppress pain and create a pleasurable effect, are
released during the act of cutting. Thus, teens learn to associate positive feelings and relief from negative feelings with cutting. In a study of women with
borderline personality disorder and repetitive cutting, Coid, Allolio, and Rees[68]
reported that higher enkephalin levels were found in patients with the most
extreme and recent acts of self-cutting. The biological increase in these chemicals during cutting can help explain the seemingly counterintuitive claims by
teens that cutting provides a genuine sense of relief and well-being.

Adolescents are notorious for their moody behavior and enigmatic emotional
displays. Their experience of new and intensified feelings takes on heightened
meanings of the most personal nature during the adolescent traverse. Many
adolescents have never before experienced their bodies as alien, beyond their
control, and as such objects of scrutiny. Most have never felt romantic or sexual
longings to such a degree or such a dire need to be accepted by peers. Many
other teens are quite frightened by their lack of sexual readiness. Adolescent
self-consciousness can be all-consuming, and perceived criticisms, inadequacies, or rejections can be experienced as tantamount to annihilation. Painful
feelings of sadness, loneliness, confusion, inadequacy, fear, and the like can
become overwhelming if the teen does not develop effective strategies for self-
consoling as well as enlisting the support of others.

Imagine a 13-year-old girl who experiences herself as unattractive, socially
awkward, and lacking in valued competencies. Her basic temperament is such
that she experiences emotions immediately and intensely, and she has not yet
developed an ability to modulate or control these emotional surges. She cries,
she withdraws, she feels angry and resentful, yet nothing alleviates her overriding despair. She feels unable to express this jumble of negativity and aban-
dons any real hope of understanding or redemption. She hates herself and feels
empty and miserable night after night, alone in her room. The concentrated
focus involved in taking action by wielding a razor blade, slicing her flesh just
enough to bleed, collecting the drops of blood on a cotton ball, and enacting at
once the roles of victim and victimizer enable the troubling emotions to fade
into the background of this dramatic ritual. She is now focused on the act, the

blood, and this seemingly eloquent articulation of her suffering. A sense of calm, of emotional catharsis, is the rewarding aftermath.

In the film *Rabbit-Proof Fence*, a horrific scene is portrayed in which Aboriginal children are literally wrenched from the arms of their wailing mothers by government authorities seeking to Christianize and "purify" Australian society. In the aftermath of this unspeakable trauma, the Aboriginal mothers and grandmothers are shown grieving while banging rocks against their skulls in an act of sheer overwhelming pain. In viewing the women's bloodied scalps and almost trancelike pounding of their own skulls, there seems nothing unnatural about this expression of pain in the context of such ultimate despair. The seeming need to obliterate the emotional pain through competing physical pain appears as a vivid, apt illustration of grief. Similarly, the replication of psychic pain by producing physical pain seems sadly congruent. Although it is impossible to compare the despair of most adolescents to these cataclysmic scenes, the urge to injure oneself in an active physical expression of emotional pain takes on a more understandable nature in this context.

In general, successful treatment is incumbent upon the youth learning to differentiate and identify emotions and their source. Only once armed with concrete knowledge of their turmoil can they develop more effective means of alleviating and redirecting their distress. In the chapters on treatment, specific strategies for identifying and then alleviating distress are discussed as a critical resource for teens seeking to relinquish cutting as a coping method.

Gina is 17 and still feels empty and inadequate despite her popularity, competence, and attractiveness. She has had a series of boyfriends and blends easily with friends, yet she always feels she is acting a role. Underneath, she feels unlovable and devoid of meaningful relationships or passions. Although her peers view her as having everything going for her, she derives little true pleasure or satisfaction in her life. When Gina is alone, usually at night, she senses that nobody truly knows her; in fact, she is certain that nobody has any clue about the despair and self-blame she suffers. She feels like an actress who knows her part too well and can only get in touch with her true, less-than-perfect inner self in private. Gina cuts her thighs, generating a signature of pain that only she can read. She needs help learning to allow others to know her more fully, warts and all. But for now, she just wants the pain to subside. After cutting each of her thighs, Gina feels companionship with her sorrow and can view the evidence of her pain rather than battle it internally.

More often than not, teenagers initially will tell me that they have no idea why they are self-injuring. Self-injury is so emotionally driven that rational explanations generally elude explanation. Cutting grows out of a painfully negative emotional state that one longs to neutralize. The reason why adding pain to pain equals no pain defies logic. Nonetheless, it can work, and the logic of continuing to do something that results in tremendous relief is hard to refute. Helping both the adolescent and her family understand this fundamental fact can humanize the teen's "sick," "twisted," "disturbed," "crazy," "self-destructive," and otherwise enigmatic behavior as having a positive goal. For the adolescent to recognize this desire to alleviate distress as a worthy goal, she then can be open to exploring means other than self-injury as a way to achieve the same goal.

Adolescents who self-injure often have deficits in their ability to cope with strong emotions. They are highly emotionally reactive, and their cognitive problem-solving skills quickly become overwhelmed by the affective storm. Thus, self-injury often reflects what might be referred to as "the perfect storm": At a time of life when teens experience emotions more intensely than ever and have the fewest coping skills available to organize and process them, a collision often results in desperate acts like self-injury or drug abuse. A clear goal of treatment is to assist the adolescent in acquiring knowledge and actionable skills that they can learn to use effectively in reducing negative emotional states. Often, only substitute strategies will enable the teen to abandon a coping device they have come to rely heavily upon.

Many individuals rely on ultimately self-destructive strategies to help them quell painful emotions. We all have heard of the so-called nervous eater or nervous smoker who repetitively reaches for food or cigarettes in an attempt to stave off anxiety. Any self-destructive behavior, be it substance abuse, overeating, undereating, risk taking, gambling, sexual acting out, or cutting, stems from the same goal: the human drive to minimize pain. That negative outcomes are associated with these behaviors, such as drug addiction, obesity, anorexia, death, bankruptcy, unwanted pregnancy, HIV infection, or lifelong scarring, is too often overlooked in an ill-advised effort simply to feel better—now. Fortunately, there are many, many healthy coping strategies people can turn to that will effectively ease pain, even if not with the same instant or powerful result.

It is often striking to me how frequently parents have difficulty fathoming what a teenager would have to be in such pain about. The depth, power, and newness of so many adolescent emotions and conflicts are tremendous, and helping the adolescent communicate about them is critical. In adolescence, these feelings and needs are perhaps more all-encompassing than at any other time of life, and it is the vastness of the feelings that often breaks through the teen's developing coping resources. For example, parents often will dismiss a teen's legendary self-consciousness as trivial. But to the teen, the heightened fear of negative social evaluation is tantamount to, in the words of some, social suicide. Thus, the stakes feel huge, almost life or death, and facing one's peers feeling unattractive, different, rejected, or inferior can feel insurmountable.

COMMUNICATING TO OTHERS: WHAT ABOUT THIS BLOODY SCREAM DO YOU NOT UNDERSTAND?

A second goal of self-injury can be the conscious or unconscious wish to alert others to one's distress. Bloody scars serve quite effectively as a scream for immediate understanding and help. The sight of self-inflicted cuts is literally a red flag to parents, friends, and teachers, who inevitably become alarmed by these obvious and disturbing signs of a troubled adolescent. Often, these scars are revealed to others almost coyly or by "accident," given the teen's reticence to declare herself less than entirely healthy or independent. Indeed, though the scar screams out the teen's desire for help, the self-injurer is often decidedly resistant to intervention. It is this conflict and contradiction that can make cutting such a complicated and intractable problem. The simultaneous scream for attention with the active rejection of it is altogether confusing to those seeking to intervene. The cutting then becomes the battleground upon which conflicts related to independence and dependence are fought. The more mature ability to explicitly enlist the support of others while maintaining a strong sense of one's personal responsibility yet need for human support is still ahead on these teenagers' developmental trajectory.

In teens with relatively normative difficulties, the simple act of cutting or even merely scratching the skin earns rapid, empathetic attention. Thus, for relatively little effort, the cutting affords the teen tremendous power over others. Parents may feel panicked and guilty, rewarding the teen's anger and rebellion. Peers may be attentive and extremely caring, rewarding the teen's need for greater attention and understanding. Parents may feel they are held hostage by the teen's implicit threat of self-injury, fearing upsetting her with firm limits or disappointments. And teachers and coaches my feel pity and behave more forgivingly to a teen who is perceived as distressed and fragile. Cutting thus can become an entrenched strategy for communicating need and vulnerability, unwittingly reinforced by the concerned reactions of others. Until the adolescent can acknowledge her distress, need, and personal responsibility through direct communication and action, cutting serves a covert means of impacting important others without directly confronting painful realities. This victim stance tends to preclude successful growth and development.

Joanna feels isolated in her pain and sadness. She wants someone to understand how she feels and maybe even help pull her out of her despair. If others feel sympathy for her suffering, perhaps they will not hold such high expectations, treating her with more kindness as a result. Joanna takes a clean nail from the garage and begins scratching parallel lines on her wrist. She wonders if anyone would notice the white scratch marks and thinks perhaps not. She intently makes a slightly deeper scratch just to the point of creating a red mark and then repeats this more visible wound on her other wrist. She hopes that someone will notice at school tomorrow and consciously decides to wear a short-sleeve T-shirt.

Nonetheless, her red marks are as invisible to others as she herself feels. She is angry, dejected, and even more depressed. This time she scratches with a vengeance and is fascinated at how focused and pain-free she feels as her efforts yield blood. She makes another bloody scratch just above it, and even if nobody notices, she feels defiant in displaying her silent screams. Indeed, her basketball coach notices her wounds and expresses his alarm. He insists that she meet with the school counselor the next day or he will have to notify her parents. She is horrified; she wanted her friends to notice, not these intrusive adults. That night, she scratches *Fuck U* on her abdomen as a scream of outrage she expects no one will hear.

As one grasps the fundamental adolescent conflict of desiring independence yet fearing the relinquishment of dependence, it is easier to understand the cryptic manner used by adolescents to signal distress. They want support, yet they resent support. They long for concerned attention, yet they detest it. They hope someone can help them feel better, yet they insist on making their own decisions. They bleed, yet they become indignant at any suggestion that they need emotional first aid. For some adolescents, the "accidental" discovery of wounds by friends or parents is a secretly longed-for event. It is their private suffering that eludes any one else's comprehension that must be both an object of concern and a mystery, hoarded as a painful yet precious secret. Willfully asking for help or expressing concern over their self-injury would in some ways defeat the central purpose, the true allure, of this seemingly nonchalant behavior.

Of course, there are many self-injurers who loathe the prospect of anyone knowing about their "shameful" behavior, and these teens will go to great lengths to maintain their secret. These individuals do not want to be discovered and can hide their symptoms effectively. Shame and guilt compel them to keep their self-damaging behaviors hidden, but if discovered, these teens also can experience a surprising sense of relief at having unintentionally alerted caring help. Given the visual evidence left by self-injury, it is inevitable that teens at the very least think extensively about the implications of others knowing. A range of perversely thrilling reactions are contemplated, from horrified parent to admiring peer to achingly concerned love objects. Ironically, this private act is ultimately an interpersonal one as well, if even in the adolescent's fantasies and imaginings.

CLEANSING THE SOUL: PUNISHING HATED ASPECTS OF THE SELF

Adolescence is a time of intense self-consciousness and introspection. Many teens do not perceive themselves as meeting social standards of attractiveness, popularity, athleticism, and the like. Many do not even feel capable of managing their own impulses, finding themselves unable to control their eating, sexual behavior, or drug abuse. Few escape without experiencing some feelings of anger at themselves for perceived inadequacies, and still others become consumed by self-criticism and self-loathing.

Through the ages, self-injury has been utilized in the service of atoning for one's real or imagined sins and as a cathartic process of purification. Christianity, Islam, and Hinduism have historically accepted self-injury or mortification of the flesh as a holy and purifying act. Fasting is required on Yom Kippur, the Jewish Day of Atonement. Secular life also has embraced self-denial and seemingly masochistic endeavors as a route to feelings of self-worth, superiority, or holier-than-thou virtue and purity. Witness the marathoners, triathletes, superslim models, and other masters of pain and deprivation who populate the upper echelons of masochistic heroics. Even the everyday runner or the no-lunches-this-week dieter feels unworthy and guilt-ridden if unable to complete their proscribed ritual of redemption. For patients with anorexia nervosa, starvation rewards them with feelings of self-worth; for the bulimic, only purging can return them to any semblance of self-acceptance. Similarly, the repetitive cutter seeks to conquer internal inadequacies and generate healing in the emotional catharsis of drawing blood. Scar tissue itself symbolizes their psychological injuries and subsequent healing.

Adolescents who cut frequently describe themselves as "ugly," "unlovable," "weak," "hopeless," and otherwise woefully inadequate. Cutting serves as a declaration of war on the unwanted aspect of self, affording the teen a temporary sense of power and pride. By forcefully and violently rejecting perceived inadequacies, the adolescent can feel symbolically purged of them. Only after inflicting punishing self-injury can the teen feel relieved of their agony and self-hate. The wounds then become symbols of the suffering they are willing to undergo to overcome these internal enemies of the self. They are no longer merely the victim of their failings but also the master who wields control in the act of punishment.

Margo is 16 and has little self-esteem despite her physical attractiveness, which other girls envy and boys pursue. When she was six, her uncle sexually abused her, and she never told anyone. The other night, she went with some of her girlfriends to a party with a bunch of seniors. It got pretty wild, and she drank too much. She thinks she had sex with a guy there, but she is not sure. Word has quickly got out that she was drunk and having sex with an older guy at the party, and she is embarrassed and ashamed. She also feels overwhelmed by a confusion of memories and emotions related to "something bad happening" with her uncle as well as some subsequent sexual experiences with boys. She feels dirty, afraid, and disgusted with herself, with surges of angry rage complicating her emotional landscape. When these overwhelming feelings take hold of her, she longs desperately for some escape from the pain and the upsetting thoughts.

Margo has heard of some girls at school known as cutters, and she has never understood why they would do that to themselves. They look damaged and wounded and miserable, and given that this is exactly how she feels, there is suddenly something about it that compels her. She feels a kinship with these scarred girls and wonders what it is like to control the pain in so aggressive a manner. To her surprise, by gently slicing her skin with a knife and drawing a trickle of blood she feels cleaner, better, and somehow empowered. She even feels disconnected from any actual physical pain, as if she were watching herself from a distance during the cutting. She hates what has happened to her, and cutting severs some of her own self-hatred against a body she feels has been violated. She can punish her body, enacting the roles of victim and victimizer at will. To her enormous relief, she no longer feels so awful, her bleeding arm serving as a sign that she has been harmed and deserves sympathy and gentle care. She is soothed by the visible bleeding and carefully tends to the wounds with creams and bandages in order to help them heal.

Jenna, on the other hand, is 19 and has been bulimic since age 15. Her friends all assume she is happy and healthy, as she goes to great lengths to keep her bulimia hidden. Every day, she skips breakfast and lunch and then succumbs to an overwhelming urge to binge eat in the evening. She eats secretly, alone in her room or in her car, and seeks out public restrooms to "get rid of the food" by purging. The bingeing and purging cycle is lonely, shame-filled, sometimes painful, and always disgusting to her, yet she feels a slave to it. Her teeth are darkened, her cheeks are swollen, and she has a chronic sore throat that she does not want to tell her doctor about. Sometimes she feels such disdain for herself that she angrily cuts her "hideous" thighs and abdomen. She finds the cutting is a way to scold herself and the self-inflicted pain as a punishment for her gluttony and weakness. She says angry, degrading things to herself when she cuts but feels a numbing relief in its wake. After cutting, she feels exhausted, in a daze, and more at peace in the sense that she has rejected and punished these horrible aspects of herself. This is her penance: a difficult yet reliable ritual that provides a sort of redemption.

Clearly, then, a central goal of treatment must be to help the teenager explore the roots of her self-hate and identify the larger patterns she has unwittingly adopted to destructively maintain it. Self-esteem, lovability, body image, the proverbial whole nine yards can become wrapped up in this assumption of unworthiness. Deconstructing false assumptions, learning to embrace positive aspects of oneself, and learning tools to transform negative thoughts into more constructive ones can be integrated into treatment. Often, teens are burdened by such a deep sense of being damaged that ongoing psychotherapy is helpful to their long-term healing and ability to embrace themselves and others.

THE DECLARATION OF INDEPENDENCE: POWER AND CONTROL

There is a terrible power wielded by an adolescent who self-injures. The adolescent herself can feel empowered by the sense of strength and courage she experiences in mastering the pain of cutting her own flesh. Rather than feeling helpless and out of control, taking direct action against the oppressive feelings can help the adolescent feel some sense of agency. In addition, the threat of self-injury asserts tremendous power over others. Parents become fearful, deeply involved, eager to appease; teachers show concern, pity, and special consideration; and friends take special notice and care. By the simple act of even scratching the skin, teens immediately can alert others that they have independent control over their behavior that no one can influence. The cutting can then become the domain within which the teen declares autonomous rule and ultimately independence.

The ability to control one's pain and injury in the act of cutting provides a steadying sense of power against an otherwise overwhelming sea of emotion. Cross[69] states that self-cutting and eating disorders are both "attempts to own the body," and the drawing of blood can "demonstrate their hatred of and conquest over real and imaginary enemies." Adolescents frequently will report feeling "strong," "determined," and "more in control" by virtue of their ability to self-injure. No longer does the teen feel controlled by her distress; she can now take charge of her own pain in the ritualized cutting. In this sense, cutting can be an ill-advised effort to take action and battle threatening feelings of helplessness and defeat. Thus, though the choice itself should never be condoned, the adolescent's efforts to struggle and gain control should be acknowledged as one undeniably healthy underpinning of self-injury.

Sometimes, teens will cut themselves in an angry demonstration of their sense of persecution. Rigid parents, rejecting friends, and punitive teachers all can be put on notice as to how damaging they are to the teen. Often, the teen does not realize her sense of power until she witnesses the dramatic, even helpless reactions of those around her. It can be a way to inflict suffering on others, solicit empathy, and make demands. The implicit or even explicit threat is this: "If I can't go to the concert, I'll just sit in my room and cut myself." Or, "If you continue to ignore me, it will be your fault that I injure myself." The inescapable threat of suicide is evoked in even the mildest act of self-injury, providing a powerful impact that reaches beyond the meaning of a simple cut. Parents in particular fear that if they fail to help their child, they risk the ultimate unspeakable tragedy of losing their child to suicide.

Ironically, the power to cut or not to cut rests entirely with the teenager. Short of 24-hour observation in a hospital, if motivated, teens always can find a means of hurting themselves. Thus, though others urgently want to help, the teen can assert her powerful independence by thwarting their efforts. In short, there is nothing anyone but the teen herself can do to cease self-injuring. A complex developmental conflict is being played out; the teen is signaling the need for help yet asserting the simultaneous need for independence. The ambivalence of both wanting and rejecting dependency must be articulated and fully understood by the teen and her family in order to help diffuse the intensity of the urge to cut. The therapist and the parents need to, in effect, communicate that they hear the teen's pain and sympathize with her dilemma of wishing for help but also ultimately needing to confront her own conflicts and choices. The ability to be concerned and present while affirming the teen's ultimate power and responsibility is an exceedingly delicate tightrope to walk. The teen will, on one hand, want others to take responsibility for making things better yet insist that no one can control her. The adolescent must confront the reality of her own anxieties and difficulties along with their many options for choosing better solutions.

Ilana is a 13-year-old eighth-grader who feels lonely and desperate to secure friendships. She recently felt cruelly outcast by two of her friends and has no obvious allies at school with whom she can seek shelter. She feels humiliated and angry and abandoned and utterly helpless to resolve her social distress. She takes a lit match and presses it to her skin. The pain is acute yet oddly satisfying. She stoically sets about burning a series of ugly marks from her thigh to her ankle, feeling more in charge of her pain and anger than she has in a long time.

At school the next day, she blithely displays the burns to some of her classmates in PE. As expected, word gets around, and even her rejecting friends take notice. Instead of feeling guilty for their cruelty, these girls decide that Ilana is "weird" and turn their backs even more. Ilana's isolation becomes unbearable, and her skin burning escalates. It seems to be her only source of controlling the pain inflicted by others, becoming the inflictor rather than the victim. Eventually, she is brought into treatment and begins the long process of learning other skills for communicating and engaging with her peers in a way that provides her more success than does the act of burning herself.

Ilana is an example of a girl grasping for some semblance of social power and internal control. Her abandonment feels terrifying, the pain unbearable, and her anger silent. The self-injury helps Ilana feel in control of this onslaught of emotions, and burning herself focuses her pain in a way she can control. Although her burn marks may not have evoked the kind of sympathy and kindness she had hoped for, other teens may even inadvertently discover their power to influence others.

Eloisa is sick of her parents' nagging. They are constantly on her back about homework and never stop prying into her social life. They set rigid curfews and try to control who she can and cannot spend time with. Eloisa has been smoking marijuana more frequently lately, even between classes, and she feels behind at school and left out of late-night gatherings. She is always fighting with her mom, even occasionally throwing things across the room in anger. Otherwise, she holes up in her room for hour after lonely hour.

One night, her father smells marijuana coming from her bedroom. Her parents freak out and ground her for two weeks. The mere thought of not seeing her friends and escaping her home is agonizing, and she cries and bangs things loudly in her room. Angrily, she zips into the kitchen to grab a paring knife and brings it back to her room. She cuts a long bloody stripe down her forearm and lets it bleed onto the carpet. She leaves the knife on her desk for her nosy parents to discover the next day. Her mother does, in fact, find the blood-crusted knife and becomes panicked with fear. She locates her at school and has her called to the office to ensure that she is safe. Eloisa defiantly saunters in, and her mother asks about the knife. Eloisa flaunts the wounded arm and says, "Are you happy now?"

Eloisa's parents are horrified and frightened. Have they been too harsh with her, or is this proof that she is out of control? They beg her to talk with them, but she refuses. Eloisa has a sense that she has suddenly obtained the upper hand with her parents and has finally shown them that they do not understand her and cannot control her. Her parents are afraid to upset her further by checking in on her yet are worried that she may be harming herself more. Eloisa feels some revenge in the suffering she is causing them and writes a note saying that unless she can see her friends, she will remain hopeless and miserable and will want to cut herself. They acquiesce reluctantly but realize they need help in reaching her as her drug use and poor school performance seem to be escalating.

Frequently, adolescents are not truly conscious of their urge to control others and demonstrate their autonomy. Yet the boldness of the self-injurious act and the teen's sole and complete power to harm herself or not inevitably leaves those around her feeling helpless, defeated, and sometimes manipulated. Bringing the power struggles out into the open where they can be addressed and negotiated ultimately can provide the teen with an even more effective means of seeking and demonstrating independence.

AN IDENTITY IN TRANSITION: "I AM NOT A CHILD ANYMORE"

Adolescence is all about forming an acceptable, cohesive, and realistic identity. The transition from childhood to young adulthood requires an ongoing integration of new experiences, emotions, and complex cognitions. Sexuality and intimate relationships, though a lifelong and ever-evolving endeavor, are confronted in especially challenging ways during this adolescent period of dramatic physical, intellectual, and emotional growth. Competing regressive and progressive pulls, that is, the longing for childhood dependence and the siren call of independence, generate wild vacillations in mood and behavior. Comprehending and expressing one's changing identity are imperatives of adolescence and often take disconcerting forms, from green hair to multiple piercings to indiscretions with drugs and sex. Occasionally, the challenges prove so overwhelming as to supplant the teen's healthy identity formation in a pattern of self-destructive behaviors.

Teens love to typecast themselves and each other. Every generation has its stoner, jock, Goth, nerd, popular, loser, and fast types. For some teens, they are at a loss for how to express both the painful and exhilarating nature of their budding maturity. Scars may be a way for a teen to declare herself a child no more but a complex, unique, and mysteriously deep creature emerging from a cocoon. Cutting and scarring can represent the relinquishing of childhood's innocence and the advent of full-blown, in-your-face adolescence.

The universal use of the body as billboard has been well documented across cultures and centuries. Tattoos, scarification, adornment, hair style, and the like always have been employed toward the declaration of status, belief, affiliation, and identity. Although cutting is not socially sanctioned in the manner that many cultures condone ritualized markings, it is emerging as a message with its own language and subculture. Cutting can visibly exhibit the torment and mystery of one's private pain, and teens increasingly know how to read these signatures of angry suffering. *Cutter* is becoming a common designation of teens, often described in as off-handed a manner as *jock* or *hippie*. Wounds can be coyly revealed to a select few, hidden altogether as a cherished secret or flaunted for their power to shock and call attention.

Kahlil is known around school as a cutter. He has embellished his arms, legs, and neck with a jagged array of wounds in various phases of healing. He is well liked by his friends and plays in a heavy metal band in which outrageous appearance is encouraged. The reactions of his schoolmates range from horror and disgust to curiosity and admiration. Although the wounds are assumed to represent some outspoken combination of rage and torment, these emotions and their rebellious expression are commonplace among his peers. Although Kahlil appears more "freaky" than the average teen, his blasé attitude toward his cutting defuses his friends' concern.

Less well known to his peers is the confusion he experiences in sorting through his sexual identity. Abused as a child by an 18-year-old male neighbor, Kahlil is certain that he is attracted to females but fears that his early experience has some how damaged him and predestined him to homosexuality. He tends to be hostile to girls and avoids any sexual expectations in his relationships. He has typically strong adolescent sexual urges but equally strong fears of being sexually shamed and rejected. The cutting somehow calms his turmoil, expresses both his passion and self-hate, and sends an off-putting message to others. His cuts advertise his sense of damage, anger, and unapproachable physicality.

Another teen, Noel, similarly lacks the words to express the many changes she is going through. She used to be able to enjoy her friends and acting silly. She once felt carefree doing the things she loves, like shopping, going to movies, and rollerblading. Now, however, she feels estranged from her friends and from these lighthearted activities. Her mind is preoccupied with a heightened sense of social stakes: How she dresses, how she talks, where she goes, and with whom all seem to draw some form of positive or negative appraisal from others. Yet she cannot seem to convey on the outside the complex ways she thinks and feels and that she is so much more than what meets the eye.

Noel senses that her peers think of her as sweet and pliable, and she resents their air of authority around her. She bristles at her friends' assumptions that she will go along with whatever they do, constantly following and never in the lead. She is sick of playing along with their catty games and longs for a sense of equality and true connection with others. None of her friends seems to know her; she is preoccupied with concerns and passions that seem to glide over their heads. She has never felt so alone.

Would a self-inflicted wound convey to her friends that she has moved beyond them to a more serious and weighty place? Would it cause them to take a second look and realize that she is different from them, even more special and intriguing? Would it let them know that though they play their superficial games, she exists on a deeper plane and suffers from the isolation? She contemplates these questions when she distracts herself from unhappiness by poking her skin with a bamboo skewer, just enough so it hurts. She now has sharp angles and hidden places deep inside her heart and soul that she never knew existed and that she finds herself expressing in the sharp cuts on her skin.

Both Kahlil and Noel perceive the adolescent experience of a changing identity as one involving deepening, unspeakable emotional pain. Self-injury can be a form of inelegantly expressing this confusing phenomenon. Self-injury in these teens partly results from a need to express, own, or otherwise declare their abandonment of childhood and the uncertain reach for more adult ways of feeling, thinking, and seriously experiencing their world. They are at once both frightened and unafraid, helpless and powerful, wonderfully complex and painfully overwhelmed. By writing their signature of struggle on their flesh, the conflicts raging within them are made manifest in as concrete a way as they feel possible.

CONCLUSIONS

Self-injurious behavior is clearly much more than simply the expression of pain or a cry for help. Although it is easy to dismiss such disturbing behavior as the hostile, manipulative actions of an exasperating teen, it is absolutely imperative that parents and clinicians understand the primary motives as being rooted in otherwise healthy developmental conflicts related to independence, identity, and intimacy. Self-injury is enacted because of the need to subdue emotional pain, communicate to others, seek redemption, gain control, and forge an identity that integrates new depths of thought and feeling. For cutting not to remain the entrenched battleground upon which these titanic adolescent struggles are fought, the deeper meanings and healthy strivings need to be uncovered and made explicit. Thus, self-injury is a negative behavior perversely employed toward the ultimate goal of successful adolescent coping and development.

Chapter 5

Laying the Foundation for Intervention: Composure, Compassion, and Comprehension

If my parents find out, they'll freak. They'll totally overreact and it'll be a huge crisis. They'll act like I'm doing this to hurt them.

14-year-old who has been cutting for months

How am I supposed to know if she's going to kill herself next?

Parent

FIRST AND FOREMOST: DO NOT PANIC

The discovery of bloody scars on an adolescent's body understandably elicits a primary response of panic in parents and sometimes even clinicians. Parents and clinicians may assume that the adolescent is truly suicidal and in imminent life-threatening danger. When a parent is genuinely unable to determine if the teen is actively suicidal, a visit to the local hospital emergency room for an evaluation is certainly prudent. A crisis is often unnecessarily provoked and hospitalization sometimes sought, however, even when the adolescent has incurred minor scratches and swears up and down that they have no desire to kill themselves. The good news is that self-injuring adolescents do not typically harbor genuine suicide intent and, though posing a serious situation, rarely require dramatic reaction or action. Reacting with outright fear and panic to the discovery of cutting can have several drawbacks that are not helpful to the teen.

First, witnessing panicky responses in adults can only heighten the teen's own anxiety and sense of being out of control. It is as if the teen is looking in a mirror, and if the parents reflect a face of despair and emergency, the teen interprets her own distress as beyond resolution or help.

Second, panicked reactions also can be interpreted as anger, causing the teen to immediately make a hasty defensive retreat. If the adolescent feels attacked and criticized, she likely will become defensive and hostile in return and sense that her parents are unable to hear about and contain her turmoil. The teen may assume that the parents are more concerned about their own well-being than hers and withdraw into silence or amplify her acting out. Although feeling anxious and worried is unavoidable, parents who act out these feelings in overly dramatic reactions only exacerbate the crisis. Similarly, though parents are understandably placed on heightened alert, if they become intrusive, restrictive, and heavy-handed, the teen can feel claustrophobic and terribly threatened by her loss of autonomy. It is critical that the adolescent perceive others' deep concern yet competence, allowing her to feel secure in the strength and support around her.

Third, overreactions by others can enhance the power of the cutting as a form of indirect and undesirable communication. If an adolescent is angry at her parents, by cutting she can immediately provoke intense distress and thereby distract herself from her own. If adults panic, the teen feels an ultimately unwanted and unhealthy power to disrupt the stability and structure around her, rather than develop skills to improve her own ability to maintain internal order and control. And of course, if cutting intimidates parents into walking on eggshells or relinquishing their authority, the situation is only likely to deteriorate. Clearly, a genuinely attentive, concerned, and caring reaction provides the best groundwork for ultimately assisting the teen in abandoning self-injury as a form of coping.

Helping professionals are in no way immune from feeling unhinged by the disturbing nature of cutting in their patients. Cutting presents tremendous treatment challenges for clinicians who must manage their own feelings of anxiety, helplessness, anger, sadness, or frustration. The clinician is also faced with the weighty responsibility of accurately assessing suicide risk in each of these very complex teenagers, not to mention the challenge of trying to therapeutically assist what are often resistant or even defiant adolescents. Teenagers whose treatment is complicated by ongoing self-injury require alert, sophisticated, and time-consuming clinical care. Clinicians are thus challenged both emotionally and professionally and must feel equipped to provide a high standard of care.

EMPATHY AND UNDERSTANDING

Often, what a self-injurious teen needs to hear above all else is, "This really tells me how badly you're hurting. I'm glad that you've told me and I'm committed to helping you get through it in your own way." This seemingly simple message acknowledges the teen's private world, ultimate autonomy, intense distress, and desire for a secure but nonintrusive parental relationship. This message clearly states, "I care, I am not angry, you are your own person, and I am strong enough to support and help you." It further acknowledges that the adult now appreciates that there are highly personal complexities and difficulties experienced by the adolescent that have up until now remained invisible. It is the adult's role to invite these issues out into the open in a caring and respectful manner.

Without criticizing or making any demands, the teen is not pushed into a defensive mode or a power struggle that merely makes productive communication impossible. Although it is unlikely that the teen who has resorted to cutting will immediately open up and reveal their most sensitive conflicts, a stance of empathy, relative calm, and willingness to understand can leave the door at least ajar.

SEEKING PROFESSIONAL HELP

Without exception, an adolescent who has been self-injurious warrants professional assessment and intervention. A well-trained licensed clinician with extensive adolescent treatment experience can be located from a variety of referral sources: school counselors, physicians, clergy, friends, and local professional organizations. Generally, a psychologist, psychiatrist, or clinical social worker will be most likely to possess the skills necessary to conduct this form of sensitive and complex treatment.

In addition to establishing rapport and providing a safe and confidential environment in which to talk openly, the first task of the clinician is to assess the teen for suicide potential. Although the vast majority of teens who cut are not actively suicidal, some indeed are. Determining the teen's ideation and fantasies around suicide, formulation of a plan, and access to the means to carry out a plan (e.g., pills, guns, razor blades, nearby train tracks) is an essential component of competent treatment. Second, the teen's level of depression, impulsivity, drug and alcohol abuse, and judgment has direct implications for suicide risk. The teen's access to social support through friends, family, school, or religious organization provides a buffer that mitigates against suicide risk. And certainly assessing coexisting conditions such as psychosis, eating disorders, sexual victimization, bipolar disorder, and other major difficulties is essential to a thorough understanding of the factors endangering and impinging upon the youth.

Many assessment tools are available to augment the interview and history in directly measuring suicidality. Both self-report measures based on empirical data and more qualitative information attained in projective testing can be employed toward assessing this central area of risk. A subtle but profound determinant in the detection of suicide potential is the teen's level of impulse control and ability to exercise sound judgment when confronted with strong emotions. The ability to differentiate and modulate emotions is an aspect of personality that greatly enhances individuals' coping abilities. Projective tests, such as the Rorschach and the Thematic Apperception Test, can provide useful information in these areas. Projective tests require the person to respond to highly unstructured tasks (e.g., "Tell me a story about this picture," "What does this design look like, what might it be") and therefore project their own issues and perceptions into their responses. Projective tests have the advantage of tapping into information about which even the patient may be unaware and obtaining valuable information despite the patient's conscious or unconscious efforts to defend against revealing responses.

At the outset of treatment or evaluation, the clinician needs to make clear the rules of confidentiality. For minors under age 18, everything they tell the clinician can be held in confidence with a few notable exceptions. First, if the clinician believes that the teen is at risk of hurting either herself or others, the clinician is mandated by law and ethics to notify parents and, if necessary, police. If any information is revealed that suggests that the teen or another minor has been neglected or sexually or physically abused, or an elderly person is being abused, this also needs to be reported to child protective agencies and other appropriate authorities. These caveats need to be made crystal clear along with the equally important assurance that all other information will be kept confidential between the teen and the clinician.

A real challenge for the clinician is to build enough trust and collaboration with the teenager in order to determine an acceptable means of keeping the parents apprised of the general status and direction of treatment. Often, teens will not want specifics of their love life, cutting rituals, or experimentation with drugs disclosed to parents, and this confidence should be strictly observed. Teens are usually amenable and often eager, however, for the clinician to communicate key issues and concerns to parents that can help them better understand and interact with their youth. It is extremely rare that a parent is so destructive or dysfunctional that excluding them from treatment is indicated. Parents need and want to be guided in this process, and the adolescent greatly needs their informed understanding and support.

Most commonly, self-injurious youth will state that they are not in danger of trying to kill themselves but are nonetheless either unable or unwilling to stop self-injuring. In these cases, treatment has the luxury of not requiring a crisis-intervention approach that can be quite intrusive to the teen's sense of autonomy and safety. Whenever there is compelling evidence that the teen is at risk to seriously harm or kill herself, hospitalization is necessary, whether under voluntary or involuntary circumstances. When the clinician establishes that the teen is self-injurious but not suicidal, intervention can continue in directly addressing the root causes of the distress on an out-patient basis.

INITIATING INTERVENTION AND TREATMENT

Successful early treatment of repetitive cutting most commonly hinges on the calm recognition and articulation of the adolescent's underlying conflicts, an avoidance of a power struggle with the teen, and the development of alternative strategies that the teen can employ to more effectively attain desired outcomes. Medical professionals are sometimes needed to assess and monitor the risk of infection, need for stitching, general health, coexisting eating or substance abuse disorders, and the potential usefulness of psychotropic medication in the patient's comprehensive care. Finally, the integral involvement of the family in treatment is fundamental to successful treatment with adolescents engaged in cutting.

The key admonition is this: "Don't just do something; sit there." In other words, parents, clinicians, teachers, and friends are usually overly eager to swing into action and "fix" the immediate problem of the cutting itself. Listening and understanding and reassuring the teenager are doing something vital; launching into desperate action is not. Efforts to demand, convince, coerce, implore, or otherwise effect an end to the cutting behavior becomes the primary if not sole goal. Taking action and seeking to change, control, or stop the teens' behavior, however, rarely can produce positive results prior to the attainment of a genuine understanding of the deeper issues involved. Thus, it is incredibly challenging for those who care about the adolescent to manage their own anxiety and recognize their own need to see the cutting stop. In order to truly understand the larger motivations surrounding the behavior itself and carefully assess potential points of intervention, conscientious patience and listening must precede action. Thus, one of the greatest challenges in treating self-injury in teens is seeing, hearing, and understanding the internal wounds plaguing the teen that the cuts merely symbolize.

Thus, short of ensuring that the teen is not suicidal and locating a professional clinician, the counterintuitive intervention of just listening, understanding, and not demanding, judging, freaking out, or controlling provides the most fruitful groundwork for successful treatment. One's stance with a teen in such apparent distress and disorder is absolutely critical in facilitating the developmental goals that inevitably underlie the desperate behavior.

The first step in responding to an adolescent discovered cutting is to express appreciation and concern for their obvious insufferable pain. Helping parents to not panic and overreact is critical to the teen's ability to communicate her distress and relinquish cutting as a coping mechanism. Only when the teen feels confident that others are trying to genuinely understand and assist her, rather than control her, will she engage in a nonbelligerent dialogue. It is critical that parents, friends, and clinicians all acknowledge the stark and sobering reality: Only the teen has control over the cutting. In other words, no one can make her stop cutting; she is in charge.

When cutting is used to stave off intense emotional distress, it is important to glean information about what thoughts or events bring on the urge to cut. When, where, and why is it most likely to occur? What feelings are experienced? How does the cutting relieve the distress? Once the teen can make the association between a painful event and the urge to cut, intervention can be successful, empowering the teen with cognitive awareness and problem-solving options. Unfortunately, most teens are not amenable to engaging in this therapeutic process with their parents and thus require a professional outside the home. There, adolescents are often quite eager to discuss alternative strategies for coping with overwhelming distress. These can include journaling, calling a friend, taking a walk, listening to an inspiring song, or other individual strategies. The notion that the teen has a choice over whether to cut is extremely important, and developing some viable alternatives is essential. Only then can she begin to take responsibility for her conflicts, her actions, and their outcomes and build a bigger arsenal of coping strategies to reduce pain.

SEEING BOTH SIDES OF THE CONFLICT: MAKING SENSE OF MIXED MESSAGES

Cutting is very often a means of communicating the proverbial thousand words in a single picture: bloody self-inflicted scars. Indeed, the wounds speak volumes, but what is the adolescent saying?

Cutting invariably elicits intense attention, especially from parents who become alarmed at the realization that their beloved child is mutilating herself, often permanently. The implicit threat of suicide shocks and mobilizes parents, teachers, friends, and clinicians when words alone seem to fall on deaf ears. The self-injurer suddenly has the attention of others who have felt impossible to reach or too humiliating to reach out to.

In one fell swoop, the adolescent wields terrible power through the forcefulness of her actions and her subsequent defiance of admonishments to cease and desist the bloody behavior. At once the cutter seems to be saying, "Help me; I'm suffering," yet at the same time declaring, "You can neither control nor help me." Therein lies what is frequently the central struggle for the adolescent as she seeks to overcome a classic developmental impasse: the need to stay dependent at an unsteady time of life, yet the simultaneous need to seize and assert autonomy and independence. Cutting that is revealed to others represents that ultimate ambivalence.

The inherent irony of this mixed message makes intervention a delicate and difficult task. Parents and clinicians must strike a balance between offering support and setting limits yet demonstrating clear recognition of their ultimate lack of control over the teen's decision to cut or not. Teenagers want to know that their parents are available to support them, yet they need to assert that everything of importance is their own choice and doing. The teen needs adults to understand this ambivalence. Conveying respect for the teen's autonomy and burden of responsibility yet not causing the teen to feel abandoned is challenging to say the least. It is crucial, however, that the teen understand that she has singular control over not only her choices but also all the responsibility, and parents can only help in so far as the teen will allow. With the absolute caveat that suicidal risk will be swiftly addressed through hospitalization to assure physical safety, minor self-injury cannot be stopped by command or force. All parties must acknowledge this, offer concerned support, and yet not demand that the teen simply behave herself.

The task of containing one's own anxiety as a parent, teacher, friend, or clinician is enormous. The more adults can respond to cutting both calmly and nonjudgmentally, however, conveys their ability and willingness to tolerate the teen's intensely disturbing emotions and ability to offer competent assistance. As parents avoid becoming overwhelmed by the adolescent's pain, the power and intensity of the cutting often abates. Without effecting dramatic reactions in others, the need to advertise her message through self-injury is no longer strongly reinforced, leaving the teen more motivated to choose other modes of expression and communication.

THE IDENTITY IMPERATIVE: VALIDATING ADULTLIKE DEPTH AND COMPLEXITY

Teens rarely have the words to express the mysterious changes occurring within. When adults show sincere but nonintrusive interest in the teen's changing psychic life, the adolescdent can begin to give an explicit voice to newly discovered parts of their developing self. In general, a key psychological principle holds that the more an adolescent can talk about what she is feeling, the less the likelihood exists of her acting out her emotions in undesirable ways. Thus, once peers and adults can appreciate all the good, bad, and ugly aspects of an adolescent's transforming identity, the need to express herself through overt action decreases dramatically. Self-understanding and communication skills develop alongside experience with receptive listeners.

What could be so complicated and daunting for this seemingly well-loved and capable adolescent? The answer is simple: suddenly everything. Passions around romantic and sexual feelings are newly pressing and at once compelling and terrifying. The need to win the acceptance and approval of a stable peer group takes on an almost life-and-death imperative. The evolving ability to think with deepening complexity is suddenly strengthened by brain development advancing abstract thinking capabilities. The twin desires to maintain parental attachments yet forge an autonomous identity can clash violently, rendering the stakes in the conflict inexplicably high. Reflecting and validating these areas of rapid growth through word and deed (e.g., "Yes, you can go to the concert" and "No, you don't need us to micromanage your homework," yet "We're here whenever you need to lean on us" and "Show us that you can handle that responsibility") assist the teen's self-confidence, self-esteem, and sense of confidence that her maturity can be integrated into changing expectations rather than fought for tooth and nail.

Adolescents need to confront their own identity confusions. What are their feelings about their sexual orientation? What limits do they want to set for themselves around sexual behavior? How might they approach conflicts with others in a more mature and successful way? What are other ways to manage unbearable academic stress or to negotiate maturely with parents around desired freedoms or privileges? What do I want to do with my life? How do I feel about drug use? These are but a small sampling of the diverse issues that confronts adolescents and where clinicians need to focus their work. The self-injurious behavior is, after all, secondary to conflicts in these areas and needs to fade into the background as more active coping with developmental challenges takes hold.

Case Example: Josie, Age 16

Josie's mother was looking in her school backpack to locate a homework assignment. Inside, she discovered a small metal box, opened it, and found cigarettes and razor blades. At first, she feared that her daughter was now using cocaine (she already knew about the occasional smoking), thus explaining the razor blades, and decided to discuss this discovery with her husband prior to confronting Josie.

Josie's parents asked to speak with her after dinner. They calmly told Josie what they had found and expressed their concerns in a nonaccusatory manner. Josie responded angrily, saying, "You don't know anything! Now you think I'm a drug addict. Stay out of my things!" and then stormed off to her room. Josie's parents didn't know what to make of her volatile behavior of late, much less how to understand her defensive attitude about the razor blades. Her mother went to Josie in her room and calmly stated that she did not think Josie was a drug addict, and her only concern was that Josie was okay and why she had those razor blades. She acknowledged that Josie had been dealing with a lot of challenging situations this year, from school stress to the breakup with her boyfriend, and wanted to be able to support her in her struggles.

Josie broke down crying and told her mother that she was miserable and lonely and overwhelmed. She hated herself and her life and sometimes did not know how to escape these feelings. She then revealed the multiple shallow cuts on her wrist and said, "This is how bad I feel." Her mother inhaled sharply and tried to embrace Josie but was pushed away. She told Josie that she could see how much she was really struggling now, how much private complexity there was to her, and that whatever her parents could do to help they would do eagerly. Josie relaxed a bit upon sensing that her mother was not angry or about to ransack her room for contraband. She said that she just did not want to talk anymore right then. Her mother said that she would certainly respect that, but did have one question: Was Josie considering suicide? Josie softly said, "No," and her mother breathed a huge sigh of relief. She left Josie's room, saying that she wanted to better understand Josie's pain and was eager to be supportive and helpful in any way possible. She added that she hoped they could talk more soon.

Although both Josie and her parents were left at this point with more concerns than answers, some important groundwork had been laid in opening the lines of communication. Because her mother did not overreact or yell or threaten and managed to maintain her composure instead of dissolving into her own tears and agony, Josie sensed that these were matters within the realm of potential discussion. Although a part of Josie was disappointed that her parents had not completely freaked out, validating her own despair and sharing some of her misery, she was calmed by the notion that her secret was out but still had her own decisions to make. She fell asleep that night relieved of some tension, wondering what might come of all this in the days to come.

At school, Josie's art teacher notices the cuts, having seen others like them. She approached her privately at the end of class to state her concern. Josie was realizing how powerful the cutting was in telegraphing her distress and felt embarrassed but also relieved that her teacher could actually see her and now understand her better. Her teacher suggested that she speak to the school counselor about her troubles, but Josie declined. Sidestepping the issue of cutting itself, the teacher asked Josie how things were going at school and in her personal life. She seemed genuinely interested, concerned but not overly alarmed. Josie said that she missed Duncan, her ex-boyfriend, and her teacher said she had not known that they had broken up. The bell then rang, and though Josie had to leave, she knew that she had secured the caring interest of an important adult with whom it seemed surprisingly safe to talk.

In these early stages, it is impossible to predict whether Josie will discontinue, continue, or escalate her use of cutting. Nonetheless, it is clear that by laying a foundation of caring, calm, and open-mindedness, Josie is in a much better position to more directly verbalize her concerns rather than acting them out in solitude. Although the struggle was far from over, Josie got the message that the cutting was less important than the feelings and conflicts that caused it and discerned open minds and lines of communication around her. She also got the message that no one was going to forcibly stop her from cutting; that was up to her.

This brief case example regarding the early stages of discovery and intervention illustrate the importance of responding with composure and a desire to understand the deeper issues troubling the adolescent cutter. Genuinely comprehending the entirety of the adolescent's struggles, in the context of her developmental strengths and vulnerabilities, further provides the necessary groundwork for successful treatment.

Case Example of Avery: Identifying the Key Developmental Conflict

Avery has just turned 18 and is in the final semester of her senior year of high school. She has completed the exhaustive and exhausting college application process and has several good options from which to choose. Her first choice is a small liberal arts college in the Midwest. It offers an excellent literature and writing curriculum that fits with her current goal of becoming a writer. Because she lives in Florida, this college seems far away from home and in a climate quite alien to her. Nonetheless, she certainly wants to be free of her parents' supervision and would feel very mature taking on such an adventure.

Avery's other best college options are both reasonably close to home and in Florida. A lot of her friends will be attending these schools, and she could drive home any weekend she wanted. She has been fighting a lot lately with her parents about their nagging and intrusiveness and judgmental attitudes, yet she is not certain she wants to be so independent so soon. She is not really aware of the conflict she is in but has been overeating and partying too much with friends. She has gained weight and has been getting a reputation as a loud drunk, all of which are decreasing her self-esteem and self-confidence.

The deadline for choosing a college is fast approaching, and Avery is feeling more out of control and agitated than ever. One night, she is pulled over and cited by a police officer for driving with open containers in her carload of friends but narrowly passes the Breathalyzer test. Her license is suspended, and her parents are angry and worried and decide to ground her for two weeks.

Avery is overwhelmed by a confluence of emotions that include anxiety, indignation, shame, and despair. She finds that her friends are preoccupied with their own concerns, and the once reliable pleasures of food and partying now only add to her distress. Now that she is grounded, she feels even more trapped and helpless, having few outlets for distracting herself from her emotions. Late one night, when everyone is asleep, she starts absently and numbly scratching her thighs with a pencil. The lead leaves marks that sink into her skin. The next night, she uses a sharp knife to retrace these marks with bleeding cuts. The distraction and fascination with her cutting is quite satisfying, and she feels calmer and more in control of her frenzied emotions.

Avery does not know how to understand and integrate all her emotions, much less calm them. She is not truly conscious of the many developmental conflicts she faces in the college transition, and as a result cannot begin to resolve the conflicts in a thoughtful way. It will be important for those who intervene with Avery not only to express calm caring but also to assist her in articulating the sources of conflict. Only then can Avery truly be empowered to take positive actions that better resolve the challenges in front of her.

Once Avery's cutting is revealed to her parents (her mother having learned about it by reading her diary) and the groundwork is laid for concerned intervention, the therapist and the parents need to work together toward this critical comprehension. The therapist, who is not so emotionally caught up in the struggle, can help sort out the stressors and clarify core conflicts. Once both Avery and her parents have an explicit understanding of the developmental struggles that are compelling her destructive behavior, they can better work in tandem toward healthier coping strategies and real-life resolutions.

It becomes immediately clear to Avery's therapist that the impending college decision and specter of leaving the security of home are creating the core conflict within her. Developmentally, she is confronting a normative and age-appropriate conflict over the competing drives for secure dependence and greater independence. Avery expresses how she wants to be able to move to the Midwest for college but is ashamed that this frightens her. She wants to feel autonomous and independent, and going to a nearby college feels too safe and coddling. Her parents are appreciative of this dilemma and offer that if she goes to the Midwest she can fly home whenever she wants and have an unlimited long-distance cell phone plan provided. By the same token, if she stays in Florida, her parents agree to work hard at not prying into her life and emphasize how independent she will, in fact, be living on campus. Suddenly, the options no longer seem as stark or drastic to Avery, and she does not feel so embarrassed of her insecurities around independence. Gradually, Avery is able to choose a nearby college and is granted a deferment to the Midwestern school should she choose to transfer after her freshman year.

Although elucidating this core dependence-independence conflict is an important first step in Avery's treatment, there is much work yet to be done. What is driving all the drinking and partying? What is the role of overeating? What is at stake for Avery around her present self-esteem and acceptable body image? How can she develop alternative strategies for suppressing intense distress? And of course, what are the pros and cons of cutting herself, and what kinds of choices does she ultimately want to make and be responsible for? Thus, treatment is now under way as the chaos of emotions becomes organized into discrete and identifiable conflicts. The real work of therapy has begun, and Avery is now empowered with knowledge and tools for confronting the many challenges before her.

CONCLUSIONS

The importance of composure and comprehension in the initial treatment of cutting has been illustrated in this chapter. Avoidance of panic, harsh judgment, and anger is critical in those who receive the alarming news, as an attitude of caring, concern, and openness to understanding is projected. This type of response prepares the soil for ongoing communication and intervention, rather than forcing the teen into a defensive or combative posture.

Once the teen is at least marginally open to intervention, identification of the core conflicts is the primary goal. Only by understanding the struggles compelling destructive behavior can healthier resolutions be adopted by the teen. Discerning where developmental conflicts around independence, intimacy, and identity coalesce, the teen and family are on their way to lasting resolution and progress.

Chapter 6

Professional Treatment of Self-Injury: Understanding the Therapeutic Process

We had reached the "Arsenic Hour"; I didn't know whether to kill him or kill myself. We had to have help.

Father of "out-of-control" 16-year-old son

It's very, very hard to tell if these kids in the ER should be hospitalized or not. Some of them may truly be at risk for suicide, yet others with even worse injuries are just needing some attention and sensitive follow-up care.

Attending hospital psychiatrist

Most families find it impossible to contend with the frightening occurrence of repetitive cutting on their own. By definition, the adolescent cannot be expected to turn wholly and cooperatively to parents, and few parents are adept at the delicate process of tolerating burgeoning independence, rebellion, and distress in their children. Too often, an adversarial relationship develops that creates a power struggle and merely focuses the conflict outside the real developmental issues at stake. Involving a professional who can equally appreciate the conflicts facing both the teen and her parents can help provide equilibrium and guidance at a dangerously unstable time.

Adolescent development ultimately involves the integration of rapid changes in biological, social, emotional, and intellectual realms. Because successful integration of these changes is the mark of healthy adjustment, treatment must be integrative in addressing a number of areas, often simultaneously. Thus, optimal treatment must be multidimensional, with a number of treatment tools and approaches integrated into a comprehensive effort to assist the developing adolescent.

Each teenager and each family deserves a treatment approach that is specifically designed for them. Although fifty adolescents may all be seen by the same clinician in treatment, each and every one has his or her own unique set of circumstances and treatment needs. The initial phase of treatment is therefore incumbent upon information and history gathering by the clinician that reaches well beyond the immediate symptom of cutting. The patient's developmental, social, behavioral, and academic histories should be carefully reviewed, along with other problematic symptoms or behaviors. Equally important is an understanding of the family dynamics and of each parent's personal histories and psychological makeup. Only then can a diagnostic understanding be achieved and a truly informed and responsible treatment plan put into place.

CONTACTING A CLINICAL PROFESSIONAL

A broad and often confusing array of individuals identifies themselves as therapists. To call oneself a therapist or a psychotherapist requires no professional training or licensure and can lead to less than optimal or even destructive treatment. It is therefore important when selecting a clinician to seek a licensed professional with specific expertise with adolescents and self-injury. The professional degrees to look for include psychologists (PhDs), psychiatrists (MDs), social workers (LCSWs), and, in some states, marriage and family therapists (MFTs).

Important differences exist between these clinicians in terms of their skills and training. A psychologist has a doctorate degree in psychology after receiving five years of training in graduate school. A psychiatrist is a medical doctor with specialized training in psychiatry who can prescribe medication. Social workers and marriage and family therapists both have a two-year master's degree in their fields. Ultimately, the right choice comes down to the individual clinician best equipped to work with the particular teen and family. Excellent clinicians can be found within each of these specialties and can be located through the professional organization in your area. Also, a family physician, friend, teacher, or spiritual leader may be able to highly recommend a qualified professional.

Ideally, the adolescent should be seen first and alone by the therapist. This respects her growing independence and need to tell her side of the story. This first meeting allows the adolescent to present herself to an unbiased adult who will first and foremost be her staunchest ally. Even allowing the teen to interview two separate therapists and choose the one she prefers can be empowering and add to her buy-in or commitment to the treatment process.

During the initial referral phone contact with the parents, a brief summary of the teen's situation can be obtained in order to orient the therapist. The parents should be assured that a complete interview will be conducted with them once the adolescent has been seen. At that time, the parents can convey a detailed psychosocial and medical history of the teen, family information, and their many questions and concerns. During the initial session with the teen, and then with the parents, confidentiality should be discussed carefully.

Adolescents do not always readily agree to meet with a clinician. Often, the stigma of seeing a mental health clinician is both threatening and offensive to the youth. The parents, however, need to remain resolute in their conviction that such a meeting must take place. The teen can be provided a number of choices, however, to provide her with some sense of control and autonomy in the matter. For example, does she prefer to see a male or female clinician? Would she like to meet with two different therapists and then choose the one she likes best? Does she want the appointment set for a Tuesday or a Friday? Would she like to be in the room during the parents' first session with the clinician? These and other choices should be placed in the adolescent's court to emphasize the collaborative and participatory nature of treatment.

Furthermore, it is extremely important to emphasize the adolescent's strengths at this difficult juncture rather than focusing solely on their difficulties. Highly social adolescents can understand that they have an interpersonal gift that can be employed in an interpersonal therapy relationship toward their goals. Bright and verbal kids can be similarly encouraged that those are the kinds of strengths that bode particularly well for positive therapeutic outcome. The healthy need for teens to confide in others aside from their parents is also affirmed by this measure. Similarly, sensitive and introspective teens can understand that they have great depth and are psychologically minded, strengths that lead to particularly productive therapies. Finally, framing the therapist as a consultant is not only less threatening but accurately describes the role most therapists assume. Just as one might seek out a consultant for legal, financial, medical, educational, or home decorating issues, the therapist is a consultant for issues both social and emotional. This reframe also emphasizes the maturity of the teen and the fact that she will be seeking the help she wants through a collaborative working alliance.

Parents should not be allowed to get off the hook in terms of their perceived role in the adolescent's developmental difficulties. By sending the teen to therapy, the parents must make it clear that they are not without a problematic role in the situation. Modeling some humility and honest self-reflection, parents can assure their teenager that they, too, need help and ultimately realize they are making mistakes. Leveling the playing field helps the teen feel less blamed and pathologized and offers the golden hope that perhaps her parents will see their own errors and react in ways more helpful to the teen.

In summary, by allowing the teen control over certain choices, destigmatizing therapy, emphasizing the teen's strengths, describing the therapist as a consultant, and recognizing the parents' responsibility as part of the evolving solution, adolescents are generally greatly relieved and far more open to the therapeutic process. Secretly, if not openly, adolescents long for an adult to understand and assist them. Helping them become freed up from their fears and defensiveness can allow them to save face and eagerly begin the important work of treatment.

THE THERAPEUTIC RELATIONSHIP: IT IS ALL ABOUT THE LOVE

Probably the single most critical component in a successful treatment relationship is the simple presence of mutual respect and liking between the clinician, the teen, and her parents. As simplistic as it may sound, treatment outcome is improved when the therapist genuinely likes the patient. *Liking* also embodies a sense of compassion, positive regard, and personal engagement on the part of the therapist that reassures and bolsters the adolescent's confidence and esteem. Similarly, for treatment to progress, the teen and her parents must feel comfortable with the therapist they choose.

The therapeutic alliance between the patient and therapist is tantamount. For the adolescent to feel affirmation and support around her central struggles with identity, intimacy, and independence, she must feel genuinely understood and cared about. That is not to say that the therapist will not at times offer corrective feedback or an unpopular interpretation. In fact, the trust that develops in a sound therapeutic alliance enables the therapist to make interventions in the face of less resistance and defensiveness by the teen. The therapist's role is not to side with all the patient's views, or the parents, but to be a nonjudgmental voice of reality. In other words, whereas the patient might minimize the significance of frequent cutting, the therapist can point out the real-life consequences, such as permanent scars. Whereas the parents might demand that the youth stop cutting and take the lock off his door, the therapist is there to remind the family that the adolescent must resolve this conflict independently, and overintrusiveness is likely to backfire.

The cornerstone of the therapist-patient relationship is confidentiality. Adolescents are especially sensitive about their privacy and can be desperate to keep information from their parents. Because the parents are also both their legal guardians and important participants in the treatment process, the confidentiality arrangement must be clear and steadfast. Teens and parents should always be told the exceptions to confidentiality. These include known danger to self or others (i.e., suicidal or homicidal intentions), suspicion of child or elder abuse, and grave disability. Legally and ethically, these serious situations require the breaking of confidentiality and immediate intervention in order to protect the safety of the youth or others.

Aside from these dramatic exceptions, the teenager needs reassurance and trust in the therapist's ability to keep personal information private. Yet adolescents always seem to understand that their parents need to remain properly informed about the treatment. In fact, teens frequently want their parents to be well informed of their plight and also actively advised about how to better parent. The teen and therapist need to then negotiate a way of communicating with parents in a manner that is most comfortable to the teen. Sometimes this involves the teen being in the room during parent meetings. Developing an explicit understanding about what the therapist needs to convey and what the teen expressly wants kept confidential further provides the adolescent a sense of safety and control. Although the therapist is often in the position of safeguarding highly sensitive information, such as details about the teen's substance abuse or sexual relationships, these confidences must be protected in order for necessary trust and safety to exist in the therapeutic relationship. Often, the very process of respecting their adolescent's right to privacy requires parents to confront their own difficulties in letting go and their tendency to micromanage their adolescent's life.

THE INITIAL SESSION

Given the adolescent's tremendous drive for autonomy, the first session should ideally be a private, individual meeting with the teen. It is important for the teen to have the opportunity to present herself (and her side of the story) to the therapist without fearing that her parents have already spoiled and biased the therapist's opinion. Although some initial information should be collected during the initial phone call, more comprehensive history-gathering can be conducted after the teen and therapist have met. Often, it is useful to allow the teen to choose among two or three clinicians, affording them a sense of control and choice in this important matter. A first session can be set up as a consultation to allow the teen and the clinician to determine whether they should continue working together.

The adolescent often will assume that the clinician has been recruited by the parents as an ally in their efforts to control her. Although the therapist and parents may certainly share the goal of stopping self-injury, the teen must feel that the clinician is equally concerned about her pressing personal goals and struggles. That the cutting is a means of managing these underlying problems needs to be respected by the therapist, lest the adolescent fear that she will be stripped of the one coping strategy she has acquired.

The avoidance of a power struggle is essential. After all, the adolescent clearly holds all the power over the decision to self-injure or not. If the teenager can be disabused of the assumption that the clinician is there to make them stop and otherwise carry out her parents' orders, she can ease up her defenses and resistance. Trusting that the clinician is concerned about her pain, her side of things, and not just the seeming victory of getting her to stop cutting is an absolute requisite for successful treatment.

This is an extremely challenging position for the therapist to maintain. Knowing, seeing, and hearing vivid details of the gruesome rituals involved in self-mutilation can evoke powerful feelings of revulsion, fear, anxiety, sadness, and even anger. In the therapist's urgency to be relieved of these distressing feelings, he or she may have the impulse to respond in the same demanding, disapproving, and emotional manner as the parents. These impulses must be held in check by the therapist and the feelings and concerns of the adolescent instead cast in the limelight. Rather than acting on these emotions in a controlling manner, the therapist can be informed by his or her reactions and thereby attain insight into the distressing feelings the teen and the parents also may be experiencing.

One absolute limit that the therapist must set regards suicidal intention or behavior. The teen must agree to a no-suicide contract wherein they promise to speak with the therapist if they feel in any danger of enacting their self-destructive feelings in a truly harmful manner. If she is unable to assure the therapist that she absolutely will not attempt suicide, hospitalization is the immediate and only recourse. If the teen is unable to make a no-suicide promise, she is telling the therapist that she is, in fact, not in control of her impulses and at serious risk, thus requiring immediate measures to assure her safety. By clarifying this expectation at the outset of therapy, the teen can better understand the implications of suicidal statements. As an extra precaution with all self-injurious patients, parents should be advised to remove from the household any potentially dangerous or lethal medications and, of course, any firearms or weapons.

Once a clear structure is in place, and the so-called rules of engagement established, treatment can proceed to uncover and identify the conflicts driving the drastic recourse of self-injury. Without coercion, but with trust and compassion, the teen often can and will eagerly launch into a litany of concerns that can quickly spell out a treatment plan. Whatever the actual roots of the distress, by forging a therapeutic alliance and clear structure of boundaries and expectations, treatment can proceed with minimal resistance, defensiveness, belligerence, and, ultimately, acting out. It is not unusual for an adolescent described as "belligerent," "uncooperative," or "hostile" to maintain that posture only in the presence of her parents. I frequently have been both amused and delighted to witness a dramatic transformation once the parents leave the room, as the teen eagerly sheds her defended posture and gushes forth her litany of heartfelt concerns and problems.

CONNECTING FEELINGS WITH BEHAVIOR: MAKING EXPLICIT CHOICES

Not surprisingly, adolescents are often at a loss to explain why they have been cutting themselves. They often will report a jumble of emotions and physical states that become indecipherable and overwhelming. Frequently, not only can teens have trouble identifying what they are feeling, but they also most often are unsure what generated the distress. One of the key goals of therapy is to help the adolescent sort through and identify what they are feeling and then to make a cognitive connection between precipitating events and painful feelings. By becoming more aware of their emotional triggers, be they academic stress, peer rejection, loneliness, or parental conflict, the teen can begin to make sense of the disturbing sequence of events. Once the teen is fully conscious of the central source of her distress, she is in a far more advantageous position to resolve it in ways other than self-injury.

For example, if Sara knows that she tends to self-injure every time she has a major fight with her mother over going out at night, she can begin to problem-solve other means of achieving her goal of increased independence. For example, she could try compromise: "Well, could I go out Friday night if I stay home tonight?" She could try to reassure her mother: "How about if I promise to call you when I get there and when I'm leaving?" She could also resort to talking on the phone with friends, e-mailing, or venting her frustration in her journal. The point is that if she can not have what she wants, can she either negotiate an acceptable resolution or find some other constructive activity that will relieve her feelings of loneliness and anger more effectively or at least less destructively than cutting?

Many treatment programs emphasize the value of insight in preventing acting out. The more a teen can understand and verbalize her feelings and conflicts, the less she is likely to express them in impulsive, self-destructive ways. By helping the adolescent pinpoint and gain conscious awareness regarding the sources of her distress in conflicts over intimacy, independence, or identity, she can better understand the potential resolutions to them as well. No longer is the teen seeking to simply blot out a muddle of emotions, she is feeling challenged by a normal and identifiable developmental challenge. Ultimately, the adolescent must learn to stay in the game and fight back, making real-life decisions regarding her relationships and goals.

BUILDING AN ARSENAL OF AMMUNITION AGAINST DESPAIR: NEW STRATEGIES AND RESOURCES

In order to relinquish the rapid remedy of self-injury, patients need to develop other techniques and resources for relieving distress. What else can the teen do to achieve relief other than cutting? What else will provide some, if not total, distraction or relief from the pain? Each patient needs to develop her own personalized list of alternatives to self-injury in order to begin learning more productive strategies for confronting a host of emotional assaults that are likely to plague her for some time.

Often, the notion of just experiencing and not acting on the distress seems novel and impossible to the teen. If the adolescent can at least embrace the idea that emotions will pass and that simply sitting with them can be growthful and empowering, however, the reflexive need to find a quick fix for distress can be interrupted. By getting in touch with and integrating painful feelings into one's whole self-experience, individuals can learn the value of confronting, riding out, and not becoming overwhelmed by strong emotions.

In addition, alternative actions need to be available to the teen, and these new strategies provide a cornerstone of the treatment process. The teen can take many actions in response to emotional distress. For example, the teen can confront the person inspiring her hurt or anger; she can call a sympathetic friend, take a walk, cry, or simply do nothing but weather the emotional storm, knowing that it will indeed pass. Teenagers need to build a new arsenal of coping skills now that the childhood options of running to one's parents or throwing a tantrum no longer seem age-appropriate. Working with the teen to define her own set of alternatives to self-injury focuses the responsibility and means for coping squarely on the teen and can empower her to actively choose not to harm herself.

Common alternatives to self-injury include journaling, exercising, listening to music, leaving the room, taking a hot bath, drinking tea, watching television, calling a friend, contacting the therapist, looking at photos with positive memories, cuddling the family dog or cat, cooking or baking, or writing a letter to the friend, teacher, or family member toward whom she feels frustrated or enraged. Individualizing the list as much as possible helps the adolescent assume ownership of her coping choices and establish methods that reflect her unique identity and personality.

Not only can the adolescent develop control over her behavior, she can learn to intervene with her thoughts as well. It is frequently the negative self-statements that the teen makes internally that provoke the pain. Thoughts like "I hate myself," "I'm fat and ugly," "No one will ever love me," and "I deserve to suffer" are purely destructive and yet are fortunately alterable. Teens can learn to think in less black-and-white terms about themselves and their circumstances and to think with more complexity about their strengths and weaknesses. Replacing these thoughts with others can generate much more positive feelings: "I'm disappointed in my grades but can understand how hard things have been lately. I can improve them"; "I feel fat right now but in two hours I'll feel better. I have other things to think about"; "I'm feeling lonely now, but I am a very loving person"; and "Suffering will not make me a better person." This type of cognitive therapy, made famous by Albert Ellis[70] and his Rational Emotive Behavior Therapy approach, can be highly empowering and effective in altering painful emotional states.

ENHANCING RELATIONSHIPS: LEARNING TO COMMUNICATE ACTIVELY AND DIRECTLY

Secure attachments to friends and family members are perhaps the most precious resources a teenager can have. During the adolescent period of redefining the self and one's relationships, a great deal of tumult often clouds the teen's ability to understand and communicate her relational needs effectively. Teens are notorious for communicating their changing needs and concerns in hostile, secretive, belligerent, dramatic, or altogether confusing ways. For them to become more successful in maintaining meaningful relationships, teens need to evolve more mature means of communicating. Thus, learning to actively express, discuss, negotiate, and give and take in their verbal communications is an extremely valuable set of skills that can be developed and practiced.

Adolescents are often distressingly egocentric. Helping the teen to appreciate another's feelings and perspectives may sound basic, but empathy is often a limited skill at this age. Learning to put oneself in another's shoes and appreciate that person's perspective is a skill that can be developed and put to valuable use by the adolescent. For example, the teen needs to ask herself, "Why are my parents unwilling to let me go with Joe to the concert?" The answer is not "Because they want to make my life miserable," but mostly likely, "Because they are worried about Joe driving and the absence of any adult supervision at the enormous stadium concert." If the teen can understand that the parents' strictness is rooted in fear for her safety and can empathize with that fear, she can begin to work with the parents in negotiating a compromise. For example, she can propose that her parents drive Joe and her to the concert and point out that her friend Susan's dad will be at the concert. The parents can confirm that he will keep an eye on the group of kids and ensure that they are ready to be picked up at midnight. If the teen is willing to be flexible in her demands, the parents often can be reassured and similarly relax their restrictions to some degree. Grasping the positive intentions behind one another's concerns and needs allows for more productive and collaborative problem solving. Ultimately, it is this process of give and take that empowers teens and parents to work toward common middle ground rather than becoming stuck in polarizing positions.

Creative solutions to seemingly irreconcilable conflicts provide families with a sense of hopeful agency. Instead of dictating that curfew must be at 10:00, perhaps the teen can be entrusted with an extra half-hour if she remembers to phone home at 10:00. This compromise can reassure the parents of the teen's willingness and ability to take responsibility and respect their concerns yet simultaneously afford the teen a nod of support and confidence in her growing sense of independence. Similarly, if the teen is refusing to go on a family vacation because she wants to be home with her friends, allowing her to bring along a friend, plan some of her preferred activities, or set up an extra series of sleepovers after the trip can respect the teen's and the family's seemingly incompatible needs.

This type of understanding and negotiation can be expanded to relationships with friends, teachers, and romantic partners. For the teen to overcome the frustration of a perceived rejection and not succumb to patterns of self-defeating attributions and behaviors such as cutting, a veritable new world can be opened up simply through the power of actively engaging in a dialogue. For example, a teen might commonly complain that a teacher is a jerk and does not like her, and therefore there is no hope of getting a B in the class. If the teen can at least contemplate the notion that the teacher might be amenable, even eager, to assist her in achieving the desired B, however, it becomes incumbent upon the teen to engage the teacher in a solution. The teacher might provide some helpful suggestions about what to focus on in studying for the upcoming exam. She might offer the teen an extra-credit opportunity. Or the teacher may allow the student to redo incomplete or absent homework. If the adolescent can learn to engage others toward a solution, rather than polarizing into adversarial or defeatist positions, she can become highly effective as her own best advocate.

Most adolescents who self-injure are highly interpersonally sensitive. Perceived rejections, slights, and criticisms are quickly met with dejection, self-recrimination, and hopelessness. The adolescent must learn to make the choice to work toward rewarding connections with others rather than withdraw into depressive reveries. The teen might not always achieve the acceptance or friendship she seeks, but she can learn to communicate in a manner that will maximize her ability to gain a realistic understanding of her interactions. Approaching a friend and telling her that she feels hurt and left out and would like to understand if she has done something to put them off encourage real engagement and honest resolution. Perhaps the friend meant no offense or assumed that she was angry with the friend. Perhaps the friend is avoiding her because she has new friends who engage in activities that embarrass her. Or perhaps the friend is hurt or angry and the air needs to be cleared in order for the friendship to continue. Perhaps she is unwilling to talk honestly and is not such a valuable friend after all. Too frequently, adolescents who self-injure are prone to a knee-jerk response that involves self-recrimination and self-destructive behavior. This leads to the tremendous distress and self-loathing that is a partner to cutting and other forms of self-injury.

Therapy can focus on improved communication in vivo between the adolescent and her parents. By mediating family discussions, conflicts, and negotiations, the therapist can teach skills to be applied at home. The therapist can serve as a role model of productive communication and help each individual rephrase or articulate the message he or she wants received. In individual session, teens can role-play how they might try to negotiate with their parents, and the therapist can provide corrective feedback to enhance the potential success at home. Similarly, the expression of conflicts and emotional issues involving friends and love interests can be practiced and polished through role-playing with the therapist in the safe confines of treatment sessions.

It is extremely instructive for the adolescent to witness the therapist's communications with her parents. Often, teens are bolstered by the therapist's efforts to hold the parents accountable, offer novel suggestions, or help negotiate resolutions. Not only does the teen feel powerfully supported, she also can respond more openly to similar messages directed toward her. The teen can gradually learn to delete inflammatory statements and utilize more effective communication strategies simply through watching and listening.

ADDRESSING PAST WOUNDS: TRAUMA AND DISSOCIATIVE CUTTING

As discussed in chapter 1, childhood traumas often resurface during adolescence, creating intensely disturbing emotions. Adolescents' emerging sexuality forces them to confront past sexual experiences in a new light, and victims of sexual abuse can be especially overwhelmed by their painful memories and conflicts. Similarly, adolescents who suffered significant losses, such as the death of a parent or sibling in childhood, are forced to reintegrate these traumas at a time of self-redefinition. In other words, as the teenager begins to establish an identity separate from parents and develop important peer attachments, past losses and traumas are revisited.

Children who are sexually abused or suffer other major traumas often cope with the overwhelming nature of the event by cutting off emotionally in a process called *dissociation*. Dissociation involves the numbing of emotional pain and awareness and can even entail complete amnesia of an event. By numbing and forgetting, the individual manages to stave off the pain, humiliation, sadness, and fear associated with a loss, humiliation, or trauma. Cutting in these individuals serves a similar purpose in creating a dissociated state in which intense distress is replaced with a feeling of numbness and ultimately of desired disconnection from painful thoughts and feelings.

Treatment with adolescents who have experienced such traumas is often more challenging and long-term. These teens require an especially safe and trusting therapeutic relationship that often takes time, and considerable attention to resistance and fears, in order to evolve. Trust issues, fear of vulnerability, and shame all make opening up to the therapist particularly daunting. The revisiting of painful memories and feelings is actively resisted until the adolescent can discover that discussing them in a safe environment does not need to overwhelm her like it did in the past. This process of uncovering past wounds can take place only when the adolescent (or adult, for that matter) discovers that she is safe from her past victimizer and less vulnerable to the shocking grief of sudden loss. Discovering that as maturing teenagers they have more agency and power to cope than they did as children is a productively empowering process.

Adolescents who use numbing during self-injury to "disappear" or otherwise soothe themselves fundamentally need to acquire new resources for withstanding strong emotions. Frequently, distress is experienced as an on or off switch; either it is full-blown and overwhelming or essentially absent. Learning to modulate or regulate emotional intensity is a critical skill. Often, simply the discussion of taboo subjects in a relatively calm state in therapy helps diffuse the long-suppressed emotional intensity and teaches the individual that he or she can survive the feelings. Therapeutic intervention in tandem with maturation can help the teen develop strategies outside of sessions to stay with feelings and ride them out or choose nondestructive alternative behaviors that provide relief or distraction.

The ultimate work with trauma victims involves repairing damaged self-images and dysfunctional relationship patterns. Learning to invoke new insights and behaviors toward managing feelings and relationships becomes an ongoing process that can save the adolescent from becoming entrenched in negative patterns. This core work can progress as more immediate concerns and crises are addressed but cannot be accomplished overnight. The safety and continuity of a long-term therapeutic relationship, though costly in terms of money, time, and energy, can be invaluable in facilitating long-term recovery and healthy adjustment.

COLLABORATION AND CONSULTATION

Adolescents' lives are demanding on numerous fronts. School-related concerns, family issues, potential medical issues, social dramas, and an often endless array of extracurricular activities challenge adolescents on often competing fronts. It is a mistake for a clinician to treat an adolescent as an isolated entity, as other key relationships and endeavors help form the larger context of their lives. Ultimately, these need to be integrated where appropriate into a comprehensive treatment plan. For example, teachers or school officials often are extremely important resources for ongoing collaboration. Physicians or coaches must sometimes be consulted and apprised of the teen's progress. Parents, and sometimes grandparents and siblings, need to be actively included in the treatment process as well.

Legally, the clinician is required to have the parent of a minor sign a form giving his or her permission to release confidential information to specific others. This will allow, for example, the therapist and the physician treating the teen's asthma to communicate about relevant stresses and medication side effects. It also is very helpful to ask the teenager to sign the permission form in order to give her explicit consent regarding the communication of treatment information. This respects the teen's privacy, control over her personal life, and growing autonomy.

It is frequently necessary to refer adolescents to other professionals in conjunction with their ongoing therapy. For example, academic tutors often are key resources in alleviating academic conflicts at home. On occasion, medication may be deemed potentially beneficial and a consultation with a physician recommended. Collaboration enhances professional treatment by maintaining communication and a more integrative process for the adolescent.

Another commonly made referral is for psychological assessment. Clinicians often will have serious questions regarding the teenager's cognitive functioning, suicide potential, drug use, impulse control, and many other issues, and psychological testing often can shed invaluable light on these dimly understood aspects of behavior and personality. Because adolescents may be highly defended and resistant or may not be conscious of their internal conflicts and therefore unable to articulate them, psychological testing utilizes tools that pursue other avenues of accessing their psychological functioning. Paper-and-pencil tests, projective tests, empirically based objective tests, and neuropsychological/cognitive tests can be selected and combined into a battery best suited for assessing key concerns with each adolescent. Psychologists who have had specialized training and experience in psychological testing should be consulted for this type of evaluation.

WHEN IS A PSYCHIATRIC CONSULTATION FOR MEDICATION INDICATED?

Increasingly, psychoactive medications are being employed in the treatment of a huge variety of emotional problems and symptoms. This is true for adolescents as well as for children and adults. In adolescents who self-injure, a variety of specific medications can be prescribed to treat the underlying depression, anxiety, and impulsive behavior. Knowing when a teen should be referred for the possible addition of medication hinges on several key signs.

First, teens with clear symptoms of depression may benefit from antidepressant medication. Major depression in teens can manifest itself in a pattern of symptoms, including irritability, diminished pleasure or interest in previously enjoyed activities, disruption of normal eating and sleeping habits, physical lethargy, agitation, low self-esteem, difficulty concentrating, flattening of affect, and thoughts of death or suicide. A constellation of these symptoms needs to have been present for at least two weeks, cause notable difficulties in functioning, and can not be attributed to drug use, medical illness, or normal bereavement.[25] Although teens might deny or even be unaware that they are depressed, these symptoms can point toward a clinical depression that may warrant adjunctive treatment with antidepressant medication.

A second set of difficulties often amenable to medication involves impulse-control problems manifested in disordered eating, shoplifting, or self-destructive actions. Teens with bulimia, for example, may obsessively ruminate about food and dieting and become overwhelmed by the impulse to binge eat. Teens who shoplift might report an inexplicable desire and drive to steal in a well-planned or strictly spur-of-the-moment manner. Often, the same medications used to treat depression have been shown to have an inhibiting effect on impulsive symptoms.

Similarly, obsessive thinking and anxious rumination also are common in adolescents who self-injure. A tendency toward worry, tension, and endless fixation on specific conflicts can be a sign of the tremendous internal preoccupation impacting the teen. Again, serotonin selective reuptake inhibitor (SSRI) antidepressants often are employed to target these disruptive symptoms and free the adolescent from a sense of being trapped and controlled by these thoughts. Difficulties concentrating and attending often are ameliorated by these medications as well. More severe obsessive-compulsive disorders can be treated with other medications in conjunction with psychotherapy.

Occasionally, adolescents will become so overwhelmed by depression as to lose their ability to think clearly and realistically. A thought disorder, psychotic depression, or bipolar illness with psychosis occasionally is observed in adolescents whose speech and thoughts are clearly disrupted and illogical. The teen may also evidence delusional thinking and/or experience auditory hallucinations. Such symptoms of a psychotic process require immediate pharmacological intervention as well as environmental modifications to reduce stress and assure safety. Antipsychotic medications may be prescribed in these cases, with or without antidepressant medication or another mood stabilizer.

SSRIs increase the amount of the neurotransmitter serotonin in the brain. Serotonin is associated with elevated mood. Researchers have determined that by increasing the level of serotonin, patients can experience a variety of benefits, including enhanced mood and a sharp decrease in anxiety, rumination, obsessiveness, and impulsivity. Self-injurious behavior is therefore decreased as the teen's distress level is held in better biological check. Prozac, Paxil, Zoloft, and Celexa are some of the more commonly used SSRIs, and each has its own side effect profile. The physician can select an SSRI to minimize or maximize certain side effects to the benefit of the patient. For example, Celexa may be prescribed when sexual side effects are bothersome. Prozac may be prescribed in individuals who can benefit from reductions in obsessive and anxious rumination. Any medication can have negative side effects, but these newer antidepressants have represented a dramatic improvement over tricyclic antidepressants and monoamine oxidase inhibitors that can generate more bothersome and even dangerous side effects. Other antidepressants also may be selected, such as Wellbutrin, a medication with the ability to enhance mood, attention, and energy level.

Medication always should be prescribed in conjunction with psychotherapy. Although many adolescents and, indeed, parents are reluctant to use medication for understandably legitimate reasons, sometimes a thorough consultation can provide clear information and dispel certain concerns. Patients are entitled to a consultation in order to carefully assess for themselves the potential benefits or undesirability of adding medication to their treatment plan.

CONCLUSIONS

Professional treatment of self-injurious adolescents often requires an integrative approach that incorporates two or more modalities of treatment, such as individual therapy, family therapy, group therapy, medication, insight-oriented approaches, and cognitive-behavioral interventions. Each adolescent presents unique challenges and assets, and treatment must therefore be highly individualized. The development of a safe, confidential, and collaborative therapeutic relationship provides the cornerstone of effective treatment. In the following chapter, specialized approaches to treating self-injury are discussed.

Chapter 7

Specialized Approaches and Adjuncts in Treating Self-Injury

Family therapy was a nightmare. But it really helped.
16-year-old struggling with alcohol abuse and self-injury

I got the most help from my teen depression group. We were all really there for each other and it was actually fun.
Acting-out 15-year-old

Developing a sound framework of psychotherapy in the treatment of cutting provides a necessary but not always sufficient program of intervention. Sometimes, additional specialized interventions need to be integrated into the core treatment plan in order to best address the difficulties of some teens. In this chapter, specialized approaches will be discussed and their usefulness as adjuncts to the comprehensive treatment of cutting explained.

GROUP THERAPY

According to Irving Yalom,[71] a modern pioneer of group therapies, group psychotherapy imparts significant and unique therapeutic benefits. Among these is the group experience's ability to combat alienation and enable individuals to experience common ground in their struggles with others who share their experience. Groups further allow individuals to gain information, hope, interpersonal skills, catharsis, camaraderie, and the opportunity to integrate and imitate skills observed and modeled by others. Importantly, group treatment allows the patient to provide help to others as well, enhancing self-esteem and consolidating insights.

Many teen groups are available to address the relevant challenges specific to particular problems. Groups may be organized around depression, parental divorce, drug abuse, shyness, eating disorders, and, of course, the problem of self-injury. For teens with ongoing cutting, seeing peers coping with similar difficulties and similar impulses to self-injure can help adolescents feel less alone, and less "abnormal." As core issues are articulated, group members can gain an appreciation for the range of, yet commonality of, adolescent difficulties and can then begin to identify and label their own. Teens who are resistant to communicating can gain tremendous information and insight just by listening to and observing other group members. Silently, they can evaluate the cycle of self-injury in someone other than themselves and perhaps more honestly address their own problems.

The interpersonal dynamics of the group further address common themes among adolescents who cut. By hearing how someone else dealt with their anger by cutting and withdrawing rather than by talking with the offending party, teens can begin to formulate other means of coping directly with interpersonal conflict. At best, these interpersonal issues occur within the group, where they can be discussed and understood in vivo. The acceptance of peers combined with the honest confrontations of peers can mobilize self-injurers in the group to more safely address their problems head-on.

Groups can also provide a structure that many teens find missing in individual therapy. Groups may have a consistent routine: The therapist may suggest a theme for each session along with information about that theme; for example, triggers for cutting. Members might then check in by saying how they confronted their impulses to self-injure or cut themselves during the week. Then, hot topics that are immediately creating stress for individual members can be identified and addressed, followed by an open group discussion about these challenging situations. The group then might conclude with the therapist providing a summary of the issues and productive strategies raised during the meeting. The predictability of a semistructured group can be reassuring to adolescents and help make the discussion of difficulties less anxiety-provoking.

Perhaps the greatest advantage of a group is that teens care far more about what their peers think of them than what adults think of them. If challenged, affirmed, or encouraged to try different coping strategies by other adolescents, self-injurers are often far more attentive and responsive than might be merely with an adult droning at them. Also, by verbalizing insights and ideas to others in the group, teens can feel empowered and perhaps more amenable to taking their own advice. Thus, teens can often feel far more invested and engaged in a group therapy with peers than in a one-on-one therapy format.

Case Example: Samantha's Group Therapy Experience

Samantha, 16, has been burning and puncturing her skin for more than nine months, despite beginning individual and family psychotherapy three months ago. Samantha is angry and rebellious, and she and her parents either fight constantly or avoid each other altogether. She is in danger of failing three of her sophomore-year courses and has been involved with an 18-year-old who has a serious alcohol problem. Samantha's parents and therapist are quite concerned about not only her self-injurious behavior but also her self-destructive choices in regard to school and intimate relationships.

Samantha is referred to an ongoing psychotherapy group for 16- and 17-year-old girls experiencing a range of difficulties. Only one other girl in the group is a cutter, but all of the girls are having serious problems with depression, parental conflict, school failure, and impulsive behavior. Samantha is initially resistant and plans to be defiantly silent in the group but is surprised to find the other girls pretty cool. She comments that "we all have a lot in common" and engages quickly in discussions about one girl's bulimia, another's poor grades, and a third's desire to run away from the ongoing battles at home. The other girls are curious about her self-injuries, but it blends in with the many other dysfunctional coping strategies that are tripping everyone up.

Not shy girls, they are all quite comfortable providing direct feedback to one another. For example, Samantha tells one girl, "It sounds like you like fighting with your Mom," and another, "No way do you need to lose weight! Tell your boyfriend to fuck off." One girl tells Samantha, "You're gonna regret those burn marks when you're older," and "They kind of make you look like you have spots." Another comments that her boyfriend is a "loser," and she could do a lot better. They all agree on the recklessness of driving with a guy who is "always loaded." These peer-generated comments, coming as they do from other teens who have no apparent investment in controlling them, take on far more significance than the scolding admonitions they have learned to block out from adults.

Samantha seems to be able to take these remarks in stride, but they reverberate in her mind deeply. She decides for the time being to stop burning spots on her skin and only to resort to needle sticks when she feels the need to self-injure. She also starts to find her boyfriend "sort of disgusting when he's slobbery drunk," and does not leave school with him during the day that week. Although she did not really like fighting with her mom, she wonders why it seemed that way to the girls in the group until she began to notice how she provoked and pushed her mom's buttons almost reflexively.

As Samantha continued in her own therapy as well as in the group, she was able to observe others making the same choices as she, and with the same negative results. As she offered support, suggestions, and sometimes constructive feedback to others, she began to experience herself as capable of problem-solving and taking charge of her own choices. She was also more receptive to the other girls' suggestions for what she could do when she was distressed besides harm herself. In conjunction with her focused work in this area during individual sessions, Samantha began to expand her resources and venture out from the dead-end corner she had fought herself into.

The benefits of including Samantha in a teen therapy group as an adjunct to her overall treatment evolved largely from direct peer engagement. Samantha gave special credence to the observations of the other girls, stimulating more honest introspection than she had previously undertaken. She also could see herself as one of many teens struggling with common adolescent obstacles and could hear her own advice to others as wise and even applicable to herself. The other group members, being outspoken and comfortable in the safe group setting, reliably confronted her smokescreens and failure to actively take responsibility. Samantha could readily reject and defy adult interpretations of her behavior but found it impossible not to hear those offered by her peers.

FAMILY THERAPY

Few therapeutic modalities fill an adolescent with more dread than the prospect of speaking directly to their parents in a meeting facilitated by a therapist who knows their truth. Addressing one's hurt, anger, and conflict directly with one's parents is a challenge many adults and even fewer adolescents eagerly undertake. The necessity of communicating more effectively at home, however, is rarely lost on the adolescent. With the therapist's support, preparation, and promise of nonpartisanship, many adolescents and their parents can be empowered to take on the difficult work of honest, open discussion and negotiation.

It can come as quite a welcome shock to teenagers to receive confirmation that everything is not all their fault and entirely their burden; parents have work to do, too. In fact, every family is a fluid and interactive system wherein each member influences one another. A parent that is depressed can fail to support his or her spouse in parenting and feel unavailable and uncaring to the adolescent. A teenager who is obnoxious and hostile creates distance, mistrust, and tremendous tension in the entire household. And parents who lovingly want to protect their teen from unforeseen dangers inadvertently may convey rigidity, lack of respect, and unyielding control to a teen striving for age-appropriate freedoms. Bringing the family to the table, so to speak, for less obstructed communication and negotiation refocuses the real work of adolescent-parent development as an actively evolving process that requires genuine and constructive engagement.

ISSUES COMMONLY ADDRESSED IN FAMILY
THERAPY WITH SELF-INJURING ADOLESCENTS

Although every family brings its own unique constellation of resources, conflicts, and dynamics into treatment, certain key issues are frequently addressed in family treatment with self-injurers.

Privacy

Teenagers confound parents with their growing secrecy and insistence on privacy. Parents who once organized their child's backpack are suddenly forbidden to so much as touch it. Teens who once welcomed and even beckoned parents into their bedrooms suddenly have discovered the door, the lock, and the Do Not Disturb sign. And parents who have been privy to the intimate details of every social drama, school problem, and emotional high and low are heartbroken to suddenly be completely left out if not altogether shunned.

Parents of self-injurers become especially conflicted about the privacy issue when they fear that their teen may be harming herself behind closed bedroom doors or hiding matches or razors in her desk or backpack. Parents may want to respect their teen's right to privacy but feel compelled to intrude in order to ensure safety. The teen also seems to be sending mixed messages that on the one hand say "Leave me alone; I'm independent" and on the other hand imply "I'm in trouble; I hurt and need your help." This intricate dilemma is often addressed in family sessions wherein the competing tensions within each conflict can be articulated and confronted head-on. The ever-challenging issue of parent-child boundaries must be continually addressed, with appropriate roles clarified and reinforced.

Suicide and Serious Harm

Even the mildest of self-injuries raises the specter of potential risk for suicide. Perhaps nothing can be more terrifying or inspiring of a sense of ultimate helplessness in parents. A clear contract for ensuring that the teen does not intend and will not seriously harm herself is often committed to writing in a signed No Suicide Contract, with the conditions for immediate hospitalization spelled out. Parents often can feel manipulated by implicit threats, however, and held hostage to fears of provoking their teen to hurt herself. And teens can feel confused by their own ambivalence, being tugged and pulled by the conflicting feelings of power and helplessness they experience with their ability to choose to self-harm or not.

Parents need to be supported in continuing to set limits, say no, and regulate restrictions on the teen's freedoms, despite their worries of sparking a self-harm impulse. Once it has been understood that they can not stop their teen from cutting, only the teen can make that decision, they must not allow themselves to be intimidated into a position of passivity or tiptoeing around conflict. Certainly, teens need extra support and understanding when they are distressed, but this should never be leveraged to obtain privileges otherwise not allowed. Furthermore, once the teen gets the message that parents will not respond to veiled threats, the power of the act becomes a far less compelling tool. Ultimately, teenagers need and want to feel their parents' presence and investment by virtue of their support as well as through corrective feedback and setting of limits. Even though they appear to be pushing parents away, if one listens closely, they are also pulling them toward them as well.

Adolescents who self-injure should be encouraged to verbalize their thoughts and feelings about harming themselves as opposed to enacting them. This is true as well for what may instinctively feel unmentionable and taboo: suicidal ideation. Such ideation can range from a passive, vague wish to just disappear, to more elaborate motivations associated with a specific plan. Constantly differentiating between what the teen is feeling and thinking versus what they believe she might actually do is crucial. This exercise needs to be repeated again and again with the understanding that even a false threat to kill oneself will necessitate hospitalization.

Often, adolescents harbor romantic fantasies of what it would be like to be hospitalized. This can be an alluring attraction, as the teen imagines being ministered to by caring adults in a safe and nondemanding environment. Hospitalization also can seem like a ticket out of overwhelming difficulties, for example academic problems, social humiliations, or unremitting family turmoil. Although these fantasies have some merit, the clinician should be up-front with the teen that hospitalization is no vacation and that there are many challenging and unpleasant aspects to it as well. Emphasizing the goal to help the teen maintain the highest level of freedom and choice as possible can help bring into focus the potential confinement and loss of control all individuals feel on hospital units, thereby giving pause to overly dramatic suicide threats. Ultimately, however, the hospital is there to assure medical safety and psychiatric assistance to teens who are genuinely overwhelmed and unable to control their impulses for serious self-harm.

Friends and Love Interests

Part and parcel to the developmental bombshells thrown by healthy adolescents is an often passionate need to spend time with friends or romantic partners. Teenagers are frustrated by their parents' questions, curfews, and general reticence about allowing what seems every bit as essential as breathing: access to friends.

Understandably, parents worry about the many risks posed by unsupervised teen exploits, with concerns ranging from sexual exploitation, pregnancy and AIDS, car accidents, drugs, and vulnerability to predators of all kinds. Used to careful oversight of their children's social lives and safe activities, the mobility, energy and intense social and sexual drives of teenagers utterly terrifies loving parents. Even the normal advent of sexual exploration can be frightening to parents and the impulse to place one's precious teen in lockdown almost irresistible.

Families therefore need a reality check on where to draw the line between freedom and firm limits. Should Alice be allowed to go downtown to just hang out with her friends? Is it okay for her to leave the movie her parents dropped her off at to spontaneously go to a party? What are the consequences of Jake coming home after curfew? What if he has alcohol on his breath? Or shows up in the car of a new 23-year-old friend? Is Susan's obvious sexual involvement with her new boyfriend to be obstructed or forbidden, ignored or denied, or constructively discussed? These are all very commonly confronted questions that teens, in their haste to have fun, and parents, in their urgency to protect, often have difficulty resolving. The role of the therapist is to facilitate understanding between family members as to their needs and desires and to negotiate some realistic compromise between these often competing interests. Adolescents often feel greatly supported and empowered by the therapist in getting through to parents, whereas parents inevitably appreciate the validation of their concerns and upholding of reasonable expectations.

Teenagers who self-injure may be particularly volatile around these issues. Helping families acquire strategies for communicating and negotiating even in the midst of charged emotional encounters further models to the adolescent the need to problem-solve and directly address tough issues rather than acting them out. Self-injuring teens often have excruciating difficulty in their peer and romantic relationships, and the steadying guidance of clearly established rules yet fully supported healthy involvements with peers provides the structure and support they cannot yet construct for themselves. Although adolescents will frequently make poor choices and missteps in their peer relationships, the therapist can assist the family in discerning where these should be tolerated and where safeguards should be set. Both teens and parents need to learn to choose their battles selectively, lest they become overbearing. Family therapy is often the only route toward this type of acquired wisdom when families are in genuine turmoil.

Cutting and Blame

Adolescents may attribute their need to self-injure to a variety of stressors or external forces. Indeed, the ultimate culprit from their immature viewpoint is often the parents. Teens will often articulate this in no uncertain terms: "My parents are ruining my life!"; "They won't let me do anything"; "They're always nagging, intruding, controlling, snooping, misunderstanding, freaking out, disapproving." From the perspective of a deeply unhappy adolescent who resorts to self-injury to quell distress, her parents are often perceived as ultimately failing her. Her parents can neither stay out nor intervene in any way that can possibly mitigate the developmental obstacles she faces and, as such, are often (unfairly) viewed as the most accessible scapegoats.

Parents may take this to heart and assume that they must somehow be to blame for the dysfunctions of their children. Some are so affronted or enraged by their child's glaring misbehavior that they overpathologize them and fail to assume responsibility for the impact their condemnation or excessive control can have on their teen. The goal in family therapy is to place the blame squarely where it belongs: on adolescence. Given the intruder in their midst, namely adolescent development, they need to be helped to confront its challenges as best as each is able. For the teen, this means taking responsibility for her behavior and her choices. For the parent, this means taking responsibility for their own need to grow in their ability to adapt to parenting this particular adolescent.

Family therapy requires skillful intervention to help the teenager accept responsibility without losing face. Teens are loath to appear foolish, mistaken, or accountable to their parents and often need a way to avoid humiliation. This can be accomplished in many ways. For example, parents can disclose their own missteps as adolescents. Teens also can be given deserved admiration for their honesty in accepting responsibility and making important concessions, which in itself reflects their growing maturity. And parents can be quieted in their critical, judgmental, and I-told-you-so attitudes. Neither the adolescent nor the parents benefit in any way by hurting or damaging the self-esteem of the other, and it is the therapist's job to ameliorate and reframe threats of this sort.

DIALECTICAL BEHAVIORAL THERAPY

In 1993, Marsha Linehan at the University of Washington published her influential theory and treatment approach in *Cognitive-Behavioral Treatment of Borderline Personality Disorder*.[36] In it, she specifically addressed the problem of repetitive self-injury, which she termed *parasuicidal behavior*. Though not exclusively the domain of women, or women with borderline personality disorder (BPD), the vast majority of patients whom she treated with repetitive self-injury were females who met the *DSM-IV*[25] criteria for BPD. Importantly, Linehan views such women as suffering from dysregulation of their emotions, relationships, behavior, cognition, and sense of self. She attributes this dysregulation to two key factors: (1) a biological vulnerability to extreme emotional lability and (2) chronic childhood exposure to so-called invalidating environments in which the patient's personal perceptions and responses were consistently discredited by significant caretakers. As children in such invalidating environments, they are told that their feelings are neither accurate nor sensible responses and that they are flawed in their ability to cope with stress up to the standards unrealistically expected of them. Thus, an emotionally vulnerable child never learns to accurately label and trust her own emotional responses, nor does she learn that others are reliably available to help her when she is distressed or overwhelmed. This results in a person who is subject to sudden surges of intense emotion without the concomitant skills for regulating and coping with such distress.

A classic example of an invalidating environment is seen in families in which sexual abuse occurs. The child feels frightened of the abuser, vulnerable, and angry. Yet these emotions are disqualified and invalidated as the abuse remains denied or unseen. The child cannot seek any validation of her experience of victimization and intense distress as the adults fail to acknowledge and intervene with the abuse. She self-invalidates and becomes dependent on others to solve her problems while trying to maintain the appearance of competence. Another less dramatic example of an invalidating environment might be seen in a family with high-achieving, successful parents. Perhaps they have a child who lacks self-confidence and experiences anxiety in social and performance-based realms. If the parents are unable to empathize with her insecurity and insist that there is nothing to be afraid of and, furthermore, she should therefore cope more successfully without any real assistance, the child learns that she is deficient, her feelings are wrong, and unless her emotional distress is dramatic, help will not be available.

Linehan posits that these emotionally vulnerable individuals subjected to an invalidating environment frequently develop borderline personality disorder, which is marked by problematic instability in mood, relationships, behavior, and identity. Suicidal or self-injurious behaviors are commonly manifested in such individuals when they become emotionally overwhelmed. If this description closely matches your experience with a self-injurious, volatile, confused teenager, the applicability of Linehan's dialectical behavioral therapy (DBT) approach becomes clear.

Dialectical refers to two extremes achieving a synthesis somewhere in the middle. The key dialectics to Linehan are acceptance and change; the message being, "Yes you are suffering and doing the best you can, *and*, yes, you can grow and change and cope more effectively." This synthesis communicates acceptance of the person's fearful dependency and their power to move toward more independent coping. This concept of addressing two simultaneous extremes at once is invaluable with adolescents who are all about contradiction, particularly in regard to their simultaneous need for dependence and independence. Synthesizing these multiple tensions in therapy and in the teen's development is extremely therapeutic.

DBT has four central treatment modalities: individual therapy, group skills training, telephone contact (with the therapist between sessions), and a consultation group for therapists. This is a tall order, and full-fledged DBT involves specialized training, resources, and a unique commitment by both the patient in the therapist. As a result, elements of DBT are often integrated into practice and can be highly useful in both understanding and treating self-injurers.

The focus of treatment is on skills training, and any or all of these skills can be extremely effective with self-injurers. DBT teaches patients mindfulness skills (a derivation of Buddhist meditation that enables one to gain better awareness and remain present, or in touch, with one's emotional experience), interpersonal effectiveness skills, emotion modulation skills, and distress tolerance skills. Clearly, for teens who are not aware of their emotions, have interpersonal conflicts, and have a central problem with modulating and tolerating distress, such concrete problem-solving tools are invaluable. These skills are developed while expressly conveying validation of the person's thoughts, feelings, and actions as thoroughly understandable, even if ultimately undesirable. The number one treatment focus in DBT is on developing skills to curtail self-injury, clearly an invaluable goal in any treatment program focused on reducing this destructive coping tool.

INTERPERSONAL PSYCHOTHERAPY

Interpersonal psychotherapy (IPT)[72] is a focused and time-limited treatment approach to depression, eating disorders, and relational difficulties in adolescents and adults. IPT focuses on relational issues that are viewed as central to the ongoing experience of many depressed and otherwise distressed adolescents. This treatment program is modeled on the work of earlier object relations theorists who believed that our early attachments and ongoing relationships formed our personalities and psychological functioning. Sessions address daily issues confronted by the adolescent in their relationships and assist the teen in learning to link their emotional state with their interpersonal relationships. In self-injurers, these links can be especially critical to recovery.

IPT is an empirically supported and semistructured treatment program designed to incorporate three main phases. The first phase involves assessment in order to focus treatment on interpersonal conflicts or deficits. The second phase seeks to resolve the primary area of interpersonal difficulty and alleviate troubling symptoms. The final stage addresses termination of therapy, supporting the patient's enhanced independence and equipping her with a knowledge of triggers and early warning signs that might necessitate a return to treatment. The time-limited nature of IPT is developmentally compatible with adolescence in that rather than fostering dependency, the patient is empowered with her new skills and encouraged to apply them as she proceeds independently.

This model of treatment can meld nicely with the normative adolescent goals of attaining increasing levels of coping skills, secure attachments, and independence. The time-limited context can help structure and focus the treatment and help enhance treatment motivation. IPT is not a theoretically biased approach and can therefore integrate a variety of therapeutic approaches and modalities, such as insight-oriented and cognitive-behavioral techniques. The relational focus is inevitably relevant to adolescents who are struggling to engage, maintain, and resolve a host of interpersonal relationships in concert with undertaking the daunting process of defining themselves.

EGO PSYCHOLOGY

Unlike classic psychoanalysis, which conjures images of Sigmund Freud, couches, and mysteriously distant analysts, ego psychology is less concerned with infantile conflicts and transference in the therapy. Rather, ego psychology focuses on the adaptive, healthy functions of a person's ego, or sense of self. It addresses the self-capacities central to adolescent development involving tolerance of emotion, maintenance of self-esteem, and connection to others. This approach theorizes that the ego has been compromised in its ability to cope, and therefore the goal of treatment is to strengthen its ability to adapt and manage stress. Ego strength, or the consistent sense of oneself and others across time and circumstance, is the goal of treatment. The patient and therapist join forces in a therapeutic alliance that offers both active support and insight as the patient's ego grows and strengthens in the face of inevitable obstacles. Ego psychology can be integrated into other modes of treatment in order to reap the benefits of multiple forms of intervention.

Given the imperative of identity formation during adolescence, seeking to foster increased ego strength in adolescents targets the very root of instability. In teens whose ego functioning is inadequate to the challenges being faced, symptoms or problematic behaviors can become a means of self-definition. It is almost as though the deficiencies hold the self together, be they manifested in an eating disorder, a drug problem, or repetitive self-injury. This is precisely why it is so difficult for the teenager to relinquish their seemingly destructive behaviors, as the symptoms themselves become an organizing principle for identity. Until the teen's ego strength is genuinely bolstered through insight and pragmatic skills, the symptoms can be clung to as if they were a veritable life preserver. Treatment, therefore, aims to enhance coping skills and capacities and foster increased ego strength that renders the teen less vulnerable to emotional instability.

Case Example: Eleanor

Eleanor is a 13-year-old just entering eighth grade at a local middle school. Up until beginning middle school in seventh grade, Eleanor was a happy, social, and well-behaved student and daughter. Within the past year, Eleanor has felt challenged by the shifting social and sexual tensions of middle school and less confident in her physical appearance and general competence. She feels intimidated by the aggressive social milieu, and changing from classroom to classroom throughout the day has left her feeling insecure and lacking a home base. Although her grades continue to be good, she has been withdrawn and depressed. She feels suddenly out of place in her own life, wondering where her breezy, comfortable sense of self has gone.

Eleanor begins to experience uncharacteristic ups and downs, one minute feeling cheerful and the next moment feeling morose. On some days, she feels connected to her friends and okay about her appearance, and then on other days she feels assaulted by feelings of inadequacy, loneliness, and betrayal by her own developing body. She does not have the words to express her confusion and despair to friends or family and feels helplessly buffeted by her painfully roller-coasting sense of self. In addition to launching a campaign to lose a few pounds, Eleanor discovers that pricking her legs with a needle and drawing blood inexplicably calms her rising tide of emotions.

Eventually, Eleanor is brought into treatment because of her visible weight loss and depression. It is only in therapy that she confides her pattern of self-injury. It becomes apparent that both the dieting and the self-injuring have escalated during a period of intense insecurity about both herself and her relationships with peers. A perceived slight can launch her into a spiral of self-condemnation and despair, whereas a compliment or success can have her riding high for the rest of the day. But ups and downs have become the norm, with only her dieting and injuring behavior serving as self-directed means of quelling her distress.

Eleanor and her therapist develop an understanding of her fragile ego as part of the natural yet challenging process of adolescent identity formation. Confronted with the many new stressors of adolescence, her ego has not yet built adequate defenses and coping mechanisms to allow consistency and resilience. They set their sights on building these very resources toward the goal of not only enhancing

Eleanor's ego strength but also replacing her reliance on dieting and injuring with skills that better facilitate her relationships and emotional regulation.

In therapy, Eleanor realizes how her close relationships with her parents and grade school teachers aided her sense of competence and self-esteem. She had come to rely on her parents and teachers to affirm her and to provide clear directions on how she should behave. Now, as parents and teachers encourage more independence and peers make more complex demands on her for their elusive approval, Eleanor is presently having difficulty determining her own standards and choices. She has become suddenly uncertain and tentative, having not yet mastered a new set of skills for navigating teenage relationships. She no longer has her parents or teachers to turn to as the arbiters of how to socialize effectively, as the nuances and complexities are beyond even her capacity to convey. Thus, Eleanor learned to better understand the developmental normality of her insecurities and began to learn to make her own social and personal judgments without expecting herself to be a finished and polished product. She could then better absorb the trial-and-error aspects of some of her choices and view them as learning steps rather than failures.

Eleanor also felt heartened to learn that though her relationships with dependency figures were shifting, parents and teachers were still available for support and guidance. She developed new ways of connecting with selected teachers and viewed her parents more realistically rather than as all-powerful figures who should be capable of easing most any pain. She learned to identify and talk about her emotions and their triggers, developing strategies to quell anxiety, sadness, anger, and loneliness that became even more directly effective than self-harm or dieting. Although it took months before Eleanor's gains took root enough for her to relinquish the self-harm with needles, it gradually became replaced by phone calls to friends, angry dialogues with parents, writings in her journal, and increasing engagement with all the slings and arrows of friendship and intimacy. Thus, Eleanor's ego strength began to consolidate, enabling her to rely more on an internal compass as opposed to the notoriously fickle assessments of others.

CONCLUSIONS

Treatment of self-injury inevitably involves a developmental perspective. The developmental challenges faced by the adolescent can be helpfully addressed through a variety of specialized adjunctive techniques and modalities. In this chapter, specialized approaches in group Therapy, family therapy, dialectical behavior therapy, interpersonal therapy, and ego psychology were presented as potential tools to augment the therapeutic arsenal. The key, of course, is to assess the individual strengths and needs of each teenager in designing as comprehensive and integrative a treatment plan as possible.

Chapter 8

The Brain as an Attitude Pharmacy: Neurochemical Roles and Remedies in Self-Injury

Teenagers like the idea that they can in essence prescribe their own drugs just by controlling their thought patterns.

Therapist

It helped me hate myself less knowing that there was an invisible chemical system behind my depression and obsession with cutting.

21-year-old finally seeking treatment in college

There is no denying the continual dynamic interplay between biology, psychology, and social factors in our human functioning and experience. This biopsychosocial interaction is fundamental to every sensation, thought, and behavior we experience. It can be hard to wrap one's mind around the rather abstract concept that thoughts and emotions are ultimately made of chemicals. Understanding how biology, particularly neurobiology, impacts the phenomenon of self-injury can be extremely valuable in learning to overcome it. Learning to influence the very pharmaceutical functions of our brains simply by controlling and altering our attitudes can yield dramatic improvements in mood and behavior.

CUTTING AND NEUROCHEMISTRY: WHY DOES IT PROVIDE RELIEF?

The fact that a sense of relief and well-being occurs immediately following self-injury may seem puzzling. It is directly counterintuitive that the infliction of pain can actually improve how one feels. Cutting and other forms of self-injury are almost always undertaken in an effort to alleviate emotional distress, and the sense of peace, calm, and relief it achieves is truly striking. In other words, for many individuals wrestling with intense psychic distress, cutting works. Yes, but how?

One answer to this question involves the brain's neurochemical response to pain. The brain produces chemicals called endorphins that serve as natural endogenous (or internally produced) opiates to help alleviate pain and distress. In fact, individuals who engage in self-mutilation and sadomasochistic practices point to the high they achieve as one of the sought-after rewards for their painful actions. In self-injury, an addiction like dependency can develop wherein only by inflicting pain can the individual self-medicate. That is, by behaviorally influencing their neurochemistry, they can thereby fend off unbearable pain. Self-injury then becomes an addictive form of coping as destructive as the use of alcohol or drugs to stave off distress.

The fact that the brain serves as a 24-hour pharmacy is not lost on addicts of all stripes. The neurochemically based relief sought by addicts has similarities to other problematic behaviors that individuals resort to in an effort to relieve suffering. Alcohol often is used by individuals to dull anxiety and sadness. Cocaine and amphetamines may be employed by individuals who feel bored, empty, or powerless. Bulimia and anorexia, by virtue of the brain's response to hunger and satiety, are also addictive patterns reinforced by their effectiveness in helping regulate emotions. Even gambling, shoplifting, and so-called positive addictions like exercise have been referred to as addictive behaviors that people employ in order to biochemically regulate emotions. Similarly, sex addictions provide a refuge from painful feelings in the pleasurable high of sexual gratification.

The opponent-process theory[73] also has been used to explain why something like the self-infliction of pain would result in positive feelings. This theory points to the brain's constant striving for homeostasis, or equilibrium, as the fundamental basis for why emotional highs are often followed by equally intense lows. The pleasure an addict may feel on heroin is at least equaled by the misery he experiences in withdrawal. The alcoholic's hangover, the sex addict's lonely turmoil, the coffee drinker's fatigue, and the adolescent cutter's mounting distress all inevitably follow the behavior of choice. Thus, the act of self-injury seems to invite a sense of relief and well-being in the aftermath of pain. Opponent-process theory therefore speaks to the signature ups and downs of addictive behaviors as the biological math of returning to equilibrium.

So-called positive addictions also have been scientifically shown to be associated with the release of endogenous opiates. The prototypical runner's high is one example whereby individuals may feel addicted to their daily run as a prerequisite to a feeling of well-being. Without running and achieving its neurochemical rewards, individuals often report feeling anxious, tense, depressed, and/or irritable. This dysphoria is only relieved by running, much like the drug addict's desperation for a drug as the key to achieving relief, however temporary. Other positive addictions may include meditation, prayer, or even charitable giving as sources of rewarding chemical changes in the brain.

As a clinical example, both obsessive-compulsive disorder (OCD) and self-injury have been tied to alterations in serotonin function within the brain. Both problems involve intrusive and irresistible urges to commit an act recognized by the person as senseless. For example, an individual with OCD who feels the repetitive need to take an even number of steps or wash his hands excessively generally realizes the irrationality of the behavior. Teenagers who cut frequently acknowledge that harming themselves is ultimately senseless. Yet both groups experience a mounting tension associated with efforts to resist enacting the behavior and, when they finally succumb, experience palpable relief from anxiety. Selective serotonin reuptake inhibitors (SSRIs), antidepressants that impact serotonin levels in the brain, have been employed with some success in the treatment of both OCD and self-injury by stabilizing mood and decreasing impulses to repeat undesirable actions.

BIOLOGICAL ASPECTS OF DEPRESSION AND SELF-INJURY

Underlying many forms of self-injury, be it cutting, burning, hair-pulling, anorexia, or bulimia, depression often lurks. As discussed, self-injury is largely a coping mechanism that individuals employ to manage unbearable emotions. This is why it is so critical to understand and treat the underlying conflicts and symptoms of self-injury and why depression is so often the target of intervention.

Although there is no single cause of depression, neurobiological factors increasingly have come into focus for their role in the development, maintenance, and resolution of depression. Several different mechanisms seem to play key roles. First, the chemical link between stress and depression has been well established. Stress generates release of the hormone cortisol, which acts on the limbic hypothalamo-pituitary-adrenal axis (LHPA) in the brain to effect changes in sleep, appetite, pleasure, and mood. Chronic overstimulation of the LHPA has been closely linked to depression.[74, 75] For example, in patients in whom an excess of cortisol is produced, such as in individuals with Cushing's syndrome, depression is very common. When these individuals' cortisol levels return to normal after treatment, however, their depression remits.[76]

As discussed earlier, a history of abuse or trauma is highly prevalent among self-injurers. Intriguingly, researchers have shown that early traumatic stress creates chronic changes in the HPA axis. The hormonal changes at puberty have been hypothesized to further impair HPA axis function, thereby exacerbating emotional difficulties in adolescents already impacted by early trauma.[77] Thus, in both understanding and treating adolescent self-injurers, their heightened vulnerability to stress must be offset with concrete tools, environmental modifications, and emotional supports. Often, the addition of medication is an important aspect of recovery.

It is further believed that cortisol impacts mood by effecting neurotransmitters involved in the control of mood. Serotonin, norepinephrine, and dopamine are often targeted by antidepressant medications. The newer antidepressants, the SSRIs, have been highly effective in the treatment of depression and associated conditions. Commonly prescribed medications such as Prozac, Zoloft, Celexa, and Effexor specifically target the serotonin system in order to restore its optimal balance and reduce depression. Low serotonin levels have been associated with self-injurious behavior, and some success has been reported in the ability of SSRIs to reduce it.[78]

MIND OVER BODY: EMPOWERING ADOLESCENTS TO TAKE CHARGE OF HOW THEY THINK

Even more remarkable than the pain-endorphin connection is the growing literature demonstrating that even our thoughts influence the chemicals released by our brains. Self-defeating thoughts such as "I'm hopeless," "I'm ugly," "I hate myself," and "Nobody will ever care about me" lead directly to corresponding feelings of depression, rejection, isolation, and frustration. If these feelings persist and mount, individuals may resort to self-injury in order to relieve tension and unhappiness. By the same token, when individuals learn to monitor their self-statements by replacing negative with positive thoughts, different sets of brain chemicals are stimulated that subsequently improve mood.[79] Thus, therapy of self-injury often involves helping the patient learn to willfully and proactively alter the nature of their internal self-talk in order to improve mood and functioning.

Cognitive restructuring therapies, such as the rational emotive behavior therapy of Albert Ellis[70] discussed in chapter 7, are based on the concept that stressful events do not, in fact, cause our feelings and physiological responses; the way we choose to interpret and think about those situations is what matters. In other words, it is not about what happens as much as how we perceive and respond to events. The sequence begins first with a perceived situation. Second, how we think about the situation follows. Finally, our responses, including emotions, physiology, and behavior, emerge from these thoughts and perceptions.

For example, say that Ernesto gets a D on a test. He may not perceive this grade as threatening his overall grade in the course and attributes it to the fact that he chose to play computer games last night rather than study. He thus reacts calmly and resolves to study harder next time. If Joe gets the same D on the same test, however, he may perceive this as a risk to him successfully passing the course. He may attribute the D to his belief that he is learning disabled and an inadequate student. He may thus respond with sadness, anxiety, and harsh self-condemnation, deciding to get high in order to feel better. The event itself does not determine an individual's emotional and behavioral reactions; it is the way the event is interpreted and thought about that impacts feelings and actions.

Sometimes, a negative thinking pattern becomes habitual for individuals. When something undesirable happens, instead of responding with a positive outlook and sense of agency, these individuals automatically feel helpless, victimized, or unworthy. These types of automatic negative attributions are particularly common in adolescents who self-injure; rather than confronting the difficulty proactively, they tend to wither and retreat into a self-destructive mode of thinking and behaving. We are all familiar with people who seem to view themselves as perennial victims, choosing to feel persecuted or unlucky as opposed to assuming an active role in their predicaments. By learning to think about situations in more empowered and rational ways, more productive responses inevitably follow. These new modes of thinking and choosing to respond are rewarded with more positive feelings, outcomes, and brain chemistry.

THE SENSE OF BEING IN CONTROL: IS SELF-CONFIDENCE MADE OF CHEMICALS?

Brain neurochemistry is also inextricably linked to one's sense of control in stressful situations. Researchers at UCLA, Lynn Fairbanks and Michael McGuire,[80] studied this association with dominant and submissive monkeys. Serotonin levels were twice as high in the group's dominant, or alpha, male as in the submissive males. When the alpha male was removed from the group and could only observe the other males gaining control over food supply, female attention, and social order, his serotonin levels dropped to the level of the formerly submissive males or even lower. In the meantime, as the other males gained more control, their respective serotonin levels rose to those of the original alpha male's level. Subsequently, the monkeys' serotonin levels were altered by administering drugs. Passive males responded to increased serotonin levels by acting dominant, whereas dominant males whose serotonin levels were decreased became subordinate. It is intriguing to consider the impact of subtle changes in neurochemistry on what may amount to confidence, self-esteem, and agency in people who can relinquish passivity and gain empowerment.

Perhaps the landmark studies in this area were conducted by Martin Seligman regarding the concept of learned helplessness.[81] Seligman and colleagues discovered that animals that were unable to actively avoid stress eventually gave up and became depressed. Thus, animals that could avoid a shock by taking action were able to function normally without undue anxiety or depression. Those that could not avoid the shock quickly learned that they were helpless and succumbed to the animal equivalent of despair. This phenomenon has been applied to humans, in that individuals with a sense of internal control and agency cope more effectively with stress. Those who feel helpless in the face of external stressors often respond in self-defeating and unproductive ways.

The related concept of locus of control is extremely useful in understanding why a sense of control is so important to one's healthy functioning.[82] Locus of control can be either internal or external. If an individual experiences one's locus of control as internal, he believes that his own actions can adequately cope with environmental challenges. In large part, such control entails a belief system that views challenges as opportunities for growth as opposed to hopeless predetermined outcomes. Individuals with an internal locus of control feel a sense of agency in mastering a situation and tend to make decisions that enable coping and success. Those with an external locus of control experience themselves as passive victims of external forces. Where one lies on the continuum between an internal versus an external locus of control has been closely correlated with health. Self-injurers who can develop a stronger sense of internal control over their fate are much more likely to choose and implement positive outcomes when faced with a challenge. This variable of hardiness has been shown along with control to be an important factor in health and well-being.[83]

The inextricable link between attitude and biochemistry is truly exemplified by this concept of control. An internal versus an external locus of control has a profound influence over the body's neurochemistry, in fact, impacting levels of serotonin, dopamine, and norepinephrine. These three neurotransmitters are implicated in depression and anxiety when low and contribute to a sense of pleasure and well-being when adequately elevated. Thus, as individuals learn to alter their thoughts, attitudes, and behaviors toward a greater sense of control and agency, the need for antidepressant treatment is lessened or removed altogether.

Clearly, a sense of control over one's life on a day-to-day basis has been associated with more positive mood. In teens who resort to self-injury, restoring a sense of control over their emotions, actions, and choices is critical to successful adjustment and symptom intervention. Well beyond the benefits of medication, adolescents need to learn how to take responsibility and feel that the choices they make directly impact their lives and well-being. Similarly, the negative internal thoughts that teens subconsciously repeat over and over can respond to restructuring in order to replace them with more positive self-statements and attitudes. These positive cognitions can, in turn, jointly impact mood and constructive coping decisions, eventually eclipsing the problematic need to self-injure.

EMOTION TOLERANCE AND REGULATION

One of the hallmarks of self-injurers is their great difficulty in tolerating and regulating negative emotions. Adolescent cutters notoriously become rapidly overwhelmed by volatile currents of emotion and, lacking other skills, resort to the ritual of self-injury to alleviate the emotional crisis. A true pioneer in the treatment of chronically self-injuring patients, Marsha Linehan's dialectical behavior therapy[36] provides a structured multidimensional program to assist individuals in both tolerating and managing such emotions. Her program incorporates many elements that focus on impacting the underlying biology responsible for such overreactive emotional systems. Teaching relaxation techniques that engage mental focus and imagery to calm the physiological upheaval of anxiety and distress is a central component of treatment.

Not many individuals can think rationally, productively, and wisely when experiencing intense emotional distress. Because such emotions are inevitable in life and are particularly disorganizing for teenagers who self-injure, learning how to achieve a state of relaxation prior to choosing any course of action is extremely beneficial. The proverbial admonitions to "count to ten," "take deep breaths," or "take a time out" may not always be sufficient, and therefore the acquisition of more structured techniques for achieving mental calm and positive thinking are beneficial.

Mindfulness meditation is a burgeoning practice that has been shown to improve mood, health, pain control, cardiovascular functioning, and emotional regulation.[84] The goal is to be as fully in the present moment as possible, focusing on one thing at a time without allowing judgments or distracting thoughts to interfere. Individuals learn to develop a sense of calm control as they quiet the din of competing thoughts and still their emotional reactivity. Complete concentration can be devoted to focusing on one's breathing or on a particular empowering thought, allowing all the associated sensations to be fully experienced in a nonjudgmental manner.

Imagery techniques can help individuals mentally travel to a safe, peaceful, beautiful place in their minds. Visualizing, for example, sitting by a crackling fire in a beautiful mountain setting can create sensations of actual warmth, calm, and pleasure in lieu of distress or rumination. When experiencing an undesirable overload of emotions, learning to close one's eyes and visualize this personal place in one's mind can have both emotionally and physically soothing effects.

Imagery and visualization skills also can be applied to reprogram one's attitudes and resulting behavior. For example, prior to diving in competition, some divers thoroughly visualize a perfect sequence of movements culminating in a perfect dive. This expectation and intention is often attributed to assisting in optimal performance. Similarly, by visualizing themselves successfully functioning in the manner desired, individuals can greatly assist their progress toward that very goal. By visualizing the desired outcome in detail during a relaxed state and experiencing the actions and outcome as completely as possible, a huge step toward that goal is achieved. Practicing the visualization and expectation of performing successfully, as if watching a desired outcome in a movie, can in reality alter attitudes, expectations, and actual outcomes.

CONCLUSIONS

The profound impact of neurochemistry on mood and well-being is informative in comprehending the mystery of self-injurious behavior. A biopsychosocial approach to understanding and intervening with cutting and self-injury can greatly enhance treatment efforts. Heightened endorphin levels that result from self-injury may in fact help explain why people report feeling so much better after the infliction of a painful, even damaging act. The related role of stress-induced neurotransmitter reductions in depression sheds further light on the need for self-injurers to achieve more effective coping attitudes and strategies in response to stress.

One's sense of control when faced with obstacles is highly correlated with physical and emotional health. An internal locus of control can greatly enhance one's hardiness, which in turn generates positive mood and health. Even by changing one's negative thought patterns into positive ones, individuals can greatly impact their attitudes and actual behavior. Learning, for example, how to achieve a sense of calm and relaxation on one's own can greatly mollify the need to resort to self-injury. A host of relaxation, imagery, and other emotion-tolerance techniques are available to assist adolescent cutters in coping with their distress.

Chapter 9

Intervention in Action: How It Works

I can't imagine trying to treat an adolescent cutter with one single treatment approach. It takes a flexible, eclectic mix of tools and perspectives to address all the issues.

Adolescent psychologist

An in-depth discussion of treatment approaches to cutting can be difficult to envision fully integrated into action. Discussing emotional difficulties and interventions separate from the human being in crisis renders such explanations and recommendations abstract. And discussing treatment with adolescents in crisis separate from their developmental contexts fails to ground intervention in a comprehensible framework. In this chapter, specific case illustrations will be utilized to convey how treatment can be put into action to address each patient's unique developmental challenges.

Case Example: Sharon, Age 14

Sharon is furious that her parents will not let her go the upcoming concert with all of her friends. They do not understand how important this is to her and insist she cannot go unless adults will be there to supervise. She storms off to her room, slams the door, and cries. This is her best chance to get together with Josh, the guy she has had a crush on, and if she is not there, Tanya will definitely go after him. She is not even sure that Josh likes her; she is not as thin as some of the other girls and not as fast as boys like him might prefer. Sharon has never felt this kind of longing for a boy, much less so many inexplicable feelings of desire, fear, love, and anger. She cannot stand it!

Sharon hates herself right now. She hates her parents and the horrible way she feels. No one understands her distress, least of all her parents. She thinks about those girls at school known as cutters who are either rumored or known to cut themselves. They seem mysterious, different, and obviously in some sort of distress. Sharon walks into the kitchen and takes a paring knife from the drawer. She takes it back to her room, thinking how utterly clueless her parents are. On the back of her forearm she prepares to inscribe her signature of distress. Will it hurt? Who cares; nothing is as bad as how she feels. This pain will be her doing; she can control it. She steels herself, intent on numbing herself to any pain or awareness of her own perverse behavior, and coolly observes the striking red beads of blood as they erupt beneath her barely penetrating knife blade. She is mesmerized, transfixed, and squeezes the cut to make the blood drip onto her desk. Slowly, she realizes that she feels calmer now, stronger, and more in command of her pain. This cut tells the story of her internal quagmire of frustrations, and it can only be read by those to whom she reveals it. It seems an appropriately perverse way of expressing this confluence of confusing emotions, and cutting quickly becomes a preoccupation for Sharon, resulting in a litany of scars on her arms and self-described fat stomach.

This episode of Sharon's reveals a great deal about the 14-year-old issues that overwhelm her. First, she desires more freedom and independence, but her parents constantly obstruct her in their efforts to assure her safety. Second, she does not know how to communicate her burgeoning emotional investment in peer relations and culture. She is not a little girl anymore, yet her parents do not seem to recognize the changes in her or the overwhelming new demands that face her. Third, Sharon is not yet equipped to cope with the intensity of these new emotions. Thus, with her identity, independence, and intimacy needs all feeling hopelessly thwarted, she turns to self-harm as an expression of her torment.

When her parents discover that their daughter has dozens of self-inflicted scars, they are shocked and distressed. In fact, they are terrified, worried, and yet angry that she has chosen to do this seemingly ridiculous, destructive thing. They confront her with their concerns, and the intensity of their reaction stuns even Sharon. She feels immediately attacked and defensive and withdraws into a posture of defiance and then distance. Her parents are frightened that she might be cutting herself again in her room, behind the locked door, yet feel helpless to intervene short of threatening or beseeching her to stop. Might she even try to kill herself, they wonder? What should they do?

Parents reflexively react to threats to their children with intense emotional and protective instincts. It is extremely difficult for a parent to remain calm and cogent when faced with the revelation that their daughter is engaging in truly disturbing behavior. Not only do they want the behavior to cease immediately, but also they are alarmed by the implications of emotional instability inherent to self-injurious behavior. Suddenly, concerns literally related to life and limb are brought into focus. Naturally, then, parents need professional guidance and support in treating a self-injurious teen.

After several brief phone consultations with a psychologist, Dr. Galvan, Sharon and her parents began actively confronting the developmental issues underlying the red flags of her cutting behavior. An initial evaluation was undertaken by Dr. Galvan to assess not only Sharon's psychological and behavioral status but also, importantly, her suicide risk and immediate danger from any related self-destructive activities (e.g., drug or alcohol use, sexual risk-taking, anorexia, or bulimia). In Sharon's first session, prior to Dr. Galvan meeting with her parents, Sharon strongly denied any intentions, thoughts, or plans to seriously injure or harm herself, and a no-suicide contract was developed in which Sharon promised to contact Dr. Galvan if she ever did feel the urge to harm herself more seriously. Her symptoms of depression were discussed and, pending some testing, did not appear to meet criteria for a clinical depression. A medical exam was recommended to assess the severity of her wounds and rule out any current risk of infection.

Sharon and Dr. Galvan discussed her current symptoms and her life context, including her social, emotional, familial, and academic environments. Sharon was able to describe her intense frustration with her parents along with deep-seated feelings of self-doubt regarding her appearance and competence. Her feelings for Josh and pressing needs for acceptance by both female and male peers were notable for their urgency and the anxiety they generated. In short, Dr. Galvan and Sharon began to understand the key conflicts underlying her misery and the corresponding need to injure herself. These specifically hinged on, first, her developing self-image as a maturing and social adolescent, with all its inherent anxieties. Second, the classic developmental struggle, fraught with ambivalence galore, for the teen to separate and become more independent as the parents ease controls had begun in earnest. Third, the confluence of intense, confusing emotions at a time of rapid hormonal change rendered Sharon unable to effectively cope. In addition to enhanced insight, she needed alternative strategies for contending with emotional distress that did not involve self-harm and more successfully achieved her goals.

Dr. Galvan assured Sharon that her confidentiality would be strictly maintained short of any suicidal threat. Sharon felt relieved to perceive Dr. Galvan as concerned first and foremost with the very issues that troubled her and sensed that Dr. Galvan could be an important ally. She was surprised at how much she told Dr. Galvan and by the lack of judgment or criticism. Moreover, Dr. Galvan even implied that her parents might need some help in improving how they interacted with Sharon, giving her hope that perhaps she might attain some of her goals after all.

Critical to any effective intervention with teenagers is concurrent consultation with parents. The adolescent's journey is inextricably linked to her parents', and they each must adapt to the rapid developmental changes facing them both. Although teens struggle with their own challenges, parents suddenly face a loss of control, a loss of intimacy, and a new set of behaviors and emotions emanating from their previously predictable little girl. It is a process of enormous give and take, mutual gains and losses, and huge successes and dismal setbacks. Thus, the parents need consultation and support in order to assist their teenager's successful transition through adolescence.

Sharon's parents met with Dr. Galvan and conveyed their worries and many questions. They never had seen her so moody before, never dealt with her current level of defiance, and felt unsure where and how to set limits. Dr. Galvan helped them understand the normal developmental transition that they, too, were undergoing, as their parental roles were shifting with Sharon's evolving needs. They became better able to understand the conflicts underlying her seemingly senseless fits of emotion. For example, her age-appropriate insistence on spending more time with friends and her growing ambivalence around parental control and dependency were set into a more understandable developmental context. Sharon's parents needed to first ground their understanding of Sharon's self-injurious behavior in the context of age-appropriate developmental challenges. This understanding better equipped them to support Sharon's appropriate expressions of autonomy and independence while maintaining a loving, supportive, but less hovering presence. This started with the very difficult task of accepting that Sharon was the only person in control of her own cutting and that for the time being, they needed to convey their concern yet contain their own intense emotional responses.

Sharon felt truly validated and supported by this intervention with her parents. As the notion of a two-way street of negotiation and communication took hold, Sharon finally felt that she had some avenues through which to assert her needs with her parents. She also understood a bit better that her parents were only doing what loving parents tend to do: reacting protectively and only reluctantly relinquishing intimacy and control with their daughter.

This explicit articulation of the developmental tasks facing both Sharon and her parents provided a framework within which they could better understand the individual and collective challenges facing them. This helped externalize and diffuse conflicts in the sense that they could now grasp the real issues at the heart of their struggles. That is, the inexorable process of development was the ultimate culprit in their midst rather than merely the angry behavior of a disturbed adolescent or the controlling actions of insensitive parents. Sharon and her parents were thus better able to humanize themselves and one another in this difficult process and see one another more as allies than adversaries.

Sharon insisted to Dr. Galvan that her self-injurious behavior gave her an important sense of identity, control, and means of blocking out painful feelings. Sharon felt particularly anxious about her ability to attract a boyfriend and earn a secure social niche among her friends. She witnessed major changes in many of her friends who were suddenly dressing more provocatively, becoming more aggressive in pursuing friends and boyfriends, and seemed to Sharon to be light-years ahead of her in tackling the sexuality and independence aspects of adolescence. At the same time, her body was developing, but to her the result was primarily a feeling of being fat and therefore unattractive and inferior. Her self-esteem and sense of control were diminished by the changes she observed both within and outside herself.

On the one hand, Sharon wanted her parents to let her go to concerts and stay out late and generally stop treating her like a child. On the other hand, however, she was also nervous about going to the concert and contending with the scores of teenagers, drugs, and rowdy elements characteristic of heavy metal concerts. Similarly, she wanted a later curfew but was aware that after 10:00 many of her friends started hooking up with boys, and she was not sure how she felt about that. Although she wanted her parents to stop nagging her about homework, she was deeply troubled by her poor grades. Thus, it was critical that Sharon learn to recognize and assume more responsibility for her own very natural personal fears and conflicts. Only then could she implement more effective, more honest solutions and choices. As Sharon's parents learned to listen to the quiet conflict underlying her loud protestations, they were better able to understand Sharon as simultaneously a vulnerable child and a maturing young woman struggling with increasing pressures and demands.

The central work of treatment involves assisting the teenager in finding more productive means of self-expression and control while acknowledging the even more daunting nature of the real-life challenges that cutting merely assist her in actively avoiding. Although both Sharon and her parents' psychological understanding and communication improved, the need remained to assist Sharon immediately with a means of confronting so many stressful challenges without resorting to self-injury. Cognitive-behavioral interventions that actively target specific thoughts and behaviors can be essential in the treatment of self-injurious behavior. These interventions tend to connect the precipitating cause, emotional response, and subsequent destructive behavior in the adolescent's consciousness as a related sequence that she can learn to interrupt.

The first step in this process often involves the teen recording aspects of the self-injury sequence in a log. When did you experience the urge to cut? What were you feeling at the time? How did your body feel? What events, feelings, or thoughts preceded the urge? What was the intended goal of the self-injury? What would be the intended and unintended messages communicated to others through the self-injury? What action did you finally take? What was the result? These questions can be addressed on a log sheet or in a journal and then carefully reviewed during therapy sessions. There the adolescent can begin to develop the self-knowledge that can empower her to make changes and alternative choices.

Alternatives to self-injury are a cornerstone of treatment. The teen can take many actions in response to emotional distress; for example, the teen can confront the person inspiring her anger or call a sympathetic friend or take a walk or cry or simply do nothing and weather the emotional storm knowing that it will indeed pass. Teenagers need to build a new arsenal of coping skills now that the childhood options of running to one's parents or throwing a tantrum no longer seem age-appropriate. Working with the teen to define her own set of alternatives to self-injury focuses the responsibility and the means for coping squarely on the teen and can empower her to actively choose not to cut.

Common alternatives to self-injury include journaling, exercising, listening to music, leaving the room, taking a bath, drinking tea, watching television, calling a friend, contacting the therapist, looking at photos with positive memories, cuddling with the family dog or cat, or writing a letter to the friend, teacher, or family member toward whom they may feel frustration or rage. Individualizing the list as much as possible helps the adolescent identify with her own options and take ownership over the process.

Sharon began a log of every occasion on which she felt a compelling urge to harm herself. She recorded the time, location, bodily sensations, emotions, and thoughts accompanying the urge. She also forced herself to think about what precipitated these feelings, how she expected the cutting to bring relief, and what she might ultimately be seeking to communicate through the cutting and visible scarring. She would then record at least five alternatives to actually engaging in the cutting. Finally, she would record what action she ultimately did take and the outcome.

For Sharon, strong feelings of anger, self-doubt, and/or loneliness tended to precede the episodes of self-injury. When she felt furious, her body felt hot and full of energy. When she felt worthless, she had the sensation of wanting to crawl out of her skin. And when she felt lonely, her body felt inert, tired, miserable. She learned to differentiate between these various feelings and sensations and put words to them. This exercise alone helped her feel less overwhelmed and help-less in the face of an emotional storm because she could break down the weighty burden into more identifiable pieces. She also learned to associate the events, thoughts, and interactions that preceded these intensely distressing emotions. Was she stressed out about the midterm exam? Was she feeling rejected? Was she making negative judgments about her physical appearance? Was she feeling thwarted by her parents in achieving a desired freedom? Once the picture became clearer, Sharon was able to imagine alternatives to cutting that would alleviate her distress without injury and possibly with even greater success. Her alternatives included (1) journaling about her thoughts and feelings, (2) writing a letter to her parents expressing her feelings and needs, (3) calling a friend and asking for support and reassurance, (4) playing a mindless computer game, (5) physically removing herself from her room to another location, and (6) listening to music.

Dr. Galvan made it clear that these alternatives would take some time and experimentation to work as well as her habit of self-injuring. Each week, they reviewed her log and discussed the recorded sequences. Importantly, Dr. Galvan worked with Sharon toward better understanding the healthy, positive meta-issue driving the urge to cut, such as a desire to feel loved, a desire to make independent decisions, or a self-punitive urge in regard to her perceived limita-tions. Once Sharon could see, for example, that her fears of rejection were better overcome through active communication and engagement with her friends than by the quick fix of cutting could she make more positive choices.

Sharon particularly found journaling to be a satisfying means of both sooth-ing herself and expressing her thoughts and feelings. In so doing, Sharon was able to see in black and white the evidence of her own internal and interper-sonal struggles and the maturing parts of her that were heroically grappling with the challenges inherent to adolescence. She could keep these insights wholly private or share selections with her therapist, a friend, or even a parent with whom she had trouble communicating. She also found that by simply leaving her room she could change the channel, as it were, and allow the emotional storm to subside as she watched television, prepared a snack, or sat on the front step. She also learned to rely on a friendship with Joanna that was fast becoming more intimate as she contacted her more frequently in times of distress.

Sharon was gradually accepting that she could surmount not only the cut-ting but also the larger struggles compelling it. As the focus of her energies shifted to her goals for intimacy, competence, and realistically defining herself as a complex individual with strengths and limitations, Sharon engaged less and less often in self-injury. Once her parents and friends no longer responded with alarm and urgency to fresh scars, the cutting became a less powerful tool for communicating and increasingly became viewed by Sharon as the unpleasant and useless coping strategy it was. The focus became her struggles, her goals, and her choices and she herself the only beneficiary or victim of them. Simultaneously, Sharon's parents had begun accepting their lack of control and stepping back from inserting themselves into Sharon's struggles. It became clearer to Sharon that she wanted and needed her parents' support but that she had to assume responsibility for either making good independent decisions or seeking out their assistance. This, ultimately, signifies true healthy development as the teen becomes more competently independent while remaining securely invested in supportive relationships with parents and peers.

In Sharon's case, a number of relevant social and environmental factors contributed to her distress. First of all, as an average student in a high-achieving, highly educated, and successful family, Sharon viewed herself as a de facto failure in her parents' eyes. Second, her parents had been contending with a severe strain in their marriage, and the tense, unhappy home environment created a discomforting feeling of anxiety for Sharon. Third, Sharon's peers were suddenly embracing pop culture with a vengeance, and she was feeling pressure to grow up, behave sexually, and dress in more provocative ways than with which she felt comfortable. Finally, Sharon felt new pressure to be competitively thin and attractive and saw herself as a contender in this social realm but hopelessly unexceptional in school or sports.

Dr. Galvan recommended couple's therapy for Sharon's parents and conducted several family sessions in which her parents could validate her perceptions yet reassure her that they were working on things. Sharon was also referred to group treatment with a psychologist who conducted a group with 14- and 15-year-old adolescents with similar difficulties. Sharon also was encouraged to establish a relationship with her academic counselor toward the goal of better defining her own goals and aspirations and to refocus some of her energies into finding meaningful volunteer or paid employment. As Sharon increasingly appreciated the environmental forces that impacted her thinking and behavior, she became better equipped to more actively make choices that best served and expressed her.

Frequently, adolescents present to treatment with not only extensive self-injury but also a host of other disturbances as well. Eating disorders, sexual abuse, drug abuse, overt suicidality, and depression are all too commonly associated. In such cases, treatment must inevitably be multimodal in order to address the complex psychological, social, biological, and environmental needs of the adolescent. The following case illustrates one such patient struggling with a confluence of serious difficulties.

Case Example: Andrea

Andrea already had a long history of difficulties by the time she was 16. Sexually abused from age six through nine by her stepfather (the abuse stopped only when he left the family) and both anorexic and bulimic since age 13, Andrea had been repeatedly hospitalized for her anorexic emaciation and desperate suicide threats. At age 15, she began indiscriminately abusing drugs, most recently smoking heroine (tar) and requiring detoxification for symptoms of withdrawal. Throughout this tumultuous history, she had also been an extensive cutter, and her face, arms, legs, and torso carried a litany of scars so vividly recorded that they nearly resembled tattoos.

Perhaps most shocking was Andrea's attitude, which despite this seeming horror show remained cheerful, friendly, and oddly upbeat. She seemed almost unconcerned about her many damaging difficulties, remaining strikingly disconnected from them. This contradiction was mirrored in numerous other contradictions in her behavior. For example, she was on the one hand vehemently self-loathing but on the other, frankly arrogant. She discussed deep-seated rage in a friendly, pleasant tone. Although severely afflicted, she remained extremely competent, maintaining a high grade point average and an uncanny independence in negotiating systems and transportation. Finally, though superficially cheerful, she was deeply distraught. The repetitive cutting fit into her defensive efforts to cut herself off from painful thoughts and feelings.

The cutting and its trail of scars served additional needs as well, however. Andrea's traumatic sexual abuse history was hidden and invisible, and the scarring screamed out her sense of damage, violation, and rage. Until she could begin the hard work of recovery from these internal wounds, she sought release and expression in external acting out. Her off-putting, even frightening appearance also sent a vivid message to others to stay away, affording her a sense of safe distance from intimacy or intrusion. Furthermore, her pervasive tendency to disconnect from her feelings and actions needed an alternative, safe replacement strategy in lieu of cutting. Andrea needed to develop internal resources and skills for withstanding the onslaught of emotions, making sense of them, and discovering other ways of self-soothing and self-expression.

Clearly, psychotherapy with Andrea will necessitate a long-term therapeutic relationship with adjunctive interventions as well. Psychiatric consultation is necessary to determine if medication is indicated for treating her deep depression and anxiety, despite her ability to mask these difficulties between episodes of self-injurious behavior. Inpatient treatment may be periodically indicated if overt suicide impulses reemerge. Although her behavior is so chaotic and dangerous, considering the drug abuse, sexual indiscretion, bulimia, and cutting, a residential treatment program may be necessary to ensure her safety. Ultimately, however, assisting Andrea in overcoming clear developmental obstacles formed the foundation of treatment understanding and intervention. Even in a teenager with such disturbing and destructive behavior, Andrea's conflicts needed to be normalized as her understandable response to overwhelming developmental demands. That these demands were indeed magnified and exacerbated by her traumatic abuse history deserved acknowledgement and understanding because they impacted her sense of identity, sexuality, and independence.

Andrea did in fact require residential treatment, but after six months she had stabilized enough to be discharged into outpatient treatment. In order to stave off acting out, several treatment interventions were highlighted. First, Andrea began a careful journal of her feelings, impulses, and actions. When she experienced distress, prior to routinely resorting to cutting, drugs, or other actions, she committed to at least examining and recording her feelings first. Initially, Andrea could record only "Feel horrible; can't stand it," followed by the impulse to self-injure and subsequent surrender to it. Over time, however, she was better able to identify and define her distress: "Feel shaky, agitated; started feeling this way after realizing I'd ruined my life and look like a freak. I want to get drunk or make a deep cut." The eventual action she recorded was "Wrote in my journal all the fucked up angry feelings until I got tired, then watched the tube. Finally just felt numb, spaced out, until able to read."

In twice-weekly therapy sessions, Andrea focused on identifying the antecedents to her various forms of distress, the specific sensations and feelings involved, the impulses she experienced, and the actions she finally took along with their consequences. This was a tedious exercise for several months, as it required Andrea to experience painful feelings fully enough to identify them, rather than desperately seeking to block them out at all costs. Yet gradually, Andrea began to feel a bit more in control when distress hit, as it was no longer simply a mammoth hurricane of devastating proportions but actually had a cause, specific feelings, and, most rewardingly, a variety of ways to contend. Although Andrea did not always make positive choices, and sometimes cut or drank or binged and purged, still she had important successes.

The cognitive-behavioral tools she was developing were important in empowering her with knowledge and alternative strategies. Having these as part of her coping arsenal enabled her to begin the extremely difficult work of addressing the trauma of her sexual abuse history. She was reassured that this work would only progress at her desired pace, and she was provided with additional supports during this phase of therapy. These supports consisted of weekly group therapy and more structure in her after-school time. She enrolled at the YWCA in a self-defense course on Tuesdays and Thursdays and arranged a social commitment on other days immediately after school. When she was busy, and when she was not alone, she was less likely to feel overwhelmed and out of control.

The work of integrating her sexual abuse history was, of course, difficult and painful, but Andrea was relieved to be able to speak her truth and vent her feelings rather than keep them buried. They seemed less intense and threatening out in the open with a therapist she trusted to understand and care about her, and gradually the internal pressure and chaos seemed to subside. She was able to humanize her turmoil these past many years and feel compassion for herself yet at the same time felt renewed strength and responsibility to make what she wanted of her life from here on out. She even consulted a plastic surgeon about the scars on her face and neck, as they began to feel less and less congruent with the self she experienced and wanted to portray to the world.

After a year, Andrea was ready to address her intense anger at her mother for not protecting her from the abuse. After a great deal of reflection, she drafted a letter to her mother, and this was reviewed in therapy. After making some revisions, Andrea invited her mother to a session during which she read the letter, and a tearful, painful session ensued. Andrea felt empowered by her ability to confront her mother and could begin to accept some of her mother's guilt and remorse. Subsequently, she wrote a letter confronting her stepfather, even though his mailing address was unknown.

As Andrea actively addressed dangerous emotions and seemed not only to survive but also to become stronger, she was able to revisit the abuse and its lingering impact on her tendency to block out or disassociate from emotions. She recalled feeling nothing during the abuse, trying to escape the horror by mentally taking herself far away. The cutting, drug use, sexual activity, and eating disorders all became means of numbing and disassociating from a web of seemingly insurmountable emotions. As this discussion progressed in tandem with her logging and alternative strategies, she experienced some relapses with her cutting. She now found it less effective and satisfying, however, and tended to renew her efforts to find better strategies and solutions. Andrea required long-term treatment and suffered future missteps but was able to stay out of the hospital, complete high school and college, and cautiously explore more intimate relationships.

Andrea's case illustrates just how complex the symptom constellation and corresponding treatment can be in adolescents who self-injure. Therapy can never focus solely on the cutting but must address the conflicts that generate it. Many youths who cry out with minor scratches are trying to contend with much deeper and darker wounds. As these are addressed more actively, the developmental impasses around intimacy, identity, and independence can be identified and confronted with less obstruction from acting-out behaviors.

Sometimes, even seemingly well-adjusted teenagers begin cutting, which can be particularly enigmatic to parents, teachers, and friends. The following case illustration occurred in a high-functioning 14-year-old with many friends, good grades, enthusiastic participation in sports, and loving, supportive parents. How could this seemingly thriving adolescent develop the impulse to cut and scar herself?

Case Example: Maya

Maya is a 14-year-old freshman at an elite prep school. Her history is replete with successes but no anxious perfectionism and with a rich life that includes many friends and participation in volleyball and her church choir. She and her family lead an active life and greatly enjoy spending time as a family. Why, then, did her mother discover razors and a jar containing blood-soaked cotton balls in her desk drawer?

Initially, Maya protested that it was none of her mom's business and nothing to worry about. Because her parents could not imagine that Maya would be cutting herself or feeling suicidal, they shrugged it off and tried to ignore their concerns. Soon thereafter, they received a phone call from the school counselor, informing them that Maya had been referred to her office by the volleyball coach. The reason: numerous cuts, new and healed, on her thighs.

Maya greeted her parents' concern with declarations that they "don't know anything about her" and that she was "suffering" in ways they could never understand. Mystified and worried, they insisted that Maya choose a therapist to talk with to help her with this suffering. Reluctantly, she agreed, but only if she thought the therapist "had a clue." The therapist in question (i.e., I) was met by a cheerful, bright, and friendly girl. She was actually bubbly and talkative and gradually revealed more about the roots of her distress. Her mother, she claimed, was always "up my butt," prying, controlling, and wanting to know everything about her life, activities, and friendships. Her mom was "totally straitlaced" and spoke reproachfully of teens who dyed their hair, dressed eccentrically, or, God forbid, experimented with drugs or sexual relationships. Maya could tell that her mom would disapprove of some of her new friends and, most especially, of their sexual precocity. Maya herself had had a sexual encounter with a boy and was both excited and somehow unnerved by it.

In fact, Maya felt guilty about the sexual encounter and a little angry because more had happened than she expected with this boy. But she did want to see him again, even though her parents would freak out if they saw his spiked hair. She had been devising ways to get out of the house on weekend nights to see him and his friends. Her mother, however, was like a hawk and questioned everything. Maya also was feeling a bit nervous about her new social interests, as she was venturing into unknown but exciting arenas. She was not feeling like the good little girl she was even last year and found some of her burgeoning desires and rebellious attitudes both confusing and exciting. At night, alone in her room, she felt very alone with these new and mysterious emotions and tapped into a deeper, darker part of herself than she had ever encountered. The feelings were sometimes painful, frightening, and, above all, alienating in her sense of aloneness.

Initially, Maya would ponder these emotions while absent-mindedly pricking superficially at her skin with a needle. Occasionally, she dared herself to poke deeper and found the tiny spots of blood intriguing and distracting. Soon, she was pricking and even cutting her skin with determination, and she would collect the droplets of blood on cotton balls, which she inexplicably saved. She found that this private preoccupation created a trancelike calm and a feeling of companionship with her emerging drives and identity. The scars were evidence of her private life and hidden self that she harbored as a valuable secret. She was mortified when her coach approached her and told her what her teammates had revealed to him the cuts they observed on her legs.

Treatment with Maya focused on the age-appropriate issues that were confronting her around sexuality, identity, and departure from parental values. Therapy was aimed at helping Maya understand her various feelings and sensations and make conscious choices that better achieved her goals. For example, rather than assuming her parents would not let her go out with a boy, she was encouraged to raise the issue directly. Rather than feeling isolated and alienated, she was supported in broaching her conflicts more openly with her close friends. She also was validated around her emerging sexuality and empowered to assert herself and set her own personal limits with boys. Ultimately, she was redirected toward identifying and then actively pursuing her needs rather than turning inward and shutting out feelings and self-expression.

Treatment thus incorporated individual sessions and family sessions at which Maya could discuss and negotiate openly with her parents. As her parents better understood her conflicts in the context of normal development, they also learned how they might need to adapt in addressing her changing needs. Maya was never implored, ordered, or bargained with to stop injuring herself. By acknowledging that these were actions solely under her control, the cutting and piercing did not become an overly charged area of contention. Rather, the challenges she faced and her responsibility in resolving them was highlighted and actively pursued. The cutting almost immediately abated, and suddenly Maya was a full-blown feisty teenager engaging her peers and her parents in the active evolution of her adolescence.

Although less common, self-injury in males is also a growing phenomenon. The developmental challenges faced by boys are generally similar to those faced by girls but obviously entail a different set of expectations and pressures. For example, boys may be expected to express less emotion and vulnerability than girls. Boys generally welcome the physical changes of adolescence, such as stronger muscles, a deeper voice, facial hair, and added vertical inches. Girls, in contrast, are often mortified by the advent of weight gain, bodily curves, breasts, and menstrual cycles. Boys are expected to engage more freely in sexual activity; girls are assumed to be more cautious and selective. In the following treatment of Danny, his sensitivity and dependency on his parents contributed to a painful developmental transition that was first brought to attention by his ritual of burning himself with cigarettes.

Case Example: Danny, Age 16

Danny had been tremendously unhappy since junior high school. Short in stature and late to enter puberty, Danny felt wholly inadequate among his rapidly maturing peers. In addition, Danny always had been somewhat shy and was easily brought to tears, much to his embarrassment. Although Danny had begun to undergo some pubertal changes by age 16, he already had withdrawn socially and maintained an overly harsh appraisal of himself. As a Latino, his machismo was called into question by both his peers and himself, further alienating and shaming him.

Danny was certain that he was attracted to girls and not to boys, yet he had no real interest in pursuing any intimacy for fear of being rejected. He was sometimes bullied at school, called derogatory names suggesting he was gay, and could not reconcile a stable sexual identity. Handsome, smart, and caring, Danny overlooked his many assets due to his core insecurity regarding his size and masculinity. He experienced his father as critical and rejecting, particularly regarding his lack of physical aggressiveness and stoicism, and his mother as overprotective and infantilizing.

Danny smoked cigarettes, a fairly common activity among his fellow high school students. In his misery, he would stoically inflict cigarette burns on his arms. He would dare himself to see how long he could withstand the searing pain before withdrawing the cigarette. Several of these burns were in fact quite severe, second degree, and he developed a painful infection on his left hand. He ignored it until he spiked a fever and his parents observed the infection and whisked him to the physician. He was successfully treated with powerful antibiotics and referred for psychotherapy to a local psychiatrist who specialized in working with adolescents.

His burns and infection had left a nasty trail of scars. Still, he would not stop burning himself. He was adamant also about not wanting to talk to anyone, much less a psychiatrist. After several rather fruitless sessions, the psychiatrist arranged for him to enter a psychotherapy group with other adolescents. He was assured that all he had to do was sit and listen and speak only if he wanted. The treatment group comprised adolescent girls and boys who either had attempted suicide or had engaged in repetitive self-destructive behavior, including self-injury and eating disorders. Danny listened to the stories of the others and felt shocked at the tremendous pain and difficulty these normal-looking teens endured. He felt less alone in his alienation and self-condemnation and was kindly treated by the other kids and the group leader. At the third session, he was asked, "What happened to your arms?" and found himself luridly describing his burning rituals.

He began to talk more openly with his psychiatrist, who did not indicate a primary agenda of making him stop the burning. This therapist was interested in how he felt and basically what it was like to be Danny, an experience he had never thought to put into words. Finally, somebody could bear witness to the pain he was in, and it came spilling out with words, tears, and questions. At the heart of the hurt lay his negative body image and how that sense of inadequacy seemed to spread into other parts of himself. Feeling small, emotionally vulnerable, and unwelcome by his peers, Danny seemed to want to stop time and forestall the specter of going to college, engaging his sexuality, and risking rejection outside the cocoon of his family. Gradually, Danny and his therapist could better crystallize the developmental challenges overwhelming him in each of the three critical realms of identity, intimacy, and independence.

The self-inflicted burns became understood as a form of self-punishment for his real and imagined shortcomings. Danny was so rejecting of his body that he harmed it in retribution. By rejecting these unwanted parts of himself, Danny could disown what he loathed and ultimately feel better about himself. He also felt strong and brave when he withstood the painful burns, counteracting his fear of physical smallness and weakness. Inevitably, of course, he would be faced with the truth of his limitations, and the cycle of punishment and disowning would be repeated.

Danny began to face a hard truth: He had no choice but to integrate a realistic sense of himself, all the "good, the bad, and the ugly," as he put it. He had to accept what were real limitations, such as his small stature, but also his many assets, for example, intelligence, caring, and many attractive physical traits. He could not escape what he did not like about himself that was encoded in his DNA, through burning, surgery, or sheer force of denial. Nor could he pretend that this was the reason for all his unhappiness, as he was making self-defeating choices that impacted his relationships, activities, and sense of accomplishment elsewhere. No, he would never be on *Championship Wrestling*, he said, but he could study math or engineering in college and more fully enjoy some activities and even meaningful relationships.

Danny benefited from role-playing exercises in therapy in which he developed more empowering ways to respond to teasing and taunts. He invented several funny remarks to make, which helped diffuse both his own discomfort and the sense of power the bully sought. When his machismo was challenged, he would quip, "The girls think I'm beautiful," or "Yes, being sensitive and handsome is such a curse." By not shrinking away and letting others prey on his vulnerability, he sidestepped the intended humiliation by displaying confidence and self-acceptance. His parents were also integrated into the treatment process, and Danny was able to express his feelings of rejection with his father and sense of smothering overprotectiveness with his mother. His parents became more aware of the impact of their behavior, and Danny's assertion that he deserved more respect from his father was discussed at length. His father's own parenting by a harsh and demanding father, within a culture that emphasized machismo as an essential virtue, was understood as a source of his habitual criticisms of Danny. He was able to express his true regard for his son and suppress more of his critical nature.

Therapy continued for a year with Danny, during which time his self-injury stopped but his social anxiety actually increased as he delved into friendships with both male and female peers. His cigarette smoking increased to an excessive level, and a referral to a physician was made. Danny was prescribed an antidepressant that also alleviated anxiety and was better able to handle his social stress and begin a smoking reduction program using Nicorette chewing gum. Treatment was ended when Danny had clearly begun to integrate a more healthy identity and a pattern of relating more comfortably and intimately.

CONCLUSIONS

Sharon, Andrea, Maya, and Danny each presented with unique patterns of self-injury, psychological functioning, and family dynamics. Although the particular conflicts driving the self-injury were unique in each case, the impasse in the developmental tasks of identity, intimacy, and independence were always at the core of their struggles. Once identified, be it the lingering trauma of sexual abuse or the vicissitudes of establishing greater independence from parental controls, the conflicts could be brought into direct focus and constituted the true work of therapy. By defining and normalizing these developmental obstacles; teaching new ways of coping with distress; and integrating group, family, and medical treatment where indicated, each of these teenagers were better able to confront their challenges rather than simply enact their pain through self-injury.

Chapter 10

Stepping Up to the Plate: How Parents Can Help

I needed to let go of believing it was my fault she was hurting herself.
Mother of an 18-year-old self-injurer

I know she needed me to be strong, but I was falling apart.
Mother of three adolescents, including one suicidal teen

Parents inevitably are an integral part of the treatment process. This is not because they are the culprits behind their daughters' need to self-injure, but because it takes amazing fortitude and finesse to parent an adolescent. Parents need to be reassured that not only did they not cause the problem, they cannot fix it. Rather, parents need to know when to stay out of the way as their teens develop and when to impose limits for guidance and safety. The way in which parents respond to their child's distress and belligerence is crucial to the teen's ability to negotiate the conflicts and challenges she faces.

LETTING GO OF PARENTAL GUILT AND TRANSFERRING RESPONSIBILITY TO THE ADOLESCENT

Typically, the advent of troubled behavior in one's child or adolescent sparks a process of soul-searching and self-blaming best captured in the timeless parental lament, "Where did I go wrong?" Although we should all take stock of our parenting strengths and limitations, as we inevitably possess both, it is a novel concept to most parents that they did not cause or fail to prevent their child from experiencing this developmental disturbance. Often it is a relief for parents to know that the conflicts now reside within the adolescent and her wider sphere of peer and cultural influences. Although parents must be a part of the solution and learn how not to obstruct the teen's progress, it is the teen who must take the initiative and responsibility for her own healthy adjustment. Thus, it is often sobering and even frightening for parents to realize that they can not fix the problems faced by their teen. It can be both a liberating and a helpless feeling for parents to let go of excessive control and responsibility over their child's developmental strivings.

Parents appropriately take full charge of their children's activities, playmates, emotional upsets, schooling, healthcare, diet, and even grooming. Children rely on their parents to orchestrate their lives and soothe their struggles, and most parents rise mightily to the task. In adolescence, however, teens want their parents neither to make their decisions nor to intrude into their emotional and social lives. Yet teens still retain some ambivalence that preserves their wish for rescue and parental help. Not only do parents often take far too much responsibility for their teens, but the teens themselves also look to their parents as the automatic cause or solution to their difficulties. The developmental and treatment processes necessitate that parents gradually let go while the adolescent increasingly assumes responsibility for her own well-being.

This changing allocation of responsibility and control can come as quite a shock to the adolescent as well as to the parents. It is a revelation that signals a true sea change in the adolescent's development: "Wow, I am the one in the driver's seat, and I'd better pay attention to where I'm going." The teen must realize that the good news is that she is in charge, and the bad news is that she is in charge. Therein lies the source of many core conflicts and the impetus for many of the wild swings in mood and functioning.

COMMITTING TO THE CAUSE: UNWAVERING LOVE AND SUPPORT

True finesse is required to both let go yet remain steadfastly available to the teen as a loving, supportive, and helpful parent. Conveying staunch commitment to helping the teen in any reasonable way possible helps allay the anxiety the teen experiences at the awesome burden of her growing independence. It can be a challenging tightrope walk to hold the teen accountable yet provide ongoing practical and emotional support.

Parents worry that by setting firm limits and refusing to take on the adolescent's conflicts the teen will feel abandoned and unloved. Much has been written about the similarities between the toddler's developmental process and the adolescent's; both require the child to venture tentatively toward greater levels of independence yet always feel safe to return to mom or dad for reassurance and aid. Adolescents experience their own versions of their ambivalent and unsteady forays into independence, risking autonomy yet relying on parents to ensure their overall safety and a secure harbor of love. Parents have few qualms about yelling to their three-year-old, "Stay out of the street!" or "Get down from that fence!" as guardians of their safety. Parents must also feel mandated to set limits that protect the life and limb of their adolescents. Sometimes this entails insisting they see a therapist or withholding the car keys.

In general, parents must set parameters outside of which the teen abdicates her decision-making privileges. For example, if an adolescent's drug abuse is rampant, inpatient rehabilitation may be the clear recourse. Or if an adolescent is habitually truant or sneaking out of the home at night to pursue high-risk adventures, a boarding or treatment school setting may be necessary. Similarly, driving in a car with anyone who has been drinking or engaging in unprotected sex are high-risk behaviors that must be clearly prohibited and backed up with meaningful ramifications and safeguards.

Parents routinely loathe the role of policeman with their adolescents, yet just as toddlers need their playgrounds supervised by attentive adults, the eminently more complex playground of the adolescent requires oversight and external controls. Families frequently need help in setting and executing fundamental limits, and family therapy is often a critical component of treatment. In family sessions, in which the adolescent and parents express their needs and negotiate boundaries, the therapist serves as an equal ally to every family member. The therapist should not take the side of the adolescent or of the parent but rather serve as a barometer of reality. The therapist needs to inform the parents when their rules are too restrictive and likely to generate more rebellion and convey to the teen the validity of parental concerns and desirability of more responsible choices by the teen. The therapist is thus equidistant from each of the family members, remaining unbiased yet clearly an avid advocate for all parties.

Adolescents are frequently surprised by the benefits of family sessions during which the therapist can help them convey their frustrations and validate legitimate needs. Commonly, the mere thought of speaking directly with one's parents in a closed-door session with a referee on duty can spark immediate resistance. Parents are more likely to listen to the advice of a professional who might suggest that the teen indeed needs privacy in her room and her relationships. Therapists often can intervene with overly controlling parents and encourage them to hear and dignify the teen's perspective. The adolescent is used to feeling outnumbered and overpowered by parents, and having the support of a trusted adult therapist can be highly beneficial and appreciated.

PARENTS UNDER SIEGE: KNOWING WHEN TO SEEK HELP

Rarely are the problems of the adolescent the only stresses confronted by parents. Siblings, jobs, finances, health, marital relations, extended families, and the gamut of life's stressors are often experienced concurrently with the specific stress of a self-injurious adolescent. Parents understandably can become overwhelmed and experience emotional difficulties themselves. Depression, marital conflict, anxiety, alcohol abuse, social isolation, sleep difficulties, irritability, and deflated self-esteem often can accompany the highly stressful process of having a self-injurious adolescent in treatment. For their own sake as well as for the adolescent's, parents need to know when their resources are overly taxed and when they need to focus on their own well-being.

Parents easily can become so involved in their teenager's agonies that they cease to engage in the normal behaviors that maintain their own equilibrium. Parents may cut out time for each other and give up socializing, exercising, or maintaining their health. Adolescents are invariably heartened to know that overwhelmed parents can acknowledge their own distress and take active steps toward alleviating it. This models responsible behavior to the teen and also alleviates the burden of the parents' tension, anger, tearfulness, or dysfunction on the adolescent's own functioning.

Parents often can take better care of themselves physically and emotionally with the simple permission to do so. Once parents understand that the happier and healthier they feel, the more they can contribute to their children's well-being and are often more motivated to focus on themselves. Sometimes, one parent may benefit from a therapist of his or her own to assist them through the emotional roller coaster they are on, or the couple may seek marital counseling. Adolescents can gain sorely lacking empathy for parents who can admit to their own difficulties and feel greatly supported and relieved by them seeking their own assistance.

Parents need to have their own distress addressed and normalized as they forge through the harsh terrain of their adolescent's development. As in any family system, every member affects each other, and assisting an overwhelmed parent ultimately assists the adolescent. Treatment benefits from not pointing an accusing finger at the adolescent as the so-called sick or disturbed person in the family and focusing on everyone's role in a successful developmental transition. Parents as well as adolescents deserve to be humanized and nurtured throughout these imposing challenges.

THE NARCISSISTIC INJURY: STIGMA AND SHAME

Having a son or daughter undergoing emotional difficulties often carries a perceived if not genuine stigma. Each social and ethnic culture varies in the degree to which emotional disturbance, self-injury, and professional intervention are accepted or stigmatized. In some communities, teenage acting out is considered par for the course; in others, the willful defiance of a teen is viewed as socially threatening and wholly unacceptable. And the degree to which parents are blamed for their children's misbehavior varies between cultures and communities.

Universally, however, the disappointment and responsibility parents feel for their children's difficulties can inflict an injury to one's pride, otherwise known as a *narcissistic injury*. Children are invariably narcissistic extensions of their parents, rightly or wrongly, and their behavior frequently viewed as a direct reflection of their own strengths or weaknesses. One need only to witness the humiliation experienced by the parent of a child throwing a huge public tantrum or the swelling pride of a parent seeing a child graduate to identify with this concept of narcissistic investment. Indeed, many of us question the competence of parents who allow their children to behave rudely or otherwise fail to meet social expectations. The public exposure of having a child exhibiting such apparently disturbed behavior as self-injury typically inflicts a narcissistic injury on the parents.

This injury can have benign or malignant consequences for both the parents and the adolescent. Most adults can maintain their sense of identity and esteem despite the disruption and hurt imposed by a troubled son or daughter. Indeed, the adolescent passage is largely about parents and children separating their all-too-often merged identities. Although challenging, parents usually can integrate the disappointments they experience in regard to their children without significant insult to their own sense of self-worth. Many parents feel unduly victimized by their child's difficulties, however, and even incensed that they have publicly humiliated them as parents. In these situations, intervention must actively address the parents' own injury so as to minimize an enmeshed and destructive process between the parents and child. Parents need an opportunity to voice and process their own pain and better understand how not to act out their hurt and anger in a way that can be damaging to the youth. The wrenching process of viewing one's child as a wholly separate individual, rather than as a self-reflection, must evolve in order for adolescents and parents to grow.

ADOPTING A NEW MANTRA: YOU DID NOT CAUSE THE CUTTING, AND YOU CANNOT FIX IT

Having a teenager who is self-injuring invariably causes soul-searching on the part of parents. What did I do wrong? What did I not do? Is it my fault that she is suffering and doing this horrible thing? This is where the rubber meets the road, so to speak, however, in that a paradigm shift in viewing parent-child relations is evolving. It is both a loss and a relief for parents to truly ascertain that they did not cause their child to have such difficulties nor can they fix them. It is truly the adolescent's story now, and though the parents have a continuing essential role in the life of their teen, they no longer can or should take full responsibility for their teen's choices and behavior.

Many parents I have worked with adopt this phrase as a virtual mantra, reminding themselves over and over that it is not their fault and they can not fix it. This enables them to not only stop beating themselves up unnecessarily but also helps them relinquish enough control so their teen can confront her troubles more productively. It is frightening for adolescents to realize that blaming their parents gets them nowhere and, in fact, no one but themselves can make things better. It can feel initially abandoning to the teen until the parents demonstrate their resolute support from the arm's length of respect for their child's autonomy. The core conflict between dependence and independence is thus brought explicitly into focus where the feelings it generates can be more fruitfully addressed.

Case Example: Mr. and Mrs. T.

Mr. and Mrs. T., or Lionel and Tess as they preferred to be called, have been married for 21 years. They have two teenage children, Alan, age 17, and Sara, age 15. They have encountered significant difficulties with both of their teens and wonder why they have "failed so miserably" as parents. Alan has twice been sent to a residential drug treatment facility and currently is foundering at an alternative high school with continuing drug issues. Sara, always their golden girl, has begun adolescence with a vengeance, defying their restrictions and efforts to curtail her suddenly rampant social life. In the course of one year in high school, she has morphed from a well-adjusted delight of a child into a multiply pierced, scantily clad, sexually active, and emotionally volatile stranger.

Primarily worried about her precocious sexuality, they are blindsided by the discovery of long vertical scars on her arms and legs. She is hostile and defiant about both her right to cut herself and to make her own sexual decisions, but her tearfulness, self-injury, falling grades, and lack of joy or connection in her relationships betray the true despair overwhelming her. She agrees to go into treatment "only because they are forcing her," but eagerly opens up in private with her therapist.

In the meantime, Lionel and Tess are having their own difficulties. Tess has felt it necessary to go to only part-time employment as a software engineer in order to be more available to her kids. Lionel hates his job, spends long hours at work and on overseas travel, and has been suffering from an undiagnosed depression for many months. Their marriage is sustained by genuine love and respect, but the magnitude of their stressors and their limited time together have disrupted even that. Now they talk only about the latest crisis at home and find themselves bickering out of sheer tension and grief. Although Lionel has been depressed, he has withdrawn emotionally from his family and drinks more than usual. Tess finds herself feeling helpless, isolated, terrified, and ashamed.

As Sara begins treatment, they also are included in the assessment and family therapy components. It becomes quickly apparent to the therapist that both of them are overwhelmed and becoming symptomatic in their own right. Efforts are made to secure Lionel a consultation for his own apparent depression, and he begins an antidepressant medication in conjunction with weekly psychotherapy. Tess is encouraged to bolster her social support and begins reaching out more to her friends and faith community. Sara's therapist spends time with them, exploring their own emotional statuses as well as the attributions they are making about her difficulties. Clearly, these parents are full of self-recrimination and experience intense shame and anger that their teenagers have disappointed and tormented them so. Consequently, their behavior is alternately overwrought and punitive with Sara, who needs more consistent support at this time.

Family sessions help support Lionel and Tess in setting appropriate limits despite Sara's defiance. Sara's responsibility for her own choices is highlighted, and her tendency to blame her parents for most things is framed as a smoke screen for her own insecurity and turmoil. Sara's developmental process is normalized and an effort made to emphasize that though her parents did not cause these challenges and they cannot solve them for her, they can provide an invaluable role in supporting and guiding her in a steadfast manner. Acknowledging Tess and Lionel's own degree of distress and their commitment to more productively address it help Sara see them as more human and validate her perceptions of their tendency to "way overreact." As they begin to model responsible attention to their own limitations, Sara feels less singled out as the so-called sick one and more charged with finding better ways to alleviate her own distress. Sara's brother, Alan, is integrated into selected sessions in order to address the family's overall functioning as a fluid system wherein everyone's behavior creates ripple effects that impact each family member differentially. Even the family's sadness over having to abandon the image of the perfect family gets verbalized and processed.

Although a long road lies ahead for Sara and her family, identification of parental vulnerabilities and their own deserving need for assistance helps each family member better attend to themselves. This ultimately allows them to be more effective as husband, wife, and parent and less likely to exacerbate Sara's anxiety and distress. Accepting less blame for Sara's difficulties and unhealthy choices enhances their parental authority and sense of competence and emotional strength.

Already feeling worn down and worried half to death about their son, Lionel and Tess feel that confronting such challenging behavior in their daughter is all the more overwhelming. They each need to care for themselves: Lionel with treatment of his depression and Tess with social support and exercise as a starting point. Both need opportunities to relax and decompress, and their relationship deserves attention through some scheduled time together. Ultimately, their sense of blame and inadequacy for having two teenagers facing such obstacles requires them to work through these attributions and not overly personalize their children's difficulties. Not only will these changes improve their own mood and esteem, but they also will greatly facilitate their ability to focus on their strengths and develop even more positive ways of parenting.

FAMILIES OF ORIGIN AND REFLECTING ON ONE'S OWN ADOLESCENCE

In treatment, it is always important for parents to discuss their own families of origin. Their own relationships with parents and siblings inevitably shed light on their adult sense of self and their roles as spouse and parent. Parents who grew up in cold, withholding families may understand their own overinvolvement and tenderness as partly a compensatory reaction to this early deprivation. Or they may themselves find it hard to empathize and comfort their children, continuing the less-than-empathic parenting modeled to them. It can be astounding to watch teenagers listen with great interest to their parents' own descriptions of their upbringings and its relevance to their relationship to their teen. It is quite eye-opening for teens to see their parents in a fully human light, doing the best they can with their own resources, limitations, and private hurts.

It is not uncommon for family history to reveal relatives with significant psychiatric difficulties. Depression, alcoholism, suicide, obsessive-compulsive disorder, abuse, and the gamut of human difficulties can suggest both biological and environmental factors that continue to influence them and quite possibly their adolescent as well. This history can significantly inform treatment in that a pervasive lineage of alcoholics clearly indicates high risk in this area, and multiple family members with clinical depression may suggest a preexisting vulnerability to depression in the teen.

It is useful for the adolescent to view herself as part of a larger family history and to appreciate the stresses and strengths that impinge on other family members as well. When teens can see their parents as actual flesh-and-blood human beings, with genuine assets and limitations, they can begin to develop empathy and more realistic expectations of their merely mortal parents. This is a critical component of maturation and of the evolving individuality that requires clear boundaries between oneself and others.

It also can be revelatory for adolescents to hear about their parents' own experiences as adolescents in particular. Often their parents' own adolescent histories help them better understand the concerns, fears, and lack of comprehension they express. For example, the mother of one 15-year-old patient had experienced a relatively calm, straitlaced adolescence that she in fact remembered rather fondly. She had been active on the school newspaper and student council and enjoyed numerous friendships. On the other hand, the father had experienced a more colorful youth, replete with drug and alcohol experimentation, sexual adventures, and parents who angrily denounced his poor grades and worrisome social life. He was not overly bothered by his daughter's occasional misbehavior: cutting classes, staying out past curfew, and going to parties with older teenagers. For him, this was nothing out of the ordinary and, in fact, rather tame compared to his own experience. The mother was, shall we say, freaked out by her daughter's behavior. It seemed wild, dangerous, and morally ungrounded, especially in comparison to her own self-described history as a "goody-goody kind of kid." The parents therefore sent mixed messages to their daughter and could rarely agree on rules and limits or clear expectations. Learning about her parents' backgrounds not only helped her better understand where they were coming from but also assisted the family in negotiating a consistent middle ground of expectations and limits.

Similarly, parents might be no stranger to depression, having themselves struggled with it in the past or present. These parents are perhaps better able to relate to their teenager's own experience of depression, which may have a positive or a negative impact. If the parent identifies too closely with the teen's distress, he or she is likely to inaccurately project his or her own experience onto the teen and contribute to an enmeshed relationship. At the same time, such sensitivity to the vicissitudes of depression can help parents sympathize with the tremendous difficulty their daughter is having. Few parents also have experienced repetitive self-injury, however, and this particular behavior may thoroughly confuse, appall, and frighten them. Thus, a crash course in contemporary teen culture is essential in helping parents conceptualize the seemingly bizarre symptoms of cutting and other forms of self-injury.

CONTEMPORARY TEEN CULTURE

Teen culture in the United States is as diverse as our nation's regions, politics, religions, races, sexualities, and socioeconomics. Thus, any discussion of teen culture must be interpreted through the lens of the specific sociocultural environment within which each teen is immersed. That being said, and an exhaustive discussion of such diversity being beyond the scope of this book, a number of universal themes seem to impact most teens exposed to today's powerful media, pop, and corporate influences.

Topping the list are two themes that other generations of youth have loudly broadcast: anger with a capital A and sex with a capital S. From the rock anthems of the 1960s to the punk of the '80s and onward through heavy metal and seething, sexualized rap, musical styles reflect the churning anger of many youth. Violence in film, television, music, world events, sports, and, sadly, many households seems to normalize and even celebrate overt verbal and physical aggression. Overtly sexual images, songs, ads, and messages similarly abound. These angry and sexual motifs are very much in synch with much of the frustration, driving sexuality, and clashing with authority that often define the teenage years. It is no wonder that on many levels teen culture is synonymous with rebellion and rage and self-injury erupts as a clear expression of frustration directed at both oneself and others.

Tattoos, piercings, torn jeans, sagging pants, spiked hair, and overly revealing garb defy the status quo and the powers that be in an expression of anger, autonomy, and rebellion. Thus, the marking, damaging, and adorning of the body are ready examples for such expression, and in this light, self-cutting or burning is not too far a deviance from these commonly accepted youthful actions. The ever-present emphasis on female beauty, thinness, and glamour in society further provokes deliberate defiance or exaggeration of such oppressive norms in teens struggling to meet impossible expectations.

Confusion and chaos also seem to be common themes in both adolescent development and pop culture. The lack of direction, confusion over goals, fears about self-sufficiency, and growing distance from parental protection create internal chaos that is then reflected in outward chaos. Drunken evenings, pervasive drug use, indiscriminate sex, truancy, shoplifting, binging and purging, dangerous driving, and thrill-seeking all serve as examples of the internal turmoil of adolescence made manifest in chaotic, gravely destructive behavior. Self-injury fits in seamlessly with this painful list of outlets. Of course, many youths are able to channel this chaotic energy into more productive activities, such as artistic expression, athletic competition, academic achievement, healthy romances, and prosocial public service and activism, but all too often the destructive routes are more readily accessed and more pervasively modeled in media portrayals.

Finally, we live in a curious culture wherein dysfunction and flamboyant misbehavior draw immense attention and even admiration of sorts. In teenagers, whereas it may be difficult to stand out as unique or special in typical spheres of athletics, academics, popularity, and the like, deviant behavior provides a quick route to distinction. By repetitively cutting and self-injuring, adolescents rapidly commandeer additional attention as peers begin to wonder about the complex person who must exist behind the striking behavior. Sympathy, too, elicits peer attention and kindness, a scarce resource for many teens.

In conclusion, though parents may never fully grasp or relate to the manifold influences that make up popular teen culture, that is not their job. Rather, what is required of parents is that they seek to understand and contextualize their adolescent's behavior within the seemingly bizarre norms of each generation's youth. By appreciating the powerful forces that impact their children, parents are in a much better position to avoid judgment, condemnation, or outright panic in reaction to undesirable behavior. In the larger context of teen culture and the developmental challenges before them, even self-mutilation takes on a perverse meaning and congruency that must be grasped in order to reach and walk alongside the teen on her tumultuous journey.

CONCLUSIONS

Parents with self-injurious adolescents are called upon to step up to the proverbial plate. This means both assuming responsibility and relinquishing it, offering unwavering support yet not smothering, contending with deep disappointment yet not falling victim to it, and remaining strong yet knowing when to seek help. The entry of their teenager into treatment also challenges parents to look at their own histories and vulnerabilities and develop more productive ways of interacting with difficult adolescent conflicts.

Parents suffer significant grief and pain as they support a beloved child who self-injures, and they in turn deserve assistance with their own difficulties and emotional needs. Finally, parents must separate enough from their teens to realize that they neither caused nor are capable of fixing the teen's self-destructive behavior. Enhanced understanding of the pervasive cultural forces impacting today's adolescents can help parents better appreciate the extrafamilial norms and pressures that are beyond their scope of influence. Stepping up to the plate ultimately requires parents to provide unwavering love and support yet allow the teen to assume responsibility for constructively addressing the challenges they face.

Chapter 11

Health and Happiness Are Verbs: The Responsibilities of the Adolescent in Treatment

There really are things I can do to make life better. It's just hard to have to do them over and over and over. Sometimes it seems easier to slip back into bad habits like numbing out with my razors, but then at the end of the day, I just have to do those harder things anyway.

18-year-old girl

I was tired of everyone talking about me and making decisions for me. I had to get off my butt to get everyone off my back.

15-year-old boy

It is not uncommon for clinicians and parents to feel that they are working harder to help the adolescent than the adolescent is working to help herself. It can be easy to lose sight of the teen's responsibility in her own development and symptom management, and too often adults are scurrying around frantically to help an adolescent who remains passive and resistant in the midst of the fray. Clinicians need to help the adolescent and the parents understand the responsibilities of each teen in treatment and help encourage and uphold these expectations in order for the teen to retain the right to make his or her own decisions.

Adolescents, as well as adults, can benefit greatly from the revelation that happiness and health are not static, passive states of being. In fact, they require constant cultivation through ongoing effort and action. Reframing happiness and health as verbs, as the very actions that uphold them, helps remind us that they require ongoing responsibility to achieve and maintain. For example, for some teens, happiness requires studying in order to achieve grades of which they can feel proud. It may also require fun social time that demands the nurturance of relationships and a commitment of time and energy to scheduled activities. Health may demand that one take medication, eat properly, and get some exercise day after day. Thus, as verbs, happiness and health take active responsibility to achieve and maintain. Adolescents in particular are called upon to relinquish passive childhood dependencies in order to assume increasing responsibility for the well-being of their maturing selves. The treatment process presents an excellent opportunity for self-injuring adolescents to acquire responsible skills and behaviors that can reduce their dependency on cutting as they actively confront challenges in their daily lives.

RESPONSIBILITY 1: VERBALIZE FEELINGS AND DILEMMAS BEFORE SELF-INJURING

The more individuals can talk about their feelings and impulses, the less likely they are to act them out in muddled and destructive ways. For teens who feel unbearably lonely and rejected and cut as a means of coping with pain, making a commitment to express these feelings prior to (and hopefully in lieu of) acting out is a huge step in treatment. The adolescent may need to tell the clinician, parent, or a friend about their sadness and hurt and longing, thus connecting these feelings to their self-destructive urge to cut. Often, simply by verbalizing their feelings and thoughts, much of the highly charged emotion can be expressed, relieved, and more constructively addressed.

This latter benefit to verbalizing emotions is that problem-solving inevitably enters the process when feelings are discussed. If the teen talks about not having anyone to call or about feeling rejected by a love interest, real coping strategies and active solutions are far more likely to become apparent. Also, the simple act of engaging with another human being around one's innermost feelings creates a sense of connection that in itself is rewarding and soothing. Clarifying one's feelings verbally helps counteract the sense of being overwhelmed and out of control, and once another person expresses understanding and empathy, the teen no longer feels hopelessly alienated and defeated by unnamed forces. It is no secret that talking about one's emotions and ideas forms the basis of psychotherapy. Talking also needs to become the fundamental currency teenagers rely on to communicate and contend with pain and conflict.

Explicit in every no-suicide or no-harm therapeutic contract is the express commitment to speak to the therapist prior to inflicting an injury. The teen is responsible for phoning and communicating directly with the therapist when feeling overwhelmed by the impulse to self-injure. This simple step frequently wards off the need to resort to self-injury, as the catharsis and warm understanding of the clinician who can handle hearing about the teen's most violent pain and impulses can pave the way for problem-solving and the teen's ability to constructively meet her needs. Although it is not always feasible for the teen to talk to the therapist immediately, this cultivation of an ability to delay gratification and tolerate emotion in the anticipation of forthcoming help is also critical to the teen's sense of strength and self-sufficiency in the face of distress.

RESPONSIBILITY 2: IDENTIFY THE FEELINGS ASSOCIATED WITH THE URGE TO CUT

Adolescent self-injurers often will report a global feeling of awfulness that resists more thoughtful articulation. Although feeling horrible is a legitimate sensation, one can feel horrible in a plethora of ways. Is the youth sad, hurt, angry, or desperately hungry for something (e.g., affection, validation, soothing, pleasure)? Breaking down this global sense of awfulness can help expose the underlying needs, conflicts, and, alas, resolutions as well. Although an answer of "I don't know" is a legitimate starting point in treatment, teens must struggle earnestly with these ambiguities in learning how to better define and articulate hot spots of emotion.

Individuals with depression characteristically demonstrate what is called *black-or-white* or *all-or-none* thinking. Things are all hopeless; nothing will ever feel good. They are completely despondent as opposed to not at all depressed. Learning to identify the shades of gray between black-and-white or all-or-none attitudes forms a critical shift in perspective. Teens must struggle to articulate multiple dimensions of their moods and experiences rather than resort to gross overgeneralizations such as, "I'm worthless," "School is hopeless," "Everything is awful," and the like. Learning to point to specific areas of stress at the same time as drawing upon areas of high functioning and strength, a more realistic perspective and problem-solving approach can unfold in lieu of a defeatist position. The case of Tony helps illustrate the importance of verbalizing specific feelings in order to identify what one, in fact, wants to change.

Tony reports to his therapist that his life sucks. Inarguably, a number of stress points create ongoing problems and unhappy consequences in his current situation. But when pressed, and then pressed further, Tony is able to list the top three aspects of his life that he hates. First and foremost, he feels ugly and unattractive to girls. A tall, skinny 15-year-old with acne and long, unkempt, dyed-black hair, Tony shies away from girls and spends much of his time alone in his room. Ultimately, this causes him to feel plagued by the pain of loneliness. When asked to list three positive things about his physical self, and after intense encouragement and unwillingness to accept the response of "nothing" from his therapist, Tony reluctantly points to his height, his green eyes, and his hair as being okay.

When pushed to identify three things he hates about his appearance, Tony only can point to his acne as making him "beyond hideous." As he gradually clarifies that he views his acne as his single most unattractive feature, the globally defeatist argument that he is a wholly and hopelessly ugly teen becomes less viable. In fact, the therapist challenges Tony with this question: Are you willing to look into improving your acne? Although he initially insists that it is a complete mess beyond anyone's control, he gradually begins to hear input about possible medications and skin care strategies prescribed by a dermatologist as a realistic (and undeniable) option. If Tony hates his acne so much, is he willing at least to try to alleviate it as much as possible? Gradually, Tony is compelled to abandon his passive victim stance and even feel a glimpse of hopeful empowerment as he agrees to consult with a dermatologist.

This is just one small example of an intervention targeted at specifically identifying genuine problems rather than becoming mired in paralyzing global emotional generalizations. Yet the overriding benefit of this approach is clear. Rather than a stance of learned helplessness and defeatist passivity, active problem-solving is incumbent upon anyone with a stake in his or her own well-being. This has to be true for the teenager on the road to adulthood as well. Ultimately, this empowering process begins with a clear articulation and naming of the negative emotion distressing the individual and the subsequent identification of the event, thought, or conflict that has generated it. Teenagers ultimately need to take responsibility for this aspect of their welfare.

RESPONSIBILITY 3: KNOW YOUR TRIGGERS: WHAT SPARKS YOUR DISTRESS?

The assumption that we all readily know why we feel the way we do is frequently false. Children and adolescents are notorious for being in the moment; their fully felt present experience eclipses awareness of what happened before, what will happen later, and that others may have utterly different feelings or needs. Yet adolescents, like many adults, gain wisdom from self-knowledge, the stuff of maturity. We only can come to know ourselves in part by understanding our sensitivities, our reactions, and our own emotional triggers. Knowledge can lead to mastery as we come to feel less at the mercy of events that trigger undesirable responses. Adolescents can gain insight and make choices about how to react to these triggers and thereby feel less helpless, blindsided, and cognitively ill-equipped to problem-solve when emotionally stressed.

The first step is a largely intellectual process that necessitates the adolescent's willingness to take responsibility for acquiring this self-knowledge. Once their curiosity about their inner lives and their sense of agency in determining outcomes is sparked, teens can learn to quite insightfully identify antecedents to specific negative emotional states. Although the mechanics of this process are discussed in chapter 6, "Professional Treatment of Self-Injury," the expectation that the teenager take responsibility for undertaking and gradually mastering this step can be set early on.

RESPONSIBILITY 4: LEARN TO NEGOTIATE WITH PARENTS AND TEACHERS

Adolescents frequently lament their sense of being nagged, punished, limited, or otherwise oppressed by parental figures. They may lash out in retaliation, making the home a battleground of combatants where the polarized positions ensure no victors. They may act out, cutting themselves, staying out all night, flaunting drug or alcohol use. Yet the only means of achieving any success over ongoing conflicts and competing needs between the teen and parents or teachers involves negotiation. Although teens have not yet learned to view themselves as having the power, skill, or responsibility to engage in frank give-and-take discussions with adults, this type of active debate and compromise is exactly the route to their achieving greater freedoms, independence, and trust.

Parents also are not always keen on viewing their children as equal partners in the decision-making processes. Too often, parents make the error of throwing autocratic decisions at their teenagers in a lopsided effort to assert their parental authority. Teens then feel not only resentful but helpless as well. This is the time for parents to begin modeling to their children one of life's indispensable skills: negotiation. This requires their openness and even their ability to invite the teen into negotiations that can achieve a joint resolution or compromise to conflicts.

Teens all too often will abdicate their role in the making or breaking of successful communication. They need to be supported and encouraged to constructively present their perspective while seeking to understand their parents'. They need to engage directly and productively in seeking a resolution to their desire to take the car to the beach and their parents' reluctance to give them the keys. Perhaps they need to explain their plans in detail with a promised time of return in order to reassure their parents. Or perhaps they will agree to a dry run by driving with a parent to the beach in order to demonstrate their competence behind the wheel. Or perhaps the request is simply unrealistic, and they will have to accept a lesser success, such as taking the car to a football game that same weekend. The point is that discussion and negotiation rather than confrontational and rigid clashes of perspectives need to be developed as the modi operandi for achieving their needs. When the parents give a little and the teen gives a little, a middle ground is achieved that ultimately promotes growth and empowerment during this developmental transition.

RESPONSIBILITY 5: DEAL DIRECTLY WITH FRIENDS

In other words, when lonely, hurt, angry, or otherwise frustrated in a friendship, teenagers need to learn to take responsibility for working out issues directly with their peers. Teens frequently will ally with peripheral friends, chat endlessly online, or cut themselves bloody in despair rather than confront the obvious need to communicate directly. So often the adolescent will imagine and assume and even concoct all sorts of negative motives in her peers only to discover that so much of her torment was unnecessary. For example, an adolescent may feel dreadfully rejected because a close friend is suddenly spending a lot more time with someone else. The teen may then withdraw further out of hurt or resentment and even begin to send hostile signals to the friend. Once the teen talks directly with the friend, expressing an honest desire for connection, however, she may discover that she is still loved and valued. The teen then must accommodate to this widening circle of friends and tolerate her jealously in order to maintain the friendship she so values.

At issue here is a central life question: Do you want to let life happen to you, or do you want to drive your own life? The only way to achieve the relationships and outcomes we desire is to actively pursue them. This demands engagement and face-to-face discussion of real feelings and difficult conflicts, often even without the barrier of technological devices. The beauty of finding the courage to take charge of one's own life in this manner is that relationships can be greatly enriched, conflicts resolved, and the tendency to become mired in isolating despair massively reduced. This is a key developmental task that can greatly abate the incidence of cutting and self-injury.

RESPONSIBILITY 6: TRY OUT YOUR PERSONAL ALTERNATIVES TO SELF-INJURY

Therapy is certainly about understanding and learning. It cannot operate successfully in a vacuum, however, where new options and strategies are not enacted in real-life situations. When teenagers agree to accept responsibility for making honest attempts to try out new self-harm alternatives, a huge milestone in treatment has been reached.

In treatment, each adolescent will have prepared a list with the therapist of alternative behaviors to engage in when feeling a strong urge to cut and self-injure. Everyone's list is unique and will integrate her own personality, social inclinations, and self-soothing strategies. Strategies may include journaling, playing a favorite CD, calling a friend, walking the dog, meditating, or even simply staying with the painful feelings and riding them out in a Zen manner of experiencing the moment. Not all the strategies will work, and the list gradually will get honed to a handful of alternatives that successfully distract, soothe, or otherwise supplant the need to inflict physical injury.

Structuring the commitment to actively employ these strategies in the face of self-harm impulses is important. Maintaining a written log in the initial weeks to record the sequences of feelings, impulses to cut, alternative strategies employed, and outcomes of these efforts serves to concretely chart the real-life transition from therapeutic ideas to actual behaviors. Sometimes, one attempted strategy will fail, but rather than resort immediately to a bloody quick fix by cutting, the teen will learn to try a second or even a third. The adolescent needs to understand that a process of trial and error is unavoidable as she learns what works for her. It will take time and practice for these alternatives to gain the same traction and benefits she has come to experience with self-injury. It is this willingness to take on the responsibility for building a larger repertoire that is empowering and productive.

RESPONSIBILITY 7: DO UNTO YOURSELF AS YOUR BETTER SELF DOES UNTO OTHERS

Yes, this twist on the Golden Rule is important in adolescents who typically afford themselves the harshest judgment, criticism, and condemnation. Often, simply by asking a teen what she would tell her best friend to do in the same situation yields an astonishing clarity. When she imagines consoling and counseling her best friend, she is the most compassionate, wise, and enthusiastic of consultants. Of course she would tell her friend to do this, that, or the other thing rather than harm herself. Of course, she would point out her friend's many assets and inherent worth and seek to put a problem or a limitation into perspective. And of course she would tell her friend to get off her proverbial butt and actively pursue what she needs and wants.

Teens frequently will smile as they realize the irony of their own advice. Yes, if they only listened to and treated themselves as their own best friends, they would be eminently compassionate, caring, and encouraging. They often can see the irony in how readily they condemn themselves and how harshly they treat themselves both psychically and physically. Listening to their best friend can help release them from the grip of their own unproductive and destructive internal voice in order to become their best compassionate and proactive selves.

Similarly, when teens contemplate how they would like their friends to interact with them, insights are gained into more productive ways to communicate. A sulky, resentful adolescent often can understand that if the tables were turned, she would prefer that a friend speak to her directly about the hurt and disappointment rather than withdraw and hold a grudge. How different things feel in someone else's shoes. Learning to metaphorically wear other pairs of shoes rather than the leaden and largely immobile shoes that keep her stuck and self-harming provides a refreshing and freeing perspective.

RESPONSIBILITY 8: LOOKING IN THE MIRROR

Lots and lots of things are wrong with the people in our lives. Parents can be controlling, friends can be inconsiderate, teachers can be demanding. Yet in every situation in which we find ourselves frustrated, we also play a role. We have choices to make that will determine to a large degree how the situation is perceived, resolved, escalated, or ignored. It is generally very hard to see our own contributions to difficulties that we find so overwhelming, distressing, and unfair. The problem can seem to be all out there, and we can readily point fingers and identify the person or system causing us grief. Yet we are often unwitting accomplices in our own difficulties and need to take responsibility for our half of the equation in order to achieve satisfactory resolutions.

Some examples will help to illustrate the benefits of looking at oneself in the mirror in order to honestly face our role in virtually any situation that brings us unhappiness.

Jamie was a 15-year-old patient with a history of out-of-control behavior since starting high school. She frequently was ignoring curfews, smoking pot, drinking to excess, and engaging in unprotected sex with seemingly random boys. Her parents tried everything to help her stop these destructive behaviors, especially relying on periods of grounding her during which she was not allowed to see any friends or leave the house except to attend school. In her despair at being isolated and her rage at her parents, Jamie would cut shallow but bloody gashes lengthwise down her arms. No matter how vigilant her parents were about combing her room for sharp objects, she always seemed to find something she could use to injure herself. Paper clips, cracked plastic bottle fragments, and the razor excavated from a manual pencil sharpener all served as adequate tools for cutting.

Despite individual and family therapy, there continued to be periods of improvement punctuated by outrageous episodes of deeply worrisome misbehavior (e.g., sneaking out at night to meet an 18-year-old man, needing to be picked up at a friend's home drunk and sick, dilated eyes noted at night, showing a child she babysat the scars on her arms, and shoplifting laxatives "for a friend"). Out of sincere fear for her physical safety, Jamie's parents and therapist began exploring options for residential treatment. A variety of treatment schools and wilderness-type camps were identified as good options in order to wrest Jamie from her environment and inability to change her behavior. Not surprisingly, Jamie was furious and intensely opposed to the idea of being "shipped away," voicing her attachment to her friends and threatening to kill herself if her parents sent her off.

At this critical life juncture, what would looking in the mirror involve for Jamie? What realities about her own choices and behavior does she need to face in order to productively confront the enormous challenges before her? If she truly does not want to go to a distant treatment school, what choices can she make to achieve that goal? In addition to hating her parents and therapist for posing this therapeutic intervention, what is her responsibility in this terrible dilemma? Ultimately, Jamie must acknowledge that her behaviors are problematic and demonstrate that she can get them under better control. Otherwise, can she truly argue that she is safe to stay at home? She needs to come clean with herself, even if not with others, and recognize that she and no one else is steering this ship.

A smaller example of learning to look in the mirror can illustrate how readily this responsibility can be called into service in daily life. A common teenage conflict, such as the battle over academic grades fought between parents and teens, serves as an example in the following case of Ritchie.

Ritchie is a high school senior with a nearly failing grade point average. He has received educational testing to assess whether a learning problem may contribute to his failure to complete assignments and perform on exams, yet the results yielded no significant findings to indicate a learning problem. Rather, it appears that his low motivation and almost complete absorption in computer poker for the past two years have distracted him from any genuine investment in his schoolwork.

Ritchie's parents have clashed continually with him over his grades. Ritchie's attitude is that if it is not important to him, he is willing to deal with the consequences and his parents will just have to deal with it. His parents have now removed his computer from the house, however, and he is both irate and desperate. He yells and argues and pleads and cries, but his parents are adamant that he not regain his computer until his grades improve to at least a 2.0 this quarter.

What will Ritchie's examination of himself in the mirror involve? First, he will have to admit to himself that even he is not thrilled with his abysmal record and the prospect of not having enough units to graduate at the end of the year. Second, can he look beyond his anger at his parents enough to truly see the lack of effort and the painful internal barriers to productivity that have brought him to this point? Can he see that his absorption in his computer life has been supplanting any real engagement in his social, physical, and academic lives? Ultimately, can he see that he is frightened of being rejected by his peers and of not having the smarts to succeed even if he does apply himself? For any productive pathway to emerge at this point, Ritchie will have to interrupt his tunnel vision in viewing his parents as his only life obstacle to see the true internal barriers he has imposed. Can he look at himself in the mirror and see that he is not happy, must make things better, and may need some help to dig out of the hole he has found himself in?

The ability to reflect and develop insight into oneself is a critical developmental task that even many adults fail to achieve consistently. As parents model for their adolescent's some admission of their own limitations and a willingness to alter their role in perpetuating negative interactions, teens often can utilize the support and direction of a therapist to really get it as well. They can learn both the truth and the amazing power of honestly looking at themselves as they take active responsibility in creating a life they can feel proud of and enjoy.

RESPONSIBILITY 9: LEARN THE REAL CONSEQUENCES OF RECURRENT SELF-INJURY

There is an unfortunate cliché that teenagers think of themselves as being immortal. That is, they rarely see themselves at risk for life or limb despite what appear to adults to be risky, dangerous, and downright destructive choices. This can apply to teenagers who self-injure as well. It is difficult for adolescents to project themselves into the future and appreciate the tremendous remorse they may feel for cutting permanent scars across their body. It is equally difficult for them to fathom any immediate risks, such as infections, concussions, social ostracism, or excessive bleeding caused by intense self-injury. Similar to how an adolescent may enjoy a tattoo today but loathe it by age 30, teens who self-injure are generally so fully immersed in the moment and the intensity of their discomfort that potential risks fail to enter their minds.

Although the consequences of most forms of repetitive self-injury among teens are psychological and social rather than medical, unforeseen complications do arise. The socially contagious aspect of self-injury within schools, institutions, and other groups of teens even raises the specter of HIV and hepatitis infection through the sharing of blades and needles. Permanent scarring is probably the most common long-term physical consequence of self-injury, resulting in shame, social anxiety, and both a damaged and a stigmatized sense of self.

Just as do teens in treatment for alcohol abuse or anorexia nervosa, self-injurers need to be fully aware of the risks and consequences of their actions. Assuming responsibility for becoming educated and making informed choices is a necessary aspect of treatment. Adolescents who take responsibility for acquiring the necessary knowledge in therapy to at least cognitively grasp the risks of self-injury have taken a big step toward choosing to intervene with their behavior. Adolescents should be informed matter-of-factly about the immediate risks as well as the chronic patterns of dysfunction that can result from self-harm.

Perhaps most at risk is the adolescent's ability to contend with successive developmental challenges. The more immersed the teen becomes in self-injury or any repetitive self-destructive behavior as a means of avoiding true coping, the more likely numerous aspects of her life also will suffer. Friends, health, academics, self-esteem, and life goals may become irreparably compromised, and the teen even may deteriorate to a point requiring inpatient or residential treatment. The long-term risks the adolescent takes in not assuming productive responsibility for overcoming this developmental impasse need to be clearly and bluntly spelled out by clinicians and parents.

RESPONSIBILITY 10: COMMIT TO SOLVING PROBLEMS WITH THE BRAIN, NOT THE BODY

Adolescents are a highly physical bunch. Rapidly changing bodies, intensifying drives, growing appetites, and powerful reserves of energy all combine to preoccupy teens with their physical selves. Physical appearance often is indistinguishable from identity and self-worth in many adolescents, and again, all focus can be painfully directed toward one's body.

It is no wonder, then, that so many adolescents seek to solve their emotional and interpersonal problems through mastery or manipulation of their bodies. Anorexics master their hunger and whittle their bodies to imagined ideals that will bring a magical sense of well-being. Bulimics surrender to tremendous impulses by binging, only to seek a sense of control and goodness through the cleansing ritual of purging. Average adolescents dye their hair, modify their bodies with tattoos or piercings, and seek to visually manipulate their look in keeping with their desired sense of self. The self-injurer who cuts or burns or inflicts pain on her eminently tangible body as a means of expressing emotional pain is similarly turning to the body in a futile attempt at self-regulation and self-soothing. In all these cases, it is ultimately the enlistment of mental resources that will truly provide greater self-control, connection, and diminishment of emotional pain.

Adolescents can learn to take responsibility for their decision to resolve conflict through physical or psychological means. They need to understand and accept that they can choose either to short-circuit effective resolution through immediate physical outlets or to take on the more adult, more lasting, and more productive process of utilizing their brains. Problem-solving alternatives to self-harm, altering negative self-statements, expressing pain verbally or artistically, and actively communicating with others are but a few of the cognitive tools available to every adolescent. Once teens take responsibility for making a commitment to bring their brains into the forefront of each confrontation with despair, they grow beyond the confines of physical solutions that have led only to an exacerbation of their difficulties thus far.

As anyone who has raised or worked with an adolescent knows, it can be extremely challenging to engage teens in endeavors that go beyond the imperative urgings and preoccupations with their bodies. Nonetheless, assuming responsibility for the role their minds play as the ultimate arbiter of psychological conflict and behavioral choice helps bring psychology and intellect into the arena of what can otherwise feel like a purely physical surge of unmanageable bodily sensations. Committing to enhancing the role of the mind in coping is a huge step beyond what has become to many the endless torture chamber of their own body.

CONCLUSIONS

Adolescents want ever so badly to have rights but often can lose sight of their responsibilities. Astonishingly, taking on responsibility can be remarkably empowering and liberating. Helping the adolescent take charge of more productive and mature coping approaches can empower her to break free of the repetitive cycle of self-injury. Engaging more directly with parents and peers in meeting needs and resolving conflicts can provide tremendous forward developmental momentum. Gaining genuine insight into their triggers, emotions, strengths, and foibles can develop empowering resources of knowledge and honest decision-making. Adolescents face a tall order of growing responsibility as they mature, and integrating this reality into the supportive framework of treatment can help direct and encourage them in this developmental journey.

Chapter 12

Depathologizing Adolescent Self-Injury: Cutting on a Continuum

I immediately assumed he was crazy; that he was sick, frightening, and lost to us forever. It felt like the end of the world.

Mother of 17-year-old cutter

I thought I was a freak. I felt disgusting and totally demented and was no way going to let anyone find out.

15-year-old male cutter

These catastrophic responses are all too common among parents who discover that their teenagers are self-mutilating, and teens can be similarly frightened as well. The ideas of self-inflicting pain, causing overt injury and permanent scarring, and obsessively ritualizing the blood and paraphernalia associated with cutting are completely foreign to most people's concept of health. Worse, it suddenly raises the possibility of death by suicide, an act seemingly just one small step removed from the violent self-injuries. To the adolescent, it raises an awareness of pushing the invisible envelope of normalcy and going outside the bounds of health. The immediate response to self-injury is generally fear, disgust, incomprehension, and a pathological view of these morbid acts of self-aggression.

Without a doubt, self-injury is always a cause for concern and should never be dismissed or trivialized. Cutting among today's adolescents, however, can represent radically different levels of dysfunction or even represent burgeoning healthy strivings. Cutting can, in rarer cases be a harbinger of severe psychopathology, of genuine psychosis, suicide risk, major depression, compulsivity, or violent fixation. Yet to the immense relief of the vast majority of families, far more often than not, self-injury is a symptom of a psychosocial obstacle, deficit, conflict, or even unexpected bump in the developmental process. Differentiating levels of severity represented by the phenomenon of cutting is critical to the sound assessment and effective treatment planning required in each individual case of cutting.

As a starting point, it is hugely therapeutic to adolescents and their families to depathologize and destigmatize self-injury in the vast majority of cases that warrant such a nonalarmist and nonjudgmental appraisal. It is natural to view cutting as a perverse and pathological behavior. What could be more senselessly self-destructive than self-mutilation? In today's teen culture, and much of broader pop culture as well, however, such behavior melds less conspicuously with other forms of body art, body modification, rebellion, and self-destructive behavior. In the postpunk era that brought us Sid Vicious and a fashion style best described as overtly hostile and masochistic, to a rap music era that celebrates violence, alienation, and misogyny, florid displays of anger and self-hate are increasingly commonplace. In fact, the ante has been upped, in that more and more dramatic forms of body art (e.g., tattooing, piercing, branding, and ultrarisqué dress) are now necessary to stand out from the norm. A recent 16-year-old patient of mine was wholly disappointed to arrive at school with a newly pierced tongue only to garner few stares or comments. In this context, combined with the age-old cross-cultural role of damaging and decorating one's skin, adolescent cutting is less shocking and but one of many undesirable forms of coping, self-expression, and rebellion.

Masochism is, in fact, highly celebrated in many cultures, including the sports- and beauty-crazed United States. For example, in sports, for the many stoic ultramarathoners who run an unfathomable 100 miles in a single race, boxers and football players who can withstand violent assault, and swimmers who specialize in braving subfreezing ocean temperatures, the willingness to withstand pain is synonymous with heroism. We celebrate gymnasts who compete despite excruciating injuries, and even children in sports are encouraged to suck it up, be tough, and transcend discomfort.

Furthermore, masochism in the service of improving physical appearance is quite acceptable and even encouraged around the world. From waxing and electrolysis to the *Extreme Makeover*–type of plastic surgery, cultures condone and even encourage the sacrifice of pain for beauty. Historical examples of foot binding in China, scarification in Africa, and painful coming-of-age rituals the world over attest to the virtue ascribed to those who suffer in the service of meeting cultural standards of beauty and acceptance. Sadomasochistic practices ranging from Opus Dei's religiously inspired self-abuse to the sexual practices of a sizable S-M subculture, the compelling affinity many have for suffering in a specific context speaks to the deep emotional and social implications of enacting, transcending, and ultimately mastering pain and injury. Finally, eating disorders, ranging from the self-starving anorexic whose emaciated body shivers even in warm weather and is allowed to consume a mere 100 calories each day to the violently purging bulimic, speak to the willingness to suffer in order to achieve internal peace, a sense of control, and exaggerated extremes of beauty and noble self-sacrifice.

So how do self-cutting and burning differ so significantly from the pervasive acceptance of diverse expressions of overt masochism in society? Simply put, teens who self-injure in this fashion are overwhelmed by internal pain and lack a social context for expressing it. Their voices are a lonely cry, cut off from a social framework that can provide support and ascribe acceptable meaning to their distress and actions. Individuals who pursue extreme or painful sports, strive for beauty, or conform to styles within a cultural subgroup are not specifically reacting to overwhelming distress or either consciously or unconsciously seeking help. Adolescents who self-injure are dramatizing the destructiveness of their internal pain in visible wounds. Although it can be argued that those who undergo elective plastic surgery, strive for the ultimate in physical endurance, or affiliate with certain subgroups are also trying to escape internal demons of insecurity and unhappiness, teens who self-injure in the manner discussed are invariably seeking a means of diminishing acute, intense, and unmanageable distress. The wounds articulate their deeper struggles and have the power to covertly elicit others to react and potentially rescue them from their pain.

Teens also cry out for help through a variety of other destructive behaviors. Partly because adolescents can no longer comfortably turn to parents for support at a time when their emotional lives are magnifying in complexity, their distress is manifested in the missteps and impulsive extremes of their efforts to simply feel better. Excessive drug or alcohol use, thrill-seeking in cars, sexual promiscuity, and even delinquent acts can be an expression of a teen's internal distress seeking release and distraction. Adolescents that largely remain clear of these dangers tend to have higher levels of self-esteem, less reactive emotional systems, and greater internal and interpersonal resources available to them.

One core factor can be helpful in tying all of these self-destructive behaviors together into a meaningful context: adolescent development. Whether expressed through anorexia, cutting, drug abuse, or unsafe sex, teens who resort to these behaviors are struggling to resolve developmental impasses. The three Is of identity, intimacy, and independence are fraught with such turmoil for so many adolescents that missteps are almost inevitable. Consistent patterns of self-destructive behavior, however, speak to a greater disruption in self-development and a clear need for professional intervention. Although exactly like other adolescents in terms of the issues and conflicts they face, self-destructive teens lack internal resources and interpersonal skills to more successfully meet these challenges. Rather than viewing these adolescents as pathological, their damaging behavior is actually a misguided effort of maturing teens to cope and overcome the overwhelming developmental challenges before them.

THE BROAD CONTINUUM OF SELF-HARM: ASSESSING THE DAMAGE AND DEMONS

An intuitive first step—appraising the severity of the injury—can help gauge the degree of psychological dysfunction being displayed by the teen. Deep wounds that require stitches, approximate major blood vessels, or cover large portions of the body all suggest that a more urgent treatment response is in order. In rarer instances of major self-mutilation, in which individuals inflict horrible harm by performing unthinkable acts such as gauging out eyes, amputating body parts, swallowing glass, or breaking limbs, it does not take a rocket scientist to appreciate the severity of the disturbance. In the case of Munchausen's syndrome, individuals may poison or severely injure themselves secretly and repeatedly in an effort to secure medical care and the human warmth and attention surrounding it. Individuals with psychotic disorders, hearing hallucinatory voices, for example, that beseech them to damage their bodies, also represent the extreme end of the self-harm continuum.

Teens presenting with what are essentially mild scratch marks initially may be seen as less desperate, less impulsive, less violent, and less disturbed. Many adolescents, adults, or even children may reveal a superficial self-injury in order to tell others about their internal pain. Again, although unlikely to represent a serious disturbance, even these gestures deserve appropriate understanding and support. It is really the enormous middle range of the self-harm continuum that spans from delicate self-cutting to forms of coarse cutting (which leaves deeper and more obvious scars but requires little to no medical treatment) that represents the vast and exasperating majority of adolescent self-injurers.

So, how can the inspection of mild to moderate cuts, burns, or bruises help assess the teen's psychological functioning? The answer is that it can not be; one must look to deeper internal factors to appraise the level of emotional dysfunction reflected rather than rely on the cryptic messages revealed by the surface wounds. A teen's psychological resources must be assessed in a variety of realms, such as her ability to regulate affect, control impulses, utilize reasoned judgment, and employ interpersonal channels productively. Therefore, the larger picture must be brought into focus in order to more clearly determine the teen's capacities and limitations.

IS THE SELF-INJURY A DISCRETE PROBLEM OR
ONE OF MANY PROBLEMATIC BEHAVIORS?

Often, an adolescent will be referred to me because of cutting, but I quickly discover that the cutting is but one form of a pervasive pattern of self-destructive behaviors. Frequently, the teen also will reveal combative family relationships, bulimia, drug use, and chaotic social and sexual relationships. In these cases, the cutting must be viewed as but one symptom of a frantic, deeply troubled youth struggling in a gamut of ways to staunch her intense pain. The more areas of a teen's life that are negatively impacted, the more severe her present situation should be viewed. A teen who is showing academic deterioration, unrewarding social engagements, and a host of other acting-out problems represents a significantly different situation than a teen whose only overt symptom is cutting.

Still, no teen's difficulties lack complexity and gravity. Many teens who cut are high-functioning: excellent students, socially active, athletically skilled, and behaviorally contained. Yet their cutting betrays their deeper struggles with emotions, longings, relationships, fears, and conflicts with which they have run out of resources to contend more effectively. These youth are often more accessible in treatment and able to focus on discrete areas of distress that have brought about their self-injurious behavior. Their intact areas of strength can provide much-needed stability, esteem, and motivation that can be brought to bear on addressing difficulties. In contrast, teens who have become globally unhinged present more chaotically and feel quite overwhelmed, requiring a multipronged treatment approach. Often, these more dysfunctional teens enter treatment with attitudes that are highly defensive and even combative. They already have endured a period of recrimination and conflict with authority figures related to their problematic behaviors.

In short, the larger picture is extremely telling in each case of self-injury. A discrete pattern of cutting that is isolated from other areas of behavioral dysfunction suggests a less worrisome prognosis. The more numerous and problematic the behaviors exhibited by the youth and the fewer developmental goals being achieved, a greater level of severity in the underlying disturbance should be suspected.

PREVIOUS LEVEL OF FUNCTIONING: HOW HEALTHY
WAS THE TEEN BEFORE THE CUTTING BEGAN?

Sometimes also given the unfortunate label *premorbid functioning*, understanding how well the teen has met previous developmental demands can inform diagnosis and treatment. Youth who have suffered significant trauma and long-standing histories of underachievement, social difficulty, emotional and behavioral problems, and family conflict bring less well-established resources to bear on their present difficulties. Youth who, on the other hand, have histories with positive academic, social, familial, and psychological experiences tend to possess more resiliency and both internal and external resources to draw upon.

A classic psychological tenet holds that "the best predictor of future behavior is past behavior." Although all bets seem to be off in predicting which teens will or will not develop problematic behaviors during their transition through the teens, the baseline level of functioning seems to be an important predictor of how well the teen eventually will emerge from the turmoil inherent to the adolescent passage. Thus, teens and parents can take heart in trusting that the strengths they have seen consistently displayed ultimately will prevail once the choppy adolescent waters have been navigated.

Many teens sadly are less fortunate and have lives replete with abuse, loss, disabilities, poor impulse control, and dysfunctional family relationships. These adolescents may feel less hope and less agency in overcoming self-injury and the many areas of unhappiness that overwhelm them. The tool of self-harm may be clung to as a life preserver in a turbulent sea, the teen having never acquired internal or external resources for managing a seeming onslaught of problems. Helping to shore up the adolescent's strengths and resources internally and environmentally is critical to lasting interventions that will not only lessen self-injure but also will improve functioning in multiple life areas.

STRENGTHS AND WEAKNESSES: LISTING THE TOP THREE

Routinely, I will ask adolescents to name the three things they like best about themselves and the three they like least. Invariably, this simple exercise can help focus treatment. Some youth are remarkably insightful about their assets and limitations; others can state only what they hate or like about themselves in more superficial terms. Responses run the gamut from disliking their physical attributes, poor grades, the lack of a boy or girlfriend, controlling parents, and stress around school performance. Teens often will point to physical attributes, kindness, caring, intelligence, sense of humor, and being a good friend as common assets they appreciate. Yet one way or another, the adolescent is communicating the fulcrums of inadequacy and power they currently perceive in themselves.

Sometimes all three negatives pertain to body image or hating school or one's parents. Adolescents will not uncommonly refuse to state any positives, so hell-bent are they on punishing and renouncing themselves. Helping the teen to gradually develop a more realistic appreciation and broadening definition of her strengths and limitations is critical to her ability to cope with adversity. Once the adolescent's tunnel vision is challenged enough for her to embrace the large diversity of her strengths and limitations into an integrated whole sense of self, the process of reflection, skill building, and genuine identity formation can better progress.

Another quick technique that may initially seem curious is to ask the adolescent to draw a picture of a person in the rain. The resulting image can reveal how she feels about herself, the degree of adversity she perceives in her environment, and her ability to actively contend and protect herself. For example, teens who generally feel helpless and beleaguered by a hostile world might draw a small, tentative, poorly defined image of a person standing in the middle of a deluge without umbrella or jacket. Teens with a sense of agency and competence might draw a stronger, well-defined figure with an ample umbrella fending off a nonimposing minor drizzle. This type of technique is, of course, merely a springboard to further conversation and insight into the adolescent who may not be willing or even able to articulate the level of vulnerability she feels. Using creative tools such as drawings can help the defended adolescent express herself through more fluid routes.

Outside sources often are extremely illuminating in understanding the broader functioning of the teen. Parents often can point to a number of awesome strengths to which their teen remains blind, such as her loving nature, creative abilities, self-discipline, sense of humor, or raw intelligence. Teachers who observe the adolescent in a setting removed from family dynamics may have an objective appraisal of the youth as highly engaged, friendly, charming, hardworking, or well liked by peers. Similarly, parents and teachers can be helpful in honing in on areas of difficulty that need to be addressed.

ALL IN THE FAMILY: DOES THE FAMILY HAVE POSITIVE RESOURCES TO ASSIST THE ADOLESCENT?

Parents: Adolescents complain that they cannot live with them and they cannot live without them. Although parents and teenagers constantly negotiate complexities in their changing relationships, some families are better equipped to support the adolescent on their developmental journey. These families can be critical assets in the treatment process, as they provide healthy functioning, modeling, relationships, emotional availability, boundaries, and parenting skills that can be skillfully employed on the youth's behalf. Inevitably, many families struggle with severe dysfunction and genuinely impaired abilities to parent. Clinicians need to assess where the family can provide a resource and where they need to set cautious boundaries in order to protect the adolescent from excessively controlling, hostile, suffocating, drug-addicted, and otherwise destructive parents.

Having a strong family in one's corner can generate a range of emotional, physical, social, intellectual, and other health-promoting resources. This can pertain to any family from any socioeconomic category, single- or dual-parented household, or other demographic. The fundamental benefits can not be overstated when it comes to youth who are blessed with loving parents who can maintain appropriate boundaries, set appropriate limits and consequences, advocate with schools and other systems on their child's behalf, and possess enough psychological resources to contend with the emotional challenges of parenting an adolescent. Obviously, no parent is perfect, but these resources allow them to withstand the many conflicts faced with adolescents.

Although family therapy often is a useful adjunct to psychotherapy, occasionally a parent will be so destructive as to preempt him or her from participation. Many times, a teen is faced with certain challenging deficits or offensive patterns in a parent. Although the parents can not always be changed, it is of immense value to the teen to have her experience and perceptions validated. It is not surprising that adolescents contending with highly dysfunctional families have less wherewithal with which they can confront their developmental challenges. Thus, the family environment and the resources available to the teen can further indicate the degree of difficulty likely to be experienced by the self-injurer.

CLOSE, WELL-FUNCTIONING FAMILIES THAT SUDDENLY IMPLODE: SHOCK AND AWE

A huge irony can occur in the happiest, healthiest, and most close-knit of families. Adolescents who are deeply attached to loving and competent parents often face an intensified conflict in separating from them. In order to establish independence, peer intimacy, and an acceptable identity, the teen must find a way to relinquish these cozy dependencies. For some of these adolescents, the only way they can wrench themselves free is by essentially setting off a bomb. By suddenly lurching into prohibited and dangerous behaviors, tremendous conflict is created, which ultimately helps the teen separate and the parents view the teen as separate. This shocking behavior can temporarily ease the umbilical ties between the teen and her parents, allowing the parents also to let go bit by bit of what is no longer the compliant, sweet child they have sought to preserve. These families typically enter treatment with a look of shock and awe, having seen few clues and fewer explanations for why their happy, well-functioning household suddenly has come under siege.

It is important to highlight the fact that in most cases of self-injury there is no so-called smoking gun that can direct blame at inadequate parents. The culprit is the struggle of development itself, and the advent of significant difficulties in an adolescent does not implicate the family as an insidious cause. One need only witness the dramatic hardships so many wonderful families confront when their child suddenly explodes into adolescence to appreciate the power of development itself as the ultimate trigger.

THE TEEN'S CAPACITY TO HAVE HEALTHY AND INTIMATE RELATIONSHIPS: A VITAL BAROMETER

Even the most reticent, withdrawn, or rageful adolescent wants to have friends. Often, the teenager will protest that she is perfectly happy in her isolation or superficial relationships or even bend the truth by claiming a slew of friendships that really do not exist. Most often, adolescents are forthright about their deep investment in peer relationships and will discuss connections, conflicts, and various dramas they experience with peers.

No question, teens who are plugged into a healthy group of friends have higher self-esteem and demonstrate capacities for the give-and-take and intimacy of lasting friendships. Teens may have a tight core of friends but lack rewarding relationships due to the prominence of substance abuse, sexual promiscuity, or other distancing factor that prevents healthy engagement. It is ultimately the adolescents who can reveal themselves selectively to safe peers and negotiate the inevitable demands and conflicts of ongoing friendships that carry an emotional parachute or safety net through the vicissitudes of the teenage years.

For innumerable reasons, some adolescents are not successful in their pursuit of intimacy. They may have grown up in disordered families in which it was not safe to be open, in which intimacy felt suffocating, or in which overt abuse existed. They may have such tentative self-esteem that they seek a harbor with any peer group that will accept them, regardless of the group's norms or treatment of one another. Some adolescents run into trouble through their hypersensitive, overreactive, or avoidant interpersonal tendencies. In all cases, assisting the teen in recognizing her role in each relationship and empowering her with better skills and insights is critical to overall coping and functioning.

The therapy relationship often is a good barometer of how the self-injurious teen relates, not necessarily just to an adult but in other relationships that require openness and communication. Some teens are so uncomfortable with revealing any weakness that they present a barrier of bravado and inflated confidence to the therapist. Some are so needy that they become desperately attached and dependent on the therapist for support. Many are appropriately forthcoming about their longings and disappointments in peer relationships and, of course, in the evolving relationships with their parents. Most teens somehow reveal the capacities and glitches in their ability to surmount the challenging demands of intimacy in even the early stages of treatment. In adolescents who cut, it is especially critical to address interpersonal difficulties in order to actively reengage them in productive relationships rather than in self-destructive dead ends.

UNEARTHING PASSION AND AMBITION: WHAT DOES THE ADOLESCENT WANT?

The beauty of a passionate interest, pursuit, or ambition is that it provides not only meaning and purpose in one's life but also true joy and pleasure. People who find something they love to do are fortunate, and this pursuit provides a nourishing and meaningful center to their lives. Adolescents who have genuine passions have an enormous advantage. Not only can enthusiastic involvement in art, sport, music, theater, science, or a diversity of pursuits provide a wellspring of meaning and pleasure for the teen, having a passion can be a good reason to get up in the morning. Adolescents who can identify pursuits that make their lives uniquely worth living draw esteem, identity, and refuge. These interests add resilience to adolescents who are troubled or depressed, maintaining one bright spot in their otherwise unhappy lives.

The key is to plug into the adolescent's unique and pure motivations and desires, untainted by parental pressure or dutiful participation. These passions that the adolescent can truly experience as emanating solely from inside herself are rewarded with an enhanced sense of authenticity and individuality. A lot can be said for having fun. Teens who can derive fun and enjoyment in their chosen pursuits sometimes have a pure-felt reason to value their lives. This investment is a strong motivator and reward for persevering through the many drudgeries and difficulties often posed by school and home.

It can be quite disconcerting to speak with an adolescent who seemingly has no interests or passions. It is not uncommon for unhappy teens to feel alienated from their own lives, simply going through the motions of what feels like a forced march. The absence of activities or interests that replenish their energies and esteem is a deficit that the teen needs to be gently encouraged to gradually overcome. Some adolescents are simply afraid to try out activities because they anticipate failure or rejection; others just experience a deadening global sense of boredom no matter what they are doing. Teens also may neglect passions that have not been actively encouraged by parents, peers, or teachers, such as interests beyond the standard sports, instruments, or academics. Helping the adolescent give voice to her love of animals, science fiction, cooking, or rock and roll can validate and encourage her to actualize her latent passions. This is all part of carving out an identity that may be separate from that prescribed by parents or societal norms and encouraging the teen to follow her healthy (even if quirky) desires.

Many of the self-injurious adolescents I have met are, in fact, troubled by overly intense passions. Often, these revolve around intimacy and sexuality drives but can also involve an all-consuming interest that absences them from involvement in other responsibilities, such as academics. Some of these teens need help structuring time and energy to pursue their passions and need to tolerate some boundaries between the activity and other important pursuits. The passions inherent to healthy teens in pursuit of love, sex, and acceptance can be overwhelming, and learning to manage the many pressing emotions in constructive ways can prove challenging. Kids who cut are often overwhelmed by very healthy passions they have little ability to yet understand, fulfill, or regulate. Self-injury can become a maladaptive effort to accomplish those goals.

CONCLUSIONS

Removing stigma and pathological labels from the growing phenomenon of cutting and self-injury makes its alleviation far more accessible. Understanding the similarities between cutting and a host of socially applauded activities that require the tolerance of pain and even injury can place cutting in a more reasonable context. Similarly, appreciating the spectrum of severity on the continuum of self-injury can alleviate undue alarm and overreaction. Factors that can help assess the level of underlying disturbance being exhibited by self-injuring adolescents were discussed in order to acquire a comprehensive perspective of the teens' many strengths and limitations. Capitalizing on these resources and helping to minimize deficits is ultimately what intervention is all about.

Conclusions:
Reconceptualizing Cutting

I am often asked the most obvious and straightforward of questions: "Why do adolescents intentionally harm themselves?" Alas, my answer is often less than satisfying: "For a thousand different reasons." I feel compelled to answer in this seemingly vague manner not to be evasive but to acknowledge the individuality and complexity of each case. People rarely expect a unitary answer to questions such as. "Why do teens use drugs?" or "Why do adolescent girls have eating problems?" or, for that matter, "Why do people behave self-destructively?" The truth is that adolescents misbehave and even cut their own flesh because of innumerable painful conflicts and misdirected efforts to achieve one or more of the following goals: (1) alleviate distress, (2) express their growing complexity, (3) punish and cleanse themselves, (4) garner needed attention and help, (5) control and defy those around them, (6) make the invisible pain both visible and controllable, (7) dramatize inner turmoil, (8) engage in something shocking and daring, and (8) just because other people they know are doing it. Although not an exhaustive list by any means, cutting and self-injury generally serve these purposes in developing individuals who have not otherwise developed the internal and interpersonal skills necessary to constructively overcome emotionally charged developmental hurdles.

In addition to these personal motivations, today's society may foster self-injury as a compelling means of expression, communication, and rebellion. Ancient and recent histories are replete with examples of religious mortification of the flesh, painful adolescent rites of passage the world over, scarification and tattooing, and the personal "terrorism" of cutting, mirroring the worldwide explosion of suicide as weapon, as power, and as a sort of furious and noble martyrdom. Could it be that the rising incidence of cutting among our increasingly disillusioned youth reflects the growing sense of hopelessness, violence, and alienation that explode across today's newspapers and television sets? Although adolescence always has been a challenging developmental phase of life, the life-and-death stakes, the brutal competition, the tattered social fabric, and the unbearable pressures on today's youth may be inflicting an especially destructive burden.

Against this background of a world in global political and environmental crisis, imagine the adolescent struggling to define an identity, assume independence, and develop meaningful intimate and sexual relationships. These challenges are in and of themselves daunting, but in a culture that celebrates dysfunction and violence, distinguishes only the exceptional few, and fosters a free-for-all model of nonintimacy, teens increasingly feel unmoored and overwhelmed by competing needs and expectations.

Teenagers who resort to self-injury are dramatizing their suffering, whether they hide their scars or flaunt them. The wounds are irrefutable evidence of emotional distress due to deficits in their developing ability to relate to others, assume responsible independence, and integrate a realistic and acceptable sense of identity. Adolescents need not be sick or disturbed or violent or crazy to strike out against themselves, and, indeed, the majority of the twenty-first-century cohort of self-injurers may simply be young people in search of themselves. Certainly, many youths also are enacting deep traumas, damaged souls, and serious emotional difficulties, including depression, eating disorders, sexual abuse, and disrupted personality formations. These latter adolescents require special attention and intervention to address not only the surface wounds they self-inflict but also the deep pain invisible to all but themselves.

In order to reach out and ultimately assist adolescent self-injurers, parents, teachers, friends, and clinicians need to adopt a nonjudgmental, nonalarmist, and wholly empathic attitude that dignifies the unique suffering of each teen. Although suicide risk and medical safety is the first priority, the purely human conflicts and distress of the adolescent must be highlighted. After all, it is internal injury that is being enacted in the flesh-and-blood wounds on the adolescent's body.

Professional treatment of cutting requires an integrative approach that addresses the biological, psychological, and social needs of the adolescent. Treatment invariably involves both enhancing psychological insight and teaching new skills and strategies that can eventually replace self-injury as the coping method of choice. Both cognitive and behavioral skills need to be integrated into an overall treatment relationship in which the safe and meaningful exploration of the adolescent's difficulties can unfold. Other modalities, such as family, group, or medication treatment can be employed on a case-by-case basis.

Adolescents and families undergo remarkable growth through the active, illuminating, challenging process of psychotherapy. Working with teenagers who are grappling ferociously with their developmental challenges can be an extremely rewarding and inspiring experience for clinicians as well. Understanding that none of us are finished products and adolescents who cut represent particularly poignant works in progress, their flesh-and-blood expression of pain is an exquisite opportunity for growth, change, and the development of an ultimately more rich and satisfying life. Far from being damaged or diminished by the impasse of cutting during adolescence, many teens are rewarded with greater depth and strength in subsequent life stages.

Perhaps most surprising to both parents and adolescents is the revelation that cutting often represents positive, healthy strivings screaming to be surmounted. Reframing the cutting in the context of the teen's age-appropriate conflicts and innate strivings helps shine a light on what is right about the youth as opposed to what is wrong. Avoiding the head-on collision of criticism and condemnation opens an avenue for far greater success in enlisting the adolescent's cooperation, motivation, and openness in overcoming both the cutting and the underlying developmental impasse.

Afterword

Since the original publication of this book in 2007, self-injury has lost some of its shock value and become almost commonplace in adolescent culture. Once thought to be the sole domain of deeply disturbed individuals, cutting is increasingly prevalent in teenagers with a wide range of seemingly normative concerns.[85-87] Increased awareness of the prevalence of cutting has helped clinicians, school personnel, and parents to become better equipped to spot, understand, and appropriately respond to adolescents exhibiting these distressing behaviors. At the same time, while cutting has become more prominent in the awareness and imagination of teenagers, social contagion has undoubtedly contributed to its further spread.

Nowhere is this "contagion" more apparent than in the online explosion of websites and message boards where teens exchange experiences, insights, support, and sometimes self-destructive tips regarding a range of self-injurious behaviors. As stated by Whitlock et al.:[11] these virtual sites "normalize and encourage self-injurious behavior and add potentially lethal behaviors" to teens' repertoires. Thus, the growing conversation about cutting is a double-edged sword, if you will, in that while it is essential to disseminate information, teens are exquisitely sensitive to peer influence and identification. Alas, even popular celebrities as well-known and emulated as Angelina Jolie, Johnny Depp, Courtney Love, and Princess Diana have publicly disclosed their own histories of self-injury.

In my own clinical practice, I have seen more and more "healthy," high-achieving, and heretofore thriving adolescents exhibiting mild forms of self-injury. A recent study [89] demonstrated that self harm in adolescents is associated with a wide range of typical teenage struggles around low self-esteem, anxiety, and sexual concerns. Even in comparing teens who present at hospitals versus those who do not following self-injury, very few differences between these two groups have been discerned. [85] The teenagers I treat also encompass a range of diagnostic categories, ranging from mild adjustment disorders to major depression to emerging personality disorders. This striking heterogeneity of diagnoses has been empirically reported in cases of non-suicidal self-injury.[88] Thus, self injury appears to be an increasingly common symptom among a wide variety of teens contending with a wide array of struggles. Fortunately, with treatment, the self-injurious symptoms usually remit quickly, and the teens I see are able to surmount whatever developmental obstacles had daunted them in the first place. Often the adolescent first heard about the practice of cutting on television, online, or through friends, and powerfully identified with the expression of pain it represented.

Recent surveys have determined that remarkably high rates of self-injury exist in adolescents. For example, 46.5 percent of the 663 adolescents surveyed using the Functional Assessment of Self-Mutilation (FASM) in one study acknowledged some form of self-injury within the past year.[89] As many as 60 percent of these teens (28 percent overall) admitted to moderate to severe levels of self-injury. Furthermore, these were not isolated incidents: these teens reported an average of 12.9 incidents within the past year. Self-injury occurs at a similarly high rate among "privileged" youths: 37.2 percent of high school students admitted to at least one incident of self injury within the past year in a recent study of socioeconomically advantaged youths.[90] Those teenagers experiencing high levels of conflict with others, or using drugs or alcohol, appear at most risk for repeated incidents.[87] In one college population studied, a 17 percent lifetime prevalence rate of self-injury was found.[11] Of these self-injurers, 75 percent had repeated incidents and 36 percent reported that no one knew about these behaviors.

Research has further determined that developmental differences have been found in the prevalence of self-injury among adolescents in early versus late stages of puberty. Using the Pubertal Development Scale, a large-scale survey of 3,332 students determined that late puberty was associated with a fourfold higher rate of self-harm than seen in early puberty. [91] Twice as many girls as boys had self-injured. Research is also now emerging that demonstrates that self-injury is not solely an American problem. In a study of international rates within seven European countries, studying 30,000 teens aged fifteen and sixteen, self-injury was twice as common in females as males.[92] In four of the seven countries studied, one in ten females had self harmed within the past year. Their most commonly cited reason for self-injuring was "to get relief from a terrible state of mind," echoing the primary motivation cited for their American counterparts.

This coping or affect regulation model of self-harm has garnered extensive research support.[89, 92, 93] This model deserves some brief elaboration here in light of its critical relevance to both causation and effective treatment. Many of the adolescents I see have great difficulty managing, modulating, processing, or otherwise coping effectively with strong negative emotions. Sadness can quickly expand into all-consuming feelings of despair, anger to unbridled rage, and anxiety to frank disorganization and impulsivity. These overwhelming emotions emerge in concert with hormonal changes, as well as rapid cognitive growth generating increased self-awareness, depth of emotion, and psychological insight. Thus, emotions that were previously fleeting or insignificant are suddenly experienced as if on steroids. The ramifications feel ENORMOUS. The strength of emotion feels OVERWHELMING. And the arsenal of mature coping strategies is as yet LIMITED. No wonder teenagers often act impulsively, dramatically, and alas, self-destructively.

Enabling an adolescent to gain confidence and a sense of their own agency in contending with internal forces is central to the treatment of self-injury. Cutting itself can be a controlled effort to regain a sense of equilibrium; thus this control can be directed in other ways. The development of alternate forms of self-soothing, and at-home practice with these new replacement strategies is the centerpiece of behavior change. Even helping the teen learn to experience, tolerate, observe and ride out strong emotional storms without doing anything is key to teaching them about their own resilience.

Of course none of this behavior change is possible without a strong therapeutic alliance between therapist and teen. Until the adolescent trusts that the clinician truly "gets" them and remains free of judgment, it is difficult for the teen to drop their defenses and allow an open window into better awareness and insight. Adolescents are often longing for adults to witness and respond to the many parts of themselves that are hidden, nascent, or too frequently overlooked by their parents and peers. Often these unformed, confusing, dark, or newly emerging aspects of self are responsible for the underlying conflicts and distress that seek expression through the act of self-injury. The relational context of psychotherapy provides a safe holding environment within which adolescents can begin to openly express, explore, and take responsibility for their choices.

More than ever, I feel committed to setting a developmental frame for the struggles self-injuring adolescents present. Interpreting "up"—that is, emphasizing the healthy strivings and capabilities the teen possesses—has been much more fruitful than a pathology-based approach. Showing confidence in the normalcy of the drives and the ultimate agency of the teenager in controlling and gratifying them helps reinforce the positive trajectory of these developmental struggles. Restoring within the adolescent both a sense of control and responsibility over how that process unfolds helps the teens see themselves as a work in progress, emphasizing an adaptive context for growth.

Adolescents have also benefited in my experience from a de-emphasis on the self-injury, per se. Unless the injuries are severe, of course, and require immediate medical evaluation, and once suicidality is ruled out, avoiding the trap of making the behavior the focus forces the teen and parents to dig deeper into a broader understanding of the many challenges impinging upon the teen. The potential power the teen wields with others via the threat of self-injury is important to defuse. Focusing matter-of-factly on the variety of options and real-life consequences helps to free the teenager from this self-destructive mode of self-assertion. The good news and the bad news is the sobering affirmation that the teen is the only person in control of their self-destructive behaviors.

It is also useful to help the adolescent realize that self-injury is merely a temporary, if oddly palliative measure. After they cut, burn, or otherwise harm themselves, they are still faced with the failing algebra grade, the demanding parent, or the back-stabbing friend. One fifteen-year-old patient of mine reported the following epiphany while attending a wilderness treatment program. He recounted wanting to self-injure one day because he was miserably cold and wet, but then realized he would still be cold and wet after harming himself. He immediately refocused his efforts on changing his wet clothing and finding a way to warm up. Continually refocusing on what the teen is going to do to resolve the real problem, all the while addressing fears and insecurities, forms the crux of treatment. While alternative modes of palliative coping and self-soothing are important, ultimately confronting developmental issues around intimacy, independence, and identity in the real world is where the teen needs refocusing, support, and assistance.

Of course, it is important to point out that "the problem" does not reside within the teen alone. Context is everything, and many self-injurious youths are responding to any number of environmental stressors. Inordinate academic demands, competitive pressures, divorce and family conflict, and even the steady diet of dour pessimism that has followed them through this decade regarding troubling events in the economy, jobs, global climate, terrorism, war, and other world affairs have taken a toll. While it may be impossible to alter these larger pressures, helping the teen name and compartmentalize some of these sources of strain is useful. Sometimes aggressive intervention is necessary by way of changing schools, recommending marital counseling, and otherwise demonstrating to the teen a willingness to dignify their concerns with decisive action.

At the time of this writing, self-injury remains a prevalent problem indicative of the suffering many teens cannot manage on their own. The act of intentionally harming oneself, no matter how minor or severe, should serve as a wake-up call to both the adolescent and the important adults in his or her life. Understanding the teen in their developmental context is pivotal to successful treatment and provides fertile grounds for a range of biopsychosocial interventions to take root. Hopefully, as the hidden nature and stigmatization of self-injury decreases, adolescents will experience less shame and reluctance to avail themselves of the support they deserve.

Lori G. Plante, Ph.D.
May, 2010

Notes

1. Hawton, K., Rodham, K., Evans, E., & Weatherall, R. (2002). Suicidal and deliberate self-harm in young people. *British Medical Journal, 325,* 1207–1211.

2. Olfson, M., Gameroff, M., Marcus, S., Greenberg, T., & Shaffer, D. (2005). National trends in hospitalization of youth with intentional self-inflicted injuries. *American Journal of Psychiatry, 162,* 1328–1334.

3. Conterio, K., & Lader, W. (1998). *Bodily harm.* New York: Hyperion.

4. Favazza, A. (1987). *Bodies under siege: Self-mutilation in culture and psychiatry.* Baltimore: Johns Hopkins University Press.

5. Favazza, A. (1998). The coming of age of self-mutilation. *Journal of Nervous and Mental Disease, 186,* 259–268.

6. Briere, J., & Gil, E. (1998). Self-mutilation in clinical and general population samples: Prevalence, correlates, and functions. *American Journal of Orthopsychiatry, 68,* 609–620.

7. Gratz, K. (2001). Measure of deliberate self-harm: Preliminary data on the Deliberate Self-Harm Inventory. *Journal of Psychopathology and Behavioral Assessment, 23,* 253–263.

8. Gratz, K., Conrad, S., & Roemer, L. (2002). Risk factors for deliberate self-harm among college students. *American Journal of Orthopsychiatry, 72,* 128–140.

9. Darche, M. (1990). Psychological factors differentiating self-mutilating and non-self-mutilating adolescent inpatient females. *Psychiatric Hospital, 21,* 31–35.

10. Hurry, J. (2000). Deliberate self-harm in children and adolescents. *International Review of Psychiatry, 1,* 31–36.

11. Whitlock, J., Eckenrode, J., & Silverman, D. (2006). Self-injurious behaviors in a college population. *Pediatrics, 117,* 1939–1948.

12. Favazza, A., & Conterio, K. (1989). Female habitual self-mutilators. *Acta Psychiatrica Scandinavica, 79,* 282–289.

13. Briere, J. (1996). *Therapy for those molested as children.* New York: Springer.

14. Plante, L. (2006). Helping adolescents with self-injurious behavior: Cutting in developmental context. In T. Plante (Ed.), *Mental disorders of the new millennium* (Vol. 1, pp. 189–207). Westport, CT: Praeger.

15. Osrich, E., Noll, J., & Putnam, F. (1999). The motivations for self-injury in psychiatric inpatients. *Psychiatry, 62,* 334–346.

16. Suyemoto, K. (1998). The functions of self-mutilation. *Clinical Psychology Review, 18,* 531–534.

17. Rosen, P., & Walsh, B. (1989). Patterns of contagion in self-mutilation epidemics. *American Journal of Psychiatry, 146,* 656–658.

18. Taiminen, T., Kallio-Soukainen, K., Nokso-Koivisto, H., Kaljonen, A., & Helenius, H. (1998). Contagion of deliberate self-harm among adolescent inpatients. *American Academy of Child and Adolescent Psychiatry, 37,* 211–217.

19. Schildkrout, E. (2001). Body art as visual language. *AnthroNotes, 22,* 1–8.

20. Musafar, F. (1996). Epilogue. In A. Favazza (Ed.), *Bodies under siege* (pp. 328–329). Baltimore: Johns Hopkins University Press.

21. Kiell, N. (1969). *The universal experience of adolescence.* London: University of London Press.

22. Lines, S. (1998). The secret language of pain: The psychology of cutting. In M. Strong (Ed.), *A bright red scream* (p. 29). New York: Penguin Books.

23. Menninger, K. (1938). *Man against himself.* New York: Harcourt.

24. Gruenbaum, H., & Klerman, G. (1967). Wrist slashing. *American Journal of Psychiatry, 124,* 527–534.

25. American Psychiatric Association. (1994). *Diagnostic and statistical manual of mental disorders* (4th ed.). Washington, DC: Author.

26. Cross, L. (1993). Body and self in feminine development: Implications for eating disorders and delicate self-mutilation. *Bulletin of the Menninger Clinic, 57,* 41–68.

27. Graff, H., & Mallin, R. (1967). The syndrome of the wrist cutter. *American Journal of Psychiatry, 124,* 36–42.

28. Pattison, E., & Kahan, J. (1983). The deliberate self-harm syndrome. *American Journal of Psychiatry, 140,* 867–872.

29. Morgan, H. (1979). *Death wishes? The understanding and management of deliberate self-harm.* New York: Wiley.

30. Cooper, J., Kapur, N., Webb, R., Lawlor, M., Guthrie, E., Mackway-Jones, K., et al. (2005). Suicide after deliberate self-harm: A 4-year cohort study. *American Journal of Psychiatry, 162,* 297–303.

31. Stanley, B., Gameroff, M., Michelsen, V., & Mann, J. (2001). Are suicide attempters who self-mutilate a unique population? *American Journal of Psychiatry, 158,* 427–432.

32. Foster, T., Gillespie, K., & McClelland, R. (1997). Mental disorders and suicide in Northern Ireland. *British Journal of Psychiatry, 170,* 447–452.

33. Appleby, L., Cooper, J., Amos, T., & Faragher, B. (1999). Psychological autopsy study of suicides by people aged under 35. *British Journal of Psychiatry, 175,* 168–174.

34. Spicer, R., & Miller, T. (2000).Suicide acts in 8 states: Incidence and case fatality rates by demographics and method. *American Journal of Public Health, 90,* 1885–1891.

35. Centers for Disease Control and Prevention. Retrieved November 25, 2006, from http://www.cdc.gov/ncipc/factsheets/suifacts.htm.

36. Linehan, M. (1986). *Cognitive-behavioral treatment of borderline personality disorder.* New York: Guilford Press.

37. National Institute of Mental Health. (1999). *Frequently asked questions about suicide.* Retrieved November 25, 2006, from http://www.mentalhealth.gov/suicideprevention/suicidefaq.cfm.

38. Kemperman, I., Russ, M., & Shearin, E. (1997). Self-injurious behavior and mood regulation in borderline personality disorder. *Journal of Personality Disorders, 11,* 146–157.

39. Muelenkamp, J., & Gutierrez, P. (2004). An investigation of differences between self-injurious behaviors and suicide attempts in a sample of adolescents. *Suicide and Life Threatening Behavior, 34,* 12–23.

40. Miller, D. (1994). *Women who hurt themselves: A book of hope and understanding.* New York: Basic Books.

41. Van der Kolk, B., Perry, J., & Herman, J. (1991). Childhood origins of self-destructive behavior. *American Journal of Psychiatry, 149,* 1665–1671.

42. Stong, M. (1998). *A bright red scream.* New York: Viking.

43. Zlotnick, C., Shea, M., Pearlstein, T., Simpson, E., Costello, E., & Begin, A. (1996). The relationship between dissociative symptoms, alexithymia, impulsivity, sexual abuse and self-mutilation. *Comprehensive Psychiatry, 37,* 12–16.

44. Bryer, J., Nelson, B., Miller, B., & Kroll, P. (1987). Childhood sexual and physical abuse as factors in adult psychiatric illness. *American Journal of Psychiatry, 144,* 1426–1430.

45. Hall, R., Tice, L., Beresford, T., & Wooley, B. (1989). Sexual abuse in patients with anorexia and bulimia. *Psychosomatics, 30,* 73–79.

46. Steinhausen, H. (2002). The outcome of anorexia nervosa in the 20th century. *American Journal of Psychiatry, 159,* 1284–1293.

47. Nielson, S. (2001). Epidemiology and mortality of eating disorders. *Psychiatric Clinics of North America, 24,* 201–214.

48. Kernberg, O. (1975). *Borderline conditions and pathological narcissism.* New York: Jason Aronson.

49. Offer, D., & Barglow, P. (1960). Adolescent and young adult self-mutilation incidents in a general psychiatric hospital. *Archives of General Psychiatry, 3,* 194–204.

50. Jones, H., & Daniels, B. (1996). An ethological approach to self-injury. *British Journal of Psychiatry, 169,* 263–267.

51. Hayward, C. (Ed.). (2003). *Gender differences at puberty*. Cambridge: Cambridge University Press.

52. Herman-Giddens, M., Bourdony, C., Slora, E., & Wasserman, R. (2001). Early puberty: A cautionary tale. *Pediatrics, 107*, 609–610.

53. Zacharias, L., Rand, W., & Wurtman, R. (1976). A prospective study of sexual development in American girls: The statistics of menarche. *Obstetrics and Gynecology Survey, 31*, 325–337.

54. Weichold, K., & Silbereisen, R. (2001, July). *Pubertal timing and substance use: The role of peers and leisure context*. Paper presented at the seventh European Congress of Psychology, London.

55. Barash, I., Cheung, C., Weigle, D., Ren, H., Kapiyting, J., Clifton, D., et al. (1996). Leptin is a metabolic signal to the reproductive system. *Endocrinology, 137*, 3144–3147.

56. Hartz, A., Barboriak, P., Wong, A., Katayama, K., Rimm, A. (1979). The association of obesity with infertility and related menstrual abnormalities in women. *International Journal of Obesity, 3*, 57–73.

57. Brooks-Gunn, J. (1987). Pubertal processes and girls' psychological adaptation. In R. Lerner and T. Foch (Eds.), *Biological-psychosocial interactions in early adolescence* (pp. 123–154). Hillsdale, NJ: Erlbaum.

58. Keel, P., Fulkerson, J., & Leon, G. (1997). Disordered eating precursors in pre- and early adolescent girls and boys. *Journal of Youth and Adolescence, 26*, 203–216.

59. Erikson, E. (1950). *Childhood and society*. New York: Norton.

60. McCann, I., & Pearlman, L. (1990). *Psychological trauma and the adult survivor: Theory, therapy, and transformation*. New York: Brunner/Mazel.

61. Pearlman, L., & Saakvitne, K. (1995). *Trauma and the therapist: Countertransference and vicarious traumatization in psychotherapy with incest survivors*. New York: Norton.

62. Deiter, P., Nicholls, S., & Pearlman, L. (2000). Self-injury and self capacities: Assisting an individual in crisis. *Journal of Clinical Psychology, 56*, 1173–1191.

63. Pope, D., & Simon, R. (2005). Help for stressed students. *Educational Leadership, 62*, 33–37.

64. Pope, D. (2001). *Doing school: How we are creating a generation of stressed out, materialistic, and miseducated students*. New Haven, CT: Yale University Press.

65. Stangel, L. (2006, 1 June). Student embodies success. *Palo Alto Daily News*, p. 2.

66. Kraut, R., Patterson, M., Lundmark, V., Kiesler, S., Mukophadhyay, T., & Scherlis, W. (1998). Internet paradox: A social technology that reduces social involvement and psychological well-being? *American Psychologist, 53*, 1017–1031.

67. Thomas, T., & Watzman, A. (1999). *Carnegie Mellon study reveals negative potential of heavy Internet use on emotional well being* (Press release). Retrieved November 25, 2006, from http://ncii.cs.cmv.edu/progress/pressrel.html.

68. Coid, J., Allolio, B., & Rees, L. (1983). Endorphin activity in childhood psychosis. *Archives of General Psychiatry, 42*, 780–783.

69. Cross, L. (1993). Body and self in feminine development: Implications for eating disorders and delicate self-mutilation. *Bulletin of the Menninger Clinic, 57*, 41–68.

70. Ellis, A. (2001). *Overcoming destructive beliefs, feelings and behaviors: New directions for rational emotive behavior therapy.* New York: Prometheus Books.

71. Yalom, I. (1985). *The theory and practice of group psychotherapy* (3rd ed.). New York: Basic Books.

72. Klerman, G., Weissman, M., Rounsaville, B., & Chevron, E. (1984). *Interpersonal therapy of depression: A brief, focused and specific strategy.* New York: Basic Books.

73. Solomon, R. (1980). The opponent-process theory of acquired motivation: The costs of pleasure and the benefits of pain. *American Psychologist, 35*, 691–712.

74. Carroll, B., Curtis, G., & Mendels, J. (1976). Neuroendocrine regulation in depression I: Limbic system-adrenocortical dysfunction. *Archives of General Psychiatry, 33*, 1039–1044.

75. Lopez, J., Kathol, R., Jaeckle, R., & Meller, W. (1987). The HPA response to insulin hypoglycemia in depression. *Biological Psychiatry, 22*, 153–166.

76. Murphy, B. (1991). Steroids and depression. *Journal of Steroid Biochemistry, 38*, 537–559.

77. Sanborn, K., & Hayward, C. (2003). Hormonal changes at puberty and the emergence of gender differences in internalizing disorders. In C. Hayward (Ed.), *Gender differences at puberty* (pp. 29–60). Cambridge: Cambridge University Press.

78. Grossman, R., & Siever, L. (2001). Impulsive self-injurious behaviors: Neurobiology and psychopharmacology. In D. Simeon & E. Hollander (Eds.), *Self-injurious behaviors: Assessment and treatment* (pp. 117–148). Washington, DC: American Psychiatric Publishing.

79. Seligman, M. (2002). *Authentic happiness: Using the new positive psychology to realize your potential for lasting fulfillment.* New York: Free Press.

80. Fairbanks, L., & McGuire, M. (1993). Maternal protectiveness and response to the unfamiliar in vervet monkeys. *American Journal of Primatology, 30*, 119–129.

81. Maier, S., & Seligman, M. (1976). Learned helplessness: Theory and evidence. *Journal of Experimental Psychology, 105*, 3–46.

82. Lefcourt, H. (1982). *Locus of control: Current trends in theory and research.* Hillsdale, NJ: Erlbaum.

83. Kobasa, S., Maddi, S., & Kahn, S. (1982). Hardiness and health: A prospective study. *Journal of Personality and Social Psychology, 42*, 168–177.

84. Kabat-Zinn, J. (1994). *Wherever you go, there you are: Mindfulness meditation in everyday life.* New York: Hyperion.

85. Hawton, K., Rodham, K., Evans, E., Harris, L. (2009). Adolescents who self harm: A comparison of those who go to hospital and those who do not. *Child and Adolescent Mental Health, 14*(1), 24–30.

86. O'Connor, R., Rasmussen, S., and Hawton, K. (2009). Predicting Deliberate self harm in adolescents: A six month prospective study. *Suicide and Life Threatening Behavior, 39*(4), 364–75.

87. Weismann, M. (2009). Teenaged, depressed and treatment resistant: What predicts self-harm? *American Journal of Psychiatry, 166*, 385.

88. Nock, M., Joiner, T., Gordon, K., Lloyd-Richardson, E., and Prinstein, M. (2006). Non suicidal self-injury among adolescents: Diagnostic correlates and relation to suicide attempts. *Psychiatry Research*, 144(1), 65–72.

89. Lloyd-Richardson, E., Perine, N., Dierker, L., Kelley, M. (2007). Characteristics and functions of non-suicidical self injury in a community sample of adolescents. *Psychological Medicine*, 37(8), 1183–92.

90. Yates, T., Tracy, A., and Luther, S. (2008). Non-suicidal self injury among "privileged" youths: Longitudinal and cross-sectional approaches to developmental process. *Journal of Consulting and Clinical Psychology*, 76(1), 52–62.

91. Patton, G., Hemphill, S., Beyers, J., Bond, L., and Toumbourou, J. (2007). Pubertal stage and deliberate self-harm in adolescents. *Psychological Medicine*, 37, 1183–92.

92. Madge, N., Hewitt, A., Hawton, K., Jan de Wilde, E., Corcoran, P., Fekete, S., et al (2008). Deliberate self-harm within an international community sample of young people: comparative findings from the Child and Adolescent self-harm in Europe (CASE) study. *Journal of Child Psychology and Psychiatry*, 49(6), 667–77.

93. Rodham, K., Hawton, K., and Evans, E. (2004). Reasons for deliberate self-harm: Comparison of self-poisoners and self-cutters in a community sample of adolescents. *Journal of the American Academy of Child and Adolescent Psychiatry*, 43(1), 80–87.

Bibliography

A WEALTH OF RESOURCES: HOW TO LOCATE HELP AND INFORMATION

As a testament to the growing problem of cutting and self-injury in the United States and abroad, an ever-expanding network of resources are becoming available to inform and treat sufferers and their families. With the advent of the Internet, online resources have expanded to provide support groups and information services to self-injurers. These sites need to be accessed cautiously by adolescents, given their sometimes explicit nature and teenagers' vulnerability to suggestion. In addition, a wealth of books, articles, and treatment centers has emerged to address the difficult challenges of coping with and treating cutting and self-injury. Although far from an exhaustive list, the following resources are available.

SELECTED BOOKS

Conterio, K., and Lader, W. (1998). *Bodily harm: The breakthrough healing program for self-injurers.* New York: Hyperion.

Farber, S. K. (2002). *When the body is the target: Self-harm, pain, and traumatic attachments.* Oxford: Rowman and Littlefield.

Favazza, A. (1987). *Bodies under siege: Self-mutilation in culture and psychiatry.* Baltimore: Johns Hopkins University Press.

Hayward, C. (2003). *Gender differences at puberty.* Cambridge: Cambridge University Press.

Herman, J. (1992). *Trauma and recovery.* New York: Basic Books.

Keel, P. (2005). *Eating disorders.* Upper Saddle River, NJ: Pearson Education.

Levenkron, S. (1998). *Cutting: Understanding and overcoming self-mutilation.* New York: Norton.

Linehan, M. (1993). *Cognitive-behavioral treatment of borderline personality disorder.* New York: Guilford Press.

Sanderson, C. (2006). *Counselling adult survivors of child sexual abuse.* London: Kingsley.

WEB SITES

American Professional Society on the Abuse of Children (APSAC): http://www.apsac.org or 877-402-7722
Rape, Abuse, and Incest National Network (RAINN): http://www.rainn.org or 800-656-HOPE
Both sites provide extensive information and links regarding issues related to treatment and understanding.

Bodies under Siege Web Ring: http://s.webring.com/hub?ring=bus+hom
Another extensive network of Internet sites on self-injury.

Borderline Personality Disorder: http://www.nimh.nih.gov/publicat/bpd.cfm
Provides information and resources regarding borderline personality disorder.

National Self Harm Network: http://www.nshn.co.uk
Also based in the United Kingdom, this is a survivor-led site that provides support to self-injurers and clinicians.

S.A.F.E. Alternatives Program (Self Abuse Finally Ends): http://www.selfinjury.com
Both a Web site that provides information as well as a well-established treatment program developed by Karen Conterio and Wendy Lader.

Secret Shame: http://www.selfharm.net
Regarded as the most comprehensive Internet site on cutting, Secret Shame offers information on numerous aspects of cutting as well as other resources developed by Deb Martinson. This site offers subscriptions to the Bodies under Siege Mailing List, which provides online support groups and chat rooms.

Self-Injury Resources Page: http://www.siari.co.uk
Provides an extensive listing of British treatment programs and resources.

HOW TO LOCATE TREATMENT SERVICES

American Psychiatric Association: http://www.psych.org or 703-907-7300
Provides links for referrals and resources.

American Psychological Association: http://www.apa.org or 800-374-2721
By clicking the Web site's "Find a Psychologist" link, appropriate psychologists can be located by area. Also provides links to state psychological associations and a wealth of informational resources.

Index

About the Author

Lori G. Plante, PhD, is an Adjunct Clinical Assistant Professor in the Department of Psychiatry and Behavioral Sciences at Stanford University Medical School. She is a clinical psychologist in private practice in Menlo Park, California, specializing in the assessment and treatment of adolescents and young adults. She is the author of numerous articles on eating disorders, sexuality, and sexual abuse in adolescents and young adults.